To Marcia
and the
Grand Street Boys

INTONATION, PERCEPTION, AND LANGUAGE

INTONATION, PERCEPTION, AND LANGUAGE

PHILIP LIEBERMAN

RESEARCH MONOGRAPH NO. 38
THE M.I.T. PRESS, CAMBRIDGE, MASSACHUSETTS

Second printing, July 1968
Third printing, first MIT Press paperback
edition, July 1975

Set in Times New Roman
and printed in the United States of America.

Library of Congress catalog card number: 67-13392
ISBN 0-262-12024-0 (hardcover)
ISBN 0-262-62031-6 (paperback)

Foreword

This is the thirty-eighth volume in the M.I.T. Research Monograph Series published by the M.I.T. Press. The objective of this series is to contribute to the professional literature a number of significant pieces of research, larger in scope than journal articles but normally less ambitious than finished books. We believe that such studies deserve a wider circulation than can be accomplished by informal channels, and we hope that this form of publication will make them readily accessible to research organizations, libraries, and independent workers.

HOWARD W. JOHNSON

Preface

I should like to take this opportunity to thank Morris Halle, Kenneth N. Stevens, Roman Jakobson, and Noam Chomsky of the Massachusetts Institute of Technology and Weiant Wathen-Dunn of the Air Force Cambridge Research Laboratories, who have discussed this work over the years and who have made innumerable helpful comments. Special thanks are also due to Jere Mead of the Harvard School of Public Health for making it possible to obtain the physiologic data that are essential to this study. Katherine S. Harris, Michael Studdert-Kennedy of the Haskins Laboratories, and Kerstin Hadding-Koch of the University of Lund, Sweden, likewise pointed out and made available their psychoacoustic data. I should also like to thank my colleagues who have patiently listened to many versions of this study and especially Sven Öhman and Björn Lindblom, who read and commented on earlier versions of this study.

Lexington, Massachusetts
April 22, 1966

PHILIP LIEBERMAN

Contents

Preface ix

1. Introduction 1

2. Physiologic, Acoustic, and Perceptual Criteria 5

2.1 The Speech Production Apparatus 5
2.2 Anatomy of the Larynx 8
2.3 Some Observations of Laryngeal Activity 10
2.4 The Myoelastic-Aerodynamic Theory of Phonation 14
2.5 Phonation in the Chest Register 18
2.6 The Falsetto Register and Mechanisms for Intensity Change 20
2.7 Summation — Laryngeal Activity 22
2.8 The Subglottal System and Respiration 23
2.9 The Breath-Group 26
2.10 The Effects of the Supraglottal Respiratory System and Perception 29
2.11 Secondary Effects 32

3. Intonation in Infant Speech 38

3.1 Some Observations of Adult Intonation 38
3.2 The Acquisition of Language by Children 39

3.3 Infant Cries 41
3.4 A Hypothetical Innate Referential Breath-Group 42
3.5 The Use of Intonation as a Meaningful Signal by Infants 44

4. Perceptual, Physiologic, and Acoustic Data 48

4.1 Perceptual Data for Swedish and American English 48
4.2 Physiologic and Acoustic Data for American English 61
4.3 Discussion of Data 91
4.4 Summary and Discussion of Hypotheses and Observations 103

5. The "Phonemic Phrase" 108

5.1 The Division of a Sentence into Breath-Groups 108
5.2 Suprasegmental Phonologic Features and the Syntactic Component 120
5.3 Emotion 121
5.4 Taxonomic Analyses of Intonation and the "Phonemic Phrase" 123
5.5 On the Independence of Pitch and Stress Levels 128

6. The Marked Breath-Group and Questions 129

6.1 The Formation of Questions in a Number of Languages 130
6.2 English Question Formation: Diachronic and Synchronic Aspects 133

7. Prominence, Stress, and Emphasis in American English 144

7.1 Definitions of Prominence, Stress, and Emphasis 144
7.2 Some Phonetic Manifestations of Stress 147
7.3 Categorization versus Discrimination 159

8. On the Perception and the Production of Speech 162

9. A Survey of Some Recent Linguistic Studies of Intonation 171

9.1 Henry Sweet (1892), *New English Grammar* 172
9.2 Daniel Jones (1909), *Intonation Curves* 173
9.3 H. E. Palmer and W. G. Blandford (1924), *A Grammar of Spoken English on a Strictly Phonetic Basis* 174
9.4 L. E. Armstrong and I. C. Ward (1926), *Handbook of English Intonation* 175
9.5 Daniel Jones (1932), *An Outline of English Phonetics* 178
9.6 L. Bloomfield (1933), *Language* 180
9.7 B. Bloch and G. L. Trager (1942), *Outline of Linguistic Analysis* 182
9.8 R. S. Wells (1945), "The Pitch Phonemes of English" 182
9.9 K. L. Pike (1945), *The Intonation of American English* 183
9.10 R. S. Wells (1947), "Immediate Constituents" 187
9.11 G. L. Trager and H. L. Smith (1951), *Outline of English Structure* 188
9.12 Z. Harris (1944), "Simultaneous Components in Phonology" 191
9.13 R. H. Stetson (1951), *Motor Phonetics: A Study of Speech Movements in Action* 191
9.14 M. Bierwisch (1965), "Regeln für die Intonation deutscher Sätze" 194

References 197

Index 207

1 Introduction

This study has two objectives. It undertakes a linguistic analysis of some aspects of the intonation of American English, and it also attempts to deal with the problem of intonation for all languages. The approach that we have taken with regard to the specific problems of American English is directed toward achieving both of these objectives, since we have attempted to analyze intonation in terms of mechanisms, that is, features and rules that underlie the observable phenomena. The two features that are discussed in this study are not sufficient to specify all the observable phenomena of American English. However, we have tried to show that people actually produce, perceive, and use some aspects of intonation as a linguistically referenced signal in terms of these features. The features thus characterize some aspects of human linguistic competence. Although notations have been devised that are sufficient to describe all of the observable phenomena of intonation (the standard musical notation with minor modifications, for example, is suitable), they do not reflect the mechanisms that people use when they deal with intonation as a linguistic signal. These notations tell us no more about the linguistic competence of speakers of American English than a Fourier analysis of a violin sonata would tell us about its musical structure. The physical output signal would be specified, but the notation would not reflect the underlying structure. Thus we are not trying to devise a "high fidelity" record of intonation; we are, instead, trying to see how the human mind functions.

We have also tried to show that intonation has a central, rather than a peripheral, status and that it must be the product of an innate, rather than an acquired, mechanism. Thus it should have a similar status in all languages. We have therefore attempted at each stage of the analysis to examine acoustic, perceptual, phonetic, and syntactic data for related and unrelated languages. These comparisons reveal certain general principles. We have also tried to formulate our hypothetical features in terms of the inherent anatomic, physiologic, and perceptual constraints that are common to all mankind. We have, moreover, tested our hypotheses in terms of the available data regarding the vocalizations of infants and young children, which may reflect innate human linguistic competence under certain conditions. For example, the primary feature that we discuss, the *breath-group,* has universal aspects that are manifested in the cries of newborn infants. At each step of the analysis we have tried to identify the language-specific and the universal aspects of our features and rules. Thus, though our analysis is most relevant to American English, it may also be pertinent to some degree to the general problem of intonation.

Our analysis is obviously not definitive since we cannot account for all the observable phenomena that characterize American English intonation. We have isolated only two of the features that may underlie the intonation of American English, the *breath-group* and *prominence.* We have not, for example, characterized the minute variations in the fundamental frequency of the vowels that occur within each breath-group. We do not even know whether all of these variations have a linguistic reference. In many other languages features exist that produce "tones" on individual vowels. Similar features may also exist in American English. Our study is also not definitive in the sense of having exhaustively analyzed the intonational system of every language on earth. Moreover, we have avoided, for the most part, the emotional aspect of intonation. It is apparent that emotion is manifested in the intonational signal, but this problem is beyond the scope of this study.

We have, however, attempted to resolve a number of problems in the course of this study. For example, we have tried to characterize the traditional "phonemic phrase" in terms of the breath-group. The scope of the breath-group is suprasegmental. Though it often delimits the constituent *sentence,* it can delimit any constituent in the derived phrase marker of a sentence. We have also discussed the possible implications of suprasegmental features on the syntactic component of the grammar. We have tried to characterize the production and perception of terminal fundamental frequency contours as well as the production and perception of contrastive stress and linguistic stress, and we have particularly tried to show that the perceptual recognition routines involve the listener's knowledge of the grammar as well as his knowledge of the articulatory gestures that are involved in speech production.

We have not attempted to establish any priority regarding the acoustic or the articulatory levels of description. The phonologic feature is the minimal linguistic unit in terms of which speech is coded. A phonologic feature therefore must have both acoustic and articulatory correlates. Speech must be produced by the human vocal tract, and a feature must therefore have articulatory correlates. Because speech must be transmitted through the air, acoustic correlates must also exist. Discussions of whether the acoustic or articulatory level is more "basic" often are really discussions of whether it is easier to obtain and classify acoustic or articulatory data.

The articulatory level of description is sometimes treated as more "basic" than the acoustic level because "motor theories of perception" have been hypothesized in which speech perception is related to speech production. We shall present experimental evidence that is consistent with the notion of a "motor theory of perception" in which the perceptual recognition routine involves the listener's knowledge of the constraints imposed by the speech production apparatus. However, this does not mean that the articulatory level of description is thus more "basic." The listener's recognition routine may also involve his knowledge of the derived constituent structure of the utterance, or its semantic interpretation, or the total social context. All of these factors may be involved in the perception of speech in a given situation. A listener may rely quite heavily on his knowledge of the social context when he perceives the stereotyped greeting *Hello there*. However, he must also consider the acoustic signal in perceiving this utterance. His reaction might be quite different if he heard some equally stereotyped invective. In some other situation he might not rely on the social context to any significant degree, for example, in a psychoacoustic test that involved "nonsense syllables." In still another situation the listener may not need to invoke his knowledge of the articulatory aspects of speech production in order to perceive the speech signal. In any event, the listener must always refer back to the acoustic signal. The "motor theory of perception" points to strong connections between the acoustic and articulatory aspects of speech, and the concept of a phonologic feature indeed represents in a sense an optimal coding of the articulatory and acoustic levels of description. When we speak of the acoustic and articulatory correlates of a feature, we are implicitly hypothesizing that somewhere in the brain both levels of description are coded in terms of a single mechanism. Because we have no way of directly studying the features at the neural level, we must perforce investigate both the acoustic and the articulatory aspects of speech.

One last comment on the organization and contents of Chapters 2 and 4 should be made. This study is intended for both the linguist and the experimental worker in speech analysis and synthesis. Although a detailed knowledge of the physiology of the larynx and the perception of intonation is essential to the analysis of intonation, the details are perhaps not of direct interest to many linguists. A summary of the most relevant aspects of the control of the larynx is therefore included in Chapter 2. A discussion and summary of the hypotheses and data in Chapters 2, 3, and 4 are also presented at the end of Chapter 4. The reader who studies these chapters in detail is asked to be patient with these repetitions. Other readers who are well acquainted with the techniques of experimental speech analysis and synthesis will doubtless find other unnecessary repetitions. However, the general absence of elementary expositions in this area makes it difficult otherwise to prepare the general reader.

2 Physiologic, Acoustic, and Perceptual Criteria

In this chapter we shall discuss some of the anatomical and physiologic aspects of speech production in relation to the acoustic output of the larynx. We shall also discuss some aspects of the perception of pure tones and other simple stimuli in psychoacoustic experiments. We shall then examine intonation in terms of the constraints imposed by the speech production apparatus and the auditory system.

In considering these constraints we can avoid fruitless searches for phonetic distinctions that are impossible to produce or perceptually to resolve. This is indeed the traditional approach to phonetic analysis. No one would ever expect to find a vowel that was produced by constricting the pharynx with the tip of the tongue since it is impossible to place the tip of the tongue in such a position. The physiologic properties of the vocal tract are inherent properties of every well-formulated phonetic theory. We shall begin by examining the larynx and the sublaryngeal respiratory system since these parts of the vocal tract are most important for intonation.

2.1 The Speech Production Apparatus

The larynx is the source of quasi-periodic energy that excites the vocal tract in the production of voiced sounds. Intonation, stress, and prosody are primarily responses to the periodicity, amplitude, spectral character, and duration of the output of the larynx.

The vocal tract is really defined operationally in the sense that there is no set of organs exclusively adapted to the production of speech. The chest, trachea, larynx, pharynx, mouth, and nose all form part of the respiratory system, whose main function is, of course, ventilation. The lips, teeth, jaw, and tongue are necessary to ingest food. The nose also contains olfactory sense organs, while the tongue has taste receptors. The larynx in certain lower forms is simply a valve that prevents solids and liquids from entering the lungs.

The respiratory system can be conveniently divided into three parts for the purpose of describing the production of speech (Figure 2.1).

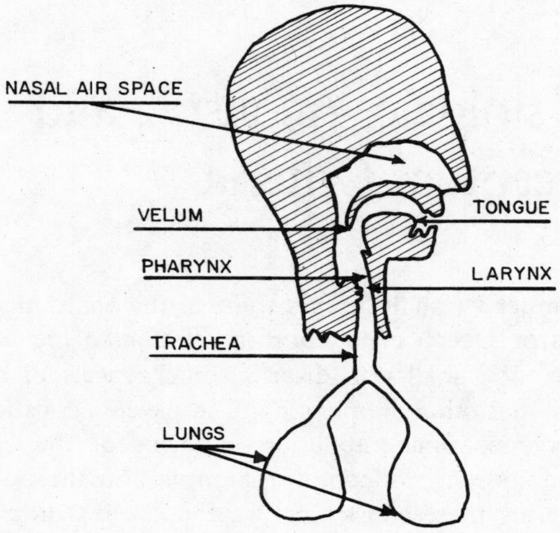

Figure 2.1 Schematic representation of the respiratory system.
The supraglottal respiratory system, which determines the phonetic quality of vowels and consonants, consists of the oral and nasal cavities and the pharynx. The sublaryngeal respiratory system consists of the trachea and lungs.

The supraglottal respiratory system consists of the oral pharynx, nasal pharynx, nose, and mouth. The jaw, lips, and tongue can all modify the interior shape and volume of the mouth, while the velum can open or close the nose to the oral cavity. It is usual to designate the upper respiratory system and the larynx as the "vocal tract," since phonetic studies are usually concerned only with articulatory gestures that distinguish different vowels and consonants. The phonetic quality of differing vowel and consonant sounds is primarily due to the configuration assumed by the upper respiratory system.

The sublaryngeal respiratory system consists of the lungs and the trachea. The larynx functions by converting the relatively steady movement of expiratory air that flows out of the lungs through the trachea into a series of "puffs" of air. The "puffs," which can occur at a relatively steady rate or fundamental frequency, excite the upper respiratory system. The upper respiratory system acts as an acoustic filter. The sequence of "puffs" of air—the volume velocity waveform that is the output of the larynx—contains energy at the fundamental frequency and many of its higher harmonics. The physical configuration of the upper respiratory system for each vowel or consonant results in an acoustic filter that has minimum attenuation at certain frequencies. Local energy maxima (Figure 2.2) therefore occur at

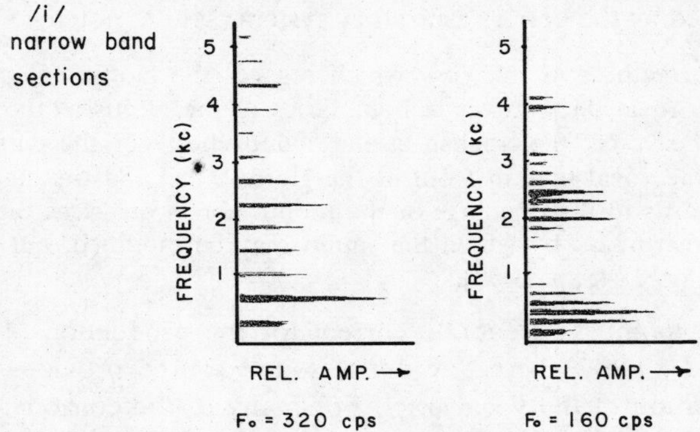

Figure 2.2 Narrow band sections of the same vowel at two different fundamental frequencies.
The local energy maxima in the vowel spectra occur in the vicinity of the formant frequencies. A speaker controls the position of the formant frequencies by varying the configuration of the supralaryngeal respiratory system.

the mouth of the speaker in the vicinity of these formant frequencies, which reflect the configuration of the upper respiratory system.

The volume velocity waveform from the larynx is always filtered by the upper respiratory system. However, the fundamental frequency and amplitude of the glottal volume velocity waveform are largely independent of the configuration of the upper respiratory system. For example, the vowel /a/ might have formant frequencies of 700, 1000, and 2500 cps for a particular talker. The talker would be able to vary his fundamental frequency between 90 and 200 cps while he preserved the vowel quality[1] of the /a/. He would vary the output of his larynx by making certain muscular adjustments in the larynx and the sublaryngeal system, keeping the configuration of his upper respiratory system unchanged. Conversely, he might maintain

[1] As a first approximation this is true. Vowel quality does change for extreme shifts in the fundamental frequency (Slawson, 1965).

the laryngeal output and vary the configuration of his upper respiratory system, producing different vowels or voiced consonants. He could, for example, produce /a/, /i/, /u/, or /l/ at a fundamental frequency of 130 cps.

2.2 Anatomy of the Larynx

We owe much of our knowledge about the larynx to the studies of Johannes Müller. Müller in 1848 pointed out that speech may be regarded as the modulation of the laryngeal source by the configuration assumed by the upper respiratory system. Müller noted

> . . . the correctness of the view which regards the glottis and the vocal cords which form the immediate boundaries of the glottis as the essential source of the voice; the trachea as the "wind chest" of the wind instrument, and the vocal tube in front of the glottis . . . and the air passages thence upwards to the openings of the mouth and nostrils, as the tube of a musical instrument by which the sound may be modified, but not generated [Müller, 1848, p. 1003].

This viewpoint is essentially correct for the production of vowels, liquids, and glides, where the glottal sound source provides the primary excitation of the vocal tract. For many of the consonants, such as /f/, /p/, /s/, the vocal tract is excited by the noiselike energy generated by air turbulence at constrictions[2] (Fant, 1960).

The larynx is a complex structure of several cartilages linked by a complicated system of muscles, ligaments, and membranes. The larynx sits on top of the trachea, or windpipe, which connects the lungs to the larynx. The cricoid cartilage, which is shaped like a signet ring, is one of the primary elements of the larynx. It is attached to the top of the trachea. Its narrow end faces the front of the neck. Two smaller cartilages called the arytenoids are flexibly attached by ligaments to the cricoid cartilage. The two arytenoids face each other since they are each attached to the opposite sides of the cricoid cartilage toward its rear (Figure 2.3). One arytenoid is attached to each side of the upper surface of the cricoid cartilage. One larger cartilage, the thyroid, is flexibly attached to the front of the cricoid. The vocal cords, each of which consists of muscular tissue (the vocalis muscle) and a ligament, extend from the thyroid cartilage to the arytenoid cartilages. One end of each vocal cord's ligament is attached to the free end (vocal process) of each arytenoid. The vocalis muscles lie

[2] Other consonants are generated by means of the glottal source and turbulent energy, such as /z/; still other consonants are generated by means of the quasi-periodic excitation of the glottal source, such as /m/.

beside the ligaments and extend to the thyroid cartilage. They form the body of the vocal cords. The arytenoid cartilages are actually embedded in the vocal cords. The opening between the vocal cords is called the glottis. The arytenoids form the margin of the rear or posterior portion of the glottis, which is the widest part of the opening during respiration. The anterior portion of the glottis, that part toward the front of the neck which is bounded by the flexible vocal ligaments, is the portion of the glottis whose motions are usually responsible for phonation.

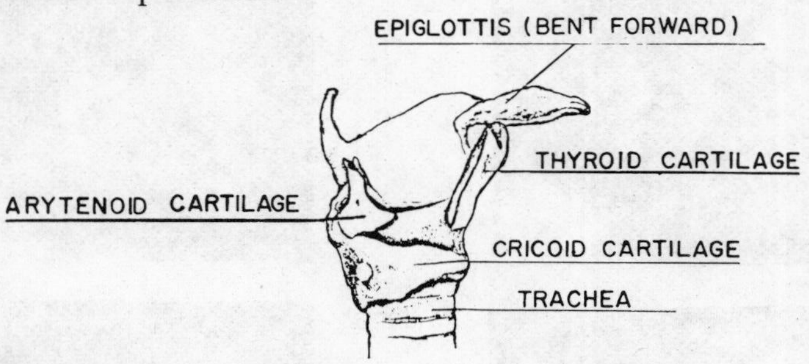

Figure 2.3 Lateral view of the larynx after removal of greater part of the right thyroid cartilage (after Piersol, 1906).
The vocal cords, which consist of muscular tissue and ligament, extend from the thyroid cartilage to the arytenoid cartilages. The end of each vocal cord's ligament is attached to the free end of each arytenoid cartilage.

In Figure 2.4 six photographs of the vocal cords are reproduced. They were taken by using a laryngeal mirror, which is a small 45-degree mirror that can be placed at the back of the mouth against the soft palate so that the vocal cords can be examined under suitable conditions.

A complex set of muscles interconnects the arytenoids, thyroid, and cricoid cartilages. The cricothyroid muscles, for example, can stretch the vocal cords. The interarytenoid muscles can draw together the arytenoid cartilages, which support the vocal cords. The posterior cricoarytenoids can separate the arytenoid cartilages. For our purposes it is sufficient to know that the laryngeal muscles can position the vocal cords within the larynx so as to enlarge or decrease the size of the glottal opening. The laryngeal muscles also can adjust the tension of the vocal cords. The thickness, or cross section, of the vocal cords is also a function of the tension applied to the vocal cords. At low tensions the cross section is comparatively large (about 2 mm for an adult male), but as tension increases, the vocal cords stretch and become thinner.

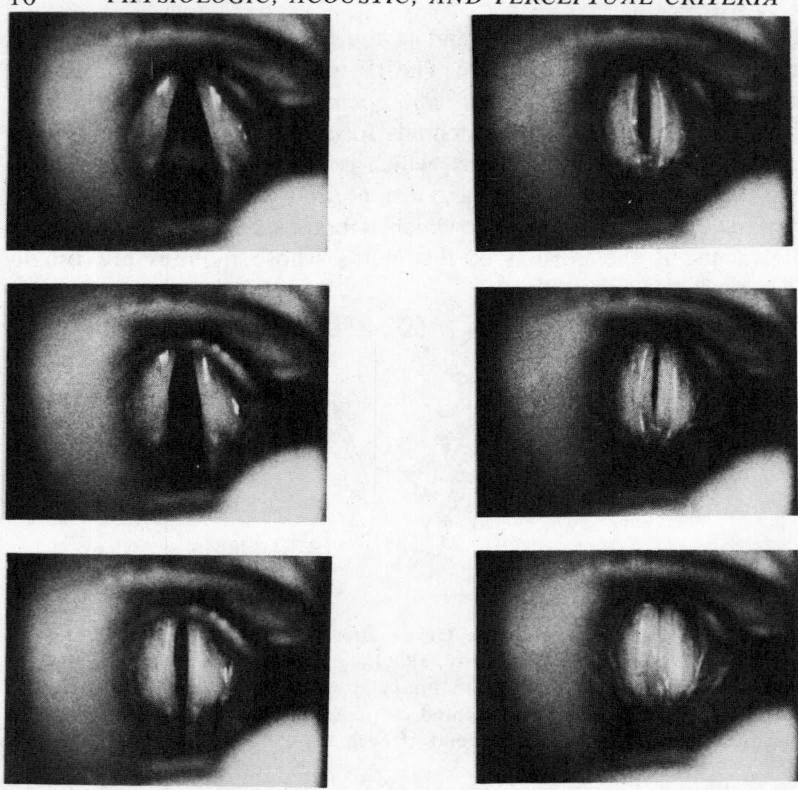

Figure 2.4 Six photographs of the larynx *in situ*.
These photographs are selected from a sequence that was exposed at a frame rate of 10,000 pictures per second using a Fastax high-speed camera. A normal male subject was uttering a series of short /a/ sounds at a fundamental frequency of 220 cps with a laryngeal mirror in place. The top left frame shows the vocal cords open in their inspiratory configuration. The anterior portion of the glottis is at the top of the picture. The middle left frame shows the vocal cords partially closed 50 msec later, and the bottom left frame shows the vocal cords 80 msec after they started to close. Phonation started 54 msec after the vocal cords moved into the position shown in the bottom left frame. The sequence of three frames in the right column shows a half cycle of the subsequent phonation. The top right frame shows the maximum glottal opening. The bottom frame shows the vocal cords completely closed, while the middle frame shows an intermediate position.

2.3 Some Observations of Laryngeal Activity

Johannes Müller first noted that the frequency at which the vocal cords vibrate is a function of both the tension of the vocal cords and the magnitude of the subglottal air pressure. Müller never saw the vocal cords operate during normal phonation, since the laryngeal mirror was not invented until 1854 (Garcia, 1855). His remarkable analysis of the larynx was instead obtained by means of experiments in which he applied tensions to the muscles of larynges excised from cadavers while he blew air through them. He formed hypotheses concerning the control of the larynx and tested these hypotheses by generating sound with an excised larynx. Müller's account of his experimental procedure is quite straightforward:

> Experiments on the separated larynx are in first attempts attended with extreme difficulty; all the parts are movable, and it is not at first apparent how the uniform tension and the uniform fixed position of the cartilages, so necessary for attaining any degree of accuracy in the experiments, can be given; and at the same time how the position once given can be made capable of alternation as the experiment may require. With a little contrivance, however, these objects can be accomplished. The first thing to be done is to obtain a fixed point in the larynx. The anterior wall is naturally mobile in the greater part of its extent, and the posterior wall at its upper part. The thyroid cartilage can be moved towards the cricoid cartilage, and the arytenoid cartilages also; and by either movement the vocal cords are rendered tense. The arytenoid cartilages being the most movable parts, and those by the wrong position of which an error in the experiments might most easily be caused, my first aim is to fix them. With this view I pass an awl or pin transversely through the base; doing this with very great care, in order that, when afterwards extended, the two vocal ligaments may have an equal degree of tension; and also making the transfixion in such a manner that, when the two cartilages are approximated on the pin, the anterior processes at their base may touch each other. The larynx, with a small portion of the trachea attached, being thus prepared, is fixed, with its posterior wall downwards, to a board by means of the cricoid cartilage; and the pin which transfixed the arytenoid cartilages (these being put into any position or degree of approximation that may be wished) is also firmly tied down to the board. The posterior wall of the larynx being thus fixed, any degree of tension required may be given to the vocal cords by exerting traction on the anterior wall formed by the thyroid cartilage. To avoid the resistance which might be offered by the attachment of the thyroid to the cricoid cartilage, it is well carefully to separate their connections. As a means of drawing away the thyroid cartilage from the posterior wall of the larynx, and thus of making tense the vocal ligaments, I fix a thin cord to the angle of the thyroid cartilage immediately above the attachment of the ligaments, and passing it over a pulley connect with it a scale; by putting different weights into this scale I can accurately regulate the tension exerted. The epiglottis,

superior ligaments of the glottis, the ventricles of the larynx, the capitula laryngis of Santorini, the ligaments aryteno-epiglottica, and even the upper portion of the thyroid cartilages, not being essential to the production of the vocal sounds, are all cut away to render the vocal cords and aperture of the glottis more easily visible. Besides, it is necessary to determine first what can be effected by the vocal cords alone, before investigating the influence of the superior part of the cavity of the larynx. A wooden tube for the experimenter to blow through is inserted into the portion of trachea left attached to the larynx.

Müller made many detailed observations of the larynx, and we shall quote only a few of the more relevant ones:

Vocal sounds can be produced not only when the lips of the glottis are separated by a narrow interval, but even when they are quite in contact especially if the chordes vocales are much relaxed . . . [p. 1010].

The height of the notes is regulated by the length and tension of the vocal cords. The notes are, caeteris paribus, lower in pitch in proportion to the length of the glottis; but deep notes may be obtained from a glottis much shortened by its lips being pressed together with forceps, if the vocal cords be at the time relaxed; and a very long glottis will yield high notes, if the chordae vocales have a great deal of tension [p. 1011].

Two perfectly distinct series of tones can be produced in a larynx separated from the body . . . one of these series of tones has the most perfect resemblance to the tones of ordinary voice; the notes of the other series are generally higher than those of the former, and are the highest that can be produced; they are in every way similar to the falsetto notes. When the vocal cords have a certain degree of tension, both these kinds of notes may be produced; sometimes one kind, and sometimes the other kind is heard. A certain tension of the cords is always productive of notes with the falsetto tone, whether the air be blown through the glottis forcefully or feebly. When the vocal ligaments are much relaxed, the tones are always those of ordinary voice, however feebly or forcefully we blow. If a slight tension of the ligaments is maintained, it depends on the manner of blowing whether the note be of the ordinary tone or falsetto (the falsetto note being most easily produced by blowing very gently); and the two different notes thus produced may be very distant from each other in the musical scale, even as much as an octave [p. 1013].

There are other modes of producing high notes, without increasing the tension of the vocal ligaments so much as to cause them to give out falsetto notes. One is to blow with greater force, by which means the notes may without difficulty be raised through a series of semitones the extent of a "fifth" . . . [p. 1014].

These observations have been quantitatively confirmed in many subsequent experiments. Van den Berg (1954, 1956, 1957, 1958,

1960*a*) has, for example, replicated Müller's experiments with excised larynxes using modern methods that permit a better approximation of the real situation. In van den Berg's experiments the arytenoid cartilages are not transfixed by a pin, and the effects of the muscular forces that are responsible for the adduction and abduction of the vocal cords can be studied. High-speed motion pictures of the human larynx during normal phonation have confirmed Müller's explanations regarding the basic pattern of activity during phonation and the difference between the falsetto and normal registers (Farnsworth, 1940; Timcke, von Leden, and Moore, 1958; Moore and von Leden, 1958; von Leden and Moore 1960; Soron and Lieberman, 1963). Acoustic analyses of the speech signal have quantitatively confirmed that fundamental frequency increases with increased vocal effort (Denes, 1959; Harris and Weiss, 1963; Draper, Ladefoged, and Whitteridge, 1959). Ladefoged (1961), for example, monitored the subglottal air pressure in normal subjects during phonation. He showed that the fundamental frequency rises as the subglottal air pressure rises.[3]

There have been many other facts noted about the activity of the larynx. The "opening quotient," for example, was defined (Farnsworth, 1940) as the fraction of each fundamental period that the glottis is open. We know that the opening quotient varies greatly during phonation. In particular, it decreases as the degree of vocal effort increases (Timcke, von Leden, and Moore, 1958). Acoustically, this means that the high-frequency content of the glottal source should increase (Flanagan, 1958), and it is no great surprise to find that independent acoustic analyses confirm that the high-frequency content of speech increases with increased vocal effort (Harris and Weiss, 1963).

Other independent experiments have determined the glottal excitation function by accounting for the effects of the upper respiratory tract (tongue, lips, jaw, nose, etc.) on the acoustic signal radiated from the speaker's lips. These experiments use a technique of inverse filtering in which the effects of formants are removed by antiresonances (Miller, 1956; Fant, 1961; Holmes, 1963). These studies, which demonstrate the extent to which the output of the glottis may vary, also show that the opening quotient decreases as the intensity increases.

[3] The relationship between intensity and pitch was known to ancient Greek science. Archytas of Tarentum, a contemporary of Plato, states: "So it is with sounds. Those that are projected by an intense breath are loud and sharp, while those projected with weak breath are soft and low" (Cohen and Drabkin, 1958).

2.4 The Myoelastic-Aerodynamic Theory of Phonation

Though the activity of the larynx has been studied in detail for more than a century, there still remains a great deal of confusion regarding the mechanism of phonation. We certainly do not know all that we might want to know about the larynx. However, much of the confusion is unwarranted and stems from the phenomenological approach of many studies. Experimental data are often not related to any explicit theory of phonation. This is often true of modern studies in which careful observations of the larynx in vivo are made. Muller had to formulate specific hypotheses regarding the mechanism of phonation, since he had to manipulate the excised larynxes to produce sounds. Müller, for example, knew that tensioning the vocal cords would produce a rise in the fundamental frequency, all other things being constant. When the larynx is observed during normal phonation by means of a laryngeal mirror, it is often difficult to infer causal relationships, especially when the experimenter has no clearly formulated model. We shall briefly outline, in a qualitative form, a theory of laryngeal activity, the myoelastic-aerodynamic theory of phonation. This theory, which derives from Müller, owes much to the recent work of van den Berg. With the exception of a few experiments that we shall discuss later, it is consistent with our present knowledge and relates many observations that are superficially incompatible.

As Stevens (1964) succinctly notes, "The vibration of the vocal folds is maintained through a rapid alternation of forces in opposite directions. . . ." For phonation to take place, the vocal cords must first be brought toward each other from the open position that is maintained during quiet breathing. The laryngeal muscles bring the vocal cords to this position, which we shall call the "phonation neutral position." This closing motion seems to be comparatively slow in comparison with the rate at which the vocal cords move during phonation. Observations from high-speed laryngeal motion pictures of three male speakers, for example, show that it takes about 100 msec for the vocal cords to move inward from their open respiratory position (Soron and Lieberman, 1963). During phonation the vocal cords will stay at their neutral position if the airflow from the lungs is interrupted (Rubin, 1960).

Two types of forces act on the vocal cords. The aerodynamic and aerostatic forces can act to displace the vocal cords from their phonation neutral position. The tissue forces always act to restore the vocal cords to their neutral position. In Figure 2.5 a schematic diagram of the vocal cords and these forces is presented. Note that the neutral position of the glottis is open. This diagram portrays the vocal cords after they have moved inward from the open breathing

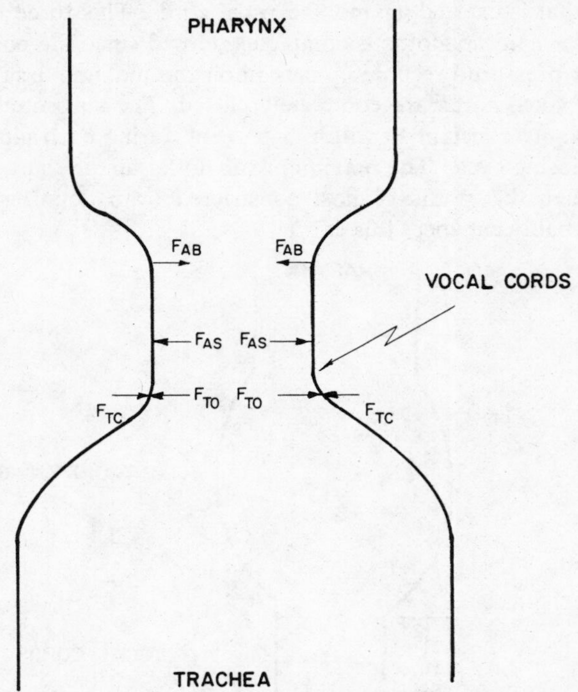

Figure 2.5 Schematic representation of the vocal cords in an open position showing some of the forces involved in phonation.
The force developed by the subglottal air pressure, which acts to displace the vocal cords outward from their "phonation neutral position," is represented by the vector $\mathbf{F}_{as}$. The vectors $\mathbf{F}_{to}$ and $\mathbf{F}_{tc}$ represent the forces due to the action of the vocal ligaments that act to restore the vocal cords to their neutral position. The Bernoulli force $\mathbf{F}_{ab}$, which is generated by the airflow through the glottal constriction, acts to pull the vocal cords inward.

position but the glottis is not completely closed. The force exerted by the positive subglottal air pressure on the vocal cords is represented by the vector $\mathbf{F}_{as}$. When the glottis is closed or almost closed, this force acts to displace the vocal cords outward from their neutral position. The vector $\mathbf{F}_{ab}$ represents the Bernoulli force that is a consequence of the negative pressure created in the glottis by the high-velocity airflow. The vectors $\mathbf{F}_{to}$ and $\mathbf{F}_{tc}$ represent the forces due to the tension of the vocal ligaments that act to restore the vocal cords to their neutral position. We shall briefly discuss these forces before turning to their interaction during phonation.

The aerostatic force $\mathbf{F}_{as}$ arises from the positive subglottal air pressure that is exerted against the vocal cords. This force reaches its maximum when the glottis is completely closed since the positive subglottal air pressure presumably acts upon the maximum surface area when the vocal cords are completely closed. The subglottal air pressure is usually constant to within 5 percent during each glottal opening and closing cycle. The maximum subglottal air pressure, however, occurs when the glottis is most constricted (van den Berg, 1956), which probably enhances this effect.

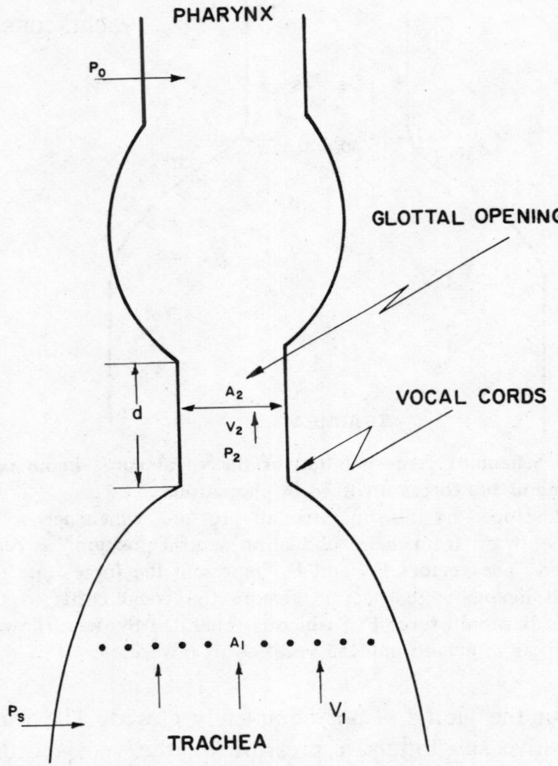

Figure 2.6 Schematic side view of the vocal cords.
Dimension d represents the length of the glottal constriction. Area A_2 is the cross-sectional area of the glottal constriction. The particle velocity and air pressure at the glottal constriction are V_2 and P_2. Area A_1 is the cross-sectional area of the trachea, and V_1 and P_1 are the particle velocity and air pressure in the trachea.

The Bernoulli effect, which generates force $\mathbf{F}_{ab}$, is a special case of the general principle of the conservation of energy. Suppose that the airflow through the glottal constriction in Figure 2.6 can be approximated by the uniform, frictionless flow of an incompressible fluid. The rate at which the fluid flows across section A_1 in Figure 2.6 is equal to $A_1V_1\rho$ where ρ is the density of the fluid. In the figure, A_1 is the cross-sectional area of the trachea, and V_1 the velocity of the fluid. If the stream is steady, the same mass must travel per unit time through the constricted portion of the pathway so that

$$A_1V_1\rho = A_2V_2\rho, \tag{2.1}$$

where A_2 and V_2 are the cross-sectional area and particle velocity at the glottal constriction. Since the density ρ is constant, $A_1V_1 = A_2V_2$.

Let us consider the rate at which energy is transferred across sections A_1 and A_2. The mass being transferred across A_1 per unit time is $A_1V_1\rho$. The kinetic energy being transferred across section A_1 is, therefore,

$$\tfrac{1}{2}\,(A_1V_1\rho)(V_1^2). \tag{2.2}$$

The rate at which work is being done by the fluid across section A_1 is equal to the force exerted by the fluid across A_1 which is A_1P_s, where P_s is the subglottal air pressure multiplied by the particle velocity V_1. The total rate at which mechanical energy is being transferred across section A_1 is, therefore,

$$\tfrac{1}{2}\,A_1\rho V_1^3 + A_1P_sV_1 \tag{2.3}$$

if we neglect the potential energy due to the force of gravity. The rate at which energy is being transferred across section A_2 is similarly

$$\tfrac{1}{2}\,A_2\rho V_2^3 + A_2P_2V_2 \tag{2.4}$$

where P_2 is the air pressure in the constriction.

Since energy is being conserved in this system,

$$\tfrac{1}{2}\,A_1\rho V_1^3 + A_1P_sV_1 = \tfrac{1}{2}\,A_2\rho V_2^3 + A_2P_2V_2, \tag{2.5}$$

but $A_1V_1 = A_2V_2$ so that

$$\tfrac{1}{2}\,\rho V_1^2 + P_s = \tfrac{1}{2}\,\rho V_2^2 + P_2. \tag{2.6}$$

The particle velocity in the glottal constriction V_2 will be larger than the particle velocity in the pharynx V_1 since

$$V_2 = \frac{A_1V_1}{A_2},$$

where A_2 is the cross-sectional area of the constriction. The kinetic energy of the fluid in the constriction

$$\frac{1}{2}\rho\left(\frac{A_1V_1}{A_2}\right)^2$$

will therefore be higher in the constricted portion of the air passage. The potential energy must decrease as the kinetic energy increases since the sum of the kinetic and potential energies must remain constant. What this means physically is that the pressure of the fluid in the constriction, P_2, decreases.

The pressure in the constriction P_2 thus may fall below atmospheric pressure as the cross section of the constriction decreases. If the walls of the air passage were flexible, they would tend to be "sucked" together by the pressure differential between P_2 and the atmospheric pressure that is maintained on the outside of the body. The pressure differential would become still greater as the walls collapsed and A_2 becomes smaller since V_2 would become larger as A_2 decreased. The flow of air through the glottis, however, is not frictionless, and the resistance of the glottis increases as it becomes more constricted (van den Berg, Zantema, and Doornenbal, 1957) so the Bernoulli force $\mathbf{F}_{ab}$ increases only up to a certain point as the glottis becomes smaller. Some of the other assumptions regarding incompressibility and laminar flow are also only approximations[4] (Flanagan, 1958). However, the idealized case predicts the correct qualitative effects.

The static tissue forces $\mathbf{F}_{to}$ and $\mathbf{F}_{tc}$ arise from the stretching of ligaments and muscles. The magnitude of these forces would be directly proportional to the displacement if the muscles and ligaments behaved like idealized springs, but this may not be the case. However, it seems safe to say that the magnitude of these forces increases as the vocal cords are displaced from the phonation neutral position.

2.5 Phonation in the Chest Register

Let us consider how these hypothetical forces might interact during normal phonation in the chest register.

The "chest register" is the range of fundamental frequencies that a person normally employs during speech. Functionally, the chest register involves the Bernoulli force in the operating cycle. The vocal cords are relatively lax, and they have an appreciable thickness (di-

[4] Flanagan points out that the incompressibility assumption is reasonably valid, "if the dimensions of the oriface are small compared with the wavelength of an acoustic disturbance in the medium, and if the mean velocity is much smaller than the speed of sound. . . ."

mension *d* in Figure 2.6) so that the airflow through the glottis involves a constricted passage in which a pressure drop can occur.

During breathing the glottal opening is quite wide, and the posterior portion of the glottis is open (Figure 2.4). Before phonation starts, the arytenoid cartilages swing inward, closing the posterior portion of the glottis and bringing the two vocal cords against each other or near to each other.

The subglottal air pressure then builds up. If the vocal cords' "neutral" position at the onset of phonation is closed, $\mathbf{F}_{as}$ initially blows them apart. But $\mathbf{F}_{as}$ is opposed by the static tissue force $\mathbf{F}_{tc}$ and the Bernoulli force $\mathbf{F}_{ab}$, which begins to act as the airflow starts through the glottis. The static air pressure force $\mathbf{F}_{as}$ decreases as the glottis opens, while the tissue force $\mathbf{F}_{tc}$ increases.

The opening motion proceeds until $\mathbf{F}_{as}$ is counterbalanced by the sum of the Bernoulli and the static tissue forces and the vocal cords start to move inward. As the vocal cords move inward, the Bernoulli force $\mathbf{F}_{ab}$ increases to a point, as the glottal opening decreases. The Bernoulli force, of course, ceases abruptly when the vocal cords close, since the airflow stops momentarily. The static pressure force $\mathbf{F}_{as}$ then reopens the glottis, and the cyclic activity continues.

If the vocal cords' "neutral" position on the onset of phonation is open, an additional component of the static tissue force is present, $\mathbf{F}_{to}$, which opposes movements that tend to move each cord inward from its neutral position. The operating cycle is similar to the simpler case where phonation starts with the vocal cords closed except that the initial movement is inward (Farnsworth, 1940; van den Berg *et al.*, 1957; Soron and Lieberman, 1963). The arytenoid cartilages move the vocal cords inward from their open breathing position, but they do not completely close the glottis. The subglottal air pressure P_s builds up, and air starts to flow through the glottis. The airflow through the constriction results in the Bernoulli force $\mathbf{F}_{ab}$, which initially draws the vocal cords together. The Bernoulli force is opposed by the static tissue force $\mathbf{F}_{to}$. As the glottis is narrowed, the Bernoulli force increases faster than the opposing tissue force so that the cords close.[5] When the vocal cords close, the Bernoulli force ceases abruptly and the static air pressure force $\mathbf{F}_{as}$, which is at its maximum, and the static tissue force $\mathbf{F}_{to}$ open the glottis. The glottis continues to open as the vocal cords move past their neutral position. The static tissue force $\mathbf{F}_{tc}$ then opposes the opening movement, the vocal cords return to their neutral position, and the cycle repeats.

[5] If the tissue forces are greater than the Bernoulli force, the vocal cords will not close.

We have grossly oversimplified many aspects of the dynamic operation of the vocal cords. There are, for example, energy losses that tend to damp the vibrations of the vocal cords. These energy losses arise from the inelastic collision of the vocal cords, the flexing of muscular tissue, and the aerodynamic resistance of the glottis (van den Berg, 1958; von Leden and Moore, 1960). When, for example, certain types of pathologic masses increase the losses caused by the collision of the vocal cords, they have marked effects on glottal activity (Lieberman, 1963*a*).

2.6 The Falsetto Register and Mechanisms for Intensity Change

The falsetto register illustrates how the laryngeal musculature can modify the basic mode of operation of the vocal cords by adjusting the effective mass that vibrates, increasing the magnitude of the static tissue forces and decreasing the importance of the aerodynamic forces (Müller, 1848; Pressman and Kelemen, 1955; van den Berg, 1960*a*; Proctor, 1964). In the falsetto register the laryngeal muscles stretch the vocal cords. Dimension *d* in Figure 2.6 becomes quite small, and the vocal cords are stretched. The Bernoulli force $\mathbf{F}_{ab}$ in Figure 2.5 therefore decreases, since there must be a relatively long constricted passage in order to generate the negative air pressure because of air resistance effects (van den Berg *et al.,* 1957). The effective mass that vibrates also decreases because of the increased tension of the laryngeal muscles, and the static tissue forces obviously are greater than they are in the chest register.

The behavior of the larynx is quite different in the chest and falsetto registers. Isshiki (1964), for example, noted that for low and medium fundamental frequencies (the chest register) the sound pressure level goes up as the subglottal pressure increases but the flow rate remains relatively constant. We may reasonably infer that the opening quotient decreases as the aerodynamic and aerostatic forces $\mathbf{F}_{ab}$ and $\mathbf{F}_{as}$ increase with the increasing subglottal pressure. This would raise the sound pressure level, while the flow rate remained relatively constant. By contrast, Isshiki notes that in the falsetto register both the sound pressure level and the flow rate rise as the subglottal air pressure rises. We may reasonably infer that for the falsetto register the opening quotient does not decrease as the subglottal air pressure increases.

Isshiki's study shows how the lack of an explicit model of phonation can lead to inappropriate conclusions from data that were obtained by extremely well planned experimental procedures. Isshiki notes that in the chest register the opening quotient must decrease as the subglottal air pressure increases, since the flow rate does not change, though the intensity increases. He states that "It appears that in order to keep the glottis closed longer [smaller opening quotient], withstanding the increasing pressure below the glottis, greater force to close the glottis is required." We know that the Bernoulli force, which tends to close the glottis, increases as the subglottal air pressure increases (van den Berg, 1957; Timcke, von Leden, and Moore, 1958). Isshiki, however, neglects the Bernoulli force in his study. He seems to believe that the only force that can close the vocal cords is the tissue force ($\mathbf{F}_{tc}$ in Figure 2.5), and he therefore concludes that ". . . at very low pitch, intensity is controlled mainly by the larynx while at very high pitch [falsetto], the expiratory muscles may be more important in controlling intensity." That is, special laryngeal gestures always control intensity in the chest register. This conclusion does not follow from Isshiki's observations. Isshiki's observations seem to support the previous indirect observations of van den Berg, Müller and Timcke, Moore and von Leden, which suggest that the decrease in the opening quotient in the chest register may be a direct consequence of the increased subglottal air pressure. The lack of an explicit model for laryngeal activity in Isshiki's study obscures this relationship.

Both our qualitative model and experimental observations thus indicate that the opening quotient may decrease as a direct consequence of an increased subglottal air pressure without any adjustment of the laryngeal muscles. However, we do not want to imply that the laryngeal muscles cannot independently change the opening quotient. Our model, for example, indicates that the force with which the glottis closes will increase if the vocal cords are fully approximated in the phonation neutral position. The only component of the static tissue force that will act will be $\mathbf{F}_{tc}$, and the mean value of the Bernoulli force $\mathbf{F}_{ab}$ will also tend to be larger than it would be if the glottis were open in the phonation neutral position, since the Bernoulli force increases as the glottal opening decreases.

Several independent experimental studies have shown that the opening quotient can be independently adjusted by the laryngeal muscles. Van den Berg (1958), for example, demonstrated this effect in his studies with excised larynges. Mead, Proctor, and Bouhuys (1965), in experiments where the subglottal air pressure was monitored during phonation, observed that the sound pressure level sometimes increased, though the subglottal pressure remained constant or decreased. The opening quotient apparently changed by means of the activity of the laryngeal muscles. Katsuki (1950) in electromyographic studies on the vocalis muscle of hemilaryngectomized talkers found that increased action potentials were observed in that muscle as the intensity of the sound increased. Fink (1962) in an independent study obtained results that supported this finding. On the other hand, Faaborg-Andersen (1957) found no significant difference in the action potentials of the intrinsic laryngeal muscles as the intensity of the sound increased. These seemingly contradictory results are explicable in terms of our model, which predicts that the intensity of the speech signal radiated from the speaker's lips can be increased by means of adjustments of the laryngeal muscles which decrease the opening quotient, or by means of increases of the subglottal air pressure which also reduce the opening quotient. Both mechanisms probably act concurrently during normal phonation. High-speed motion pictures of the vocal cords, for example, show that phonation can occur at virtually any degree of vocal effort at almost any fundamental frequency (Farnsworth, 1940; Timcke, von Leden, and Moore, 1958; Moore and von Leden, 1958; von Leden and Moore, 1960; Soron and Lieberman, 1963). It therefore would not be surprising to discover many intermediate cases. Much of the past controversy on the number of vocal registers (van den Berg, 1960a)—chest, head, falsetto, etc.—may reflect these intermediate adjustments.

2.7 Summation—Laryngeal Activity

In short, the larynx consists of a number of cartilages, connected with muscles and ligaments, which by their relative positions change the tension, position, and effective vibrating mass of the vocal cords. The larynx can be considered as a mechanical system whose activity is regulated by comparatively slow changes in the tension of its muscular system. The mechanical damping factor of this system is established by the accelerating masses of the vocal cords, the tensions of the muscular system, the airflow resistance through the glottis, and the inelastic collision of the vocal cords. The acoustic output of the larynx is determined by the air pressure against the glottis and the muscular adjustments.

The theory of laryngeal activity that we have described has come to be known as the myoelastic-aerodynamic theory of phonation. The activity of the larynx is regulated by the slowly varying tensions of its muscular system and the aerodynamic forces that result from the motion of air through it. Other theories have been proposed at various times since Ferrein compared the vocal cords to vibrating strings in 1741. Recently Husson (1950, 1955, 1957) proposed a new theory, the neurochronaxic theory. Husson assumed that a train of neural pulses was transmitted from the brain to the laryngeal muscles and that the vocalis muscle opened and closed the glottis in synchronism with this pulse train *"coup par coup."* Husson's theory is not, however, consistent with the vast body of experimental evidence that we have regarding the activity of the larynx. Other investigators, moreover, have been unable to replicate the particular experiments on which Husson based his theory (van den Berg, 1954, 1958; Rubin 1960).

2.8 The Subglottal System and Respiration

The main function of the subglottal system is gas exchange: to transfer oxygen into and carbon dioxide out of the blood stream. The trachea extends from the larynx and divides into branches that supply each lung. The normal rate of breathing during quiet wakefulness is about 16 to 18 cycles per minute. Each expiration therefore lasts about 2 to 3 seconds.[6] A volume of about 500 cc (the tidal volume) is exchanged on each breath. An additional reserve of about 1500 cc (for an adult male) can also enter into the respiratory cycle (Landois, 1923).

The pattern of muscular activity during respiration is rather complex. During inspiration the inspiratory muscles essentially expand the volume of the lungs, and the subglottal air pressure P_s falls below atmospheric pressure. The inspiratory muscles have to overcome the elastic recoil forces that tend to collapse the lungs. During expiration the elastic recoil forces act on the lungs and expel air. The expiratory muscles can augment the elastic recoil force during expiration to expel air. The inspiratory muscles can also act during expiration to oppose the elastic recoil force and reduce the subglottal air pressure. The elastic recoil force is a function of the volume of the lungs. It is largest when the lungs are expanded to their maximum capacity (Agostoni and Mead, 1964). In the absence of phonation the inspiratory and expiratory phases of phonation are nearly equal in their time and flow patterns. During rest inspiration takes slightly less than half the cycle. During moderately heavy exercise the two phases are more nearly equal. Mead and Agostoni (1964) state that ". . . the inspiratory muscles continue to act well into the expiratory

[6] It is interesting to note that the duration of a normal sentence usually does not exceed 2 seconds, which matches this ventilation rate.

phase, opposing the static recoil of the lungs and chest wall and, as it were, letting the system down gently." In Figure 2.7 the volume of the air in the lungs and the air pressure in the lungs are presented during spontaneous breathing at rest (cf. Mead and Agostoni, 1964, p. 422). Since most of the pressure drop in the respiratory system takes place at the larynx (Proctor, 1964; Negus, 1949), the subglottal air pressure P_s also gradually rises and falls as the volume of air in the lungs rises and falls.

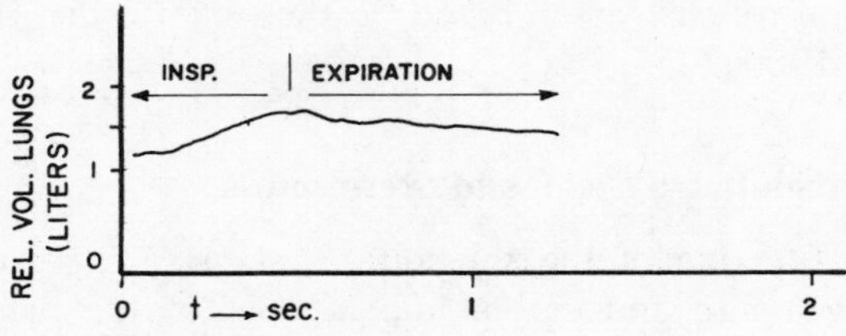

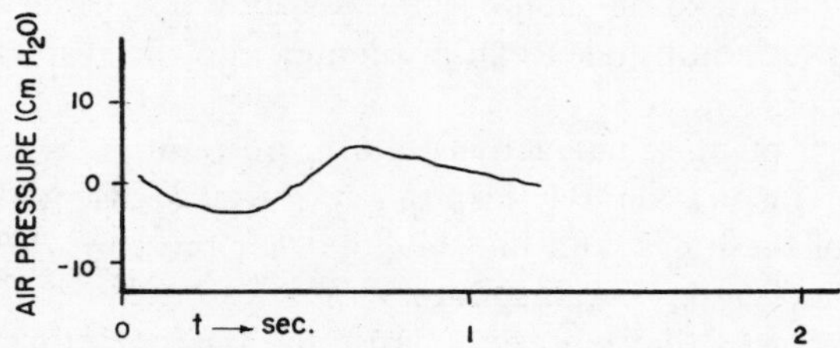

Figure 2.7 Subglottal air pressure in cm H_2O and relative volume of air in the lungs in liters during quiet respiratory activity.
Note that the inspiratory and expiratory phases have nearly the same duration.

During phonation there are several deviations from the pattern of activity characteristic of quiet nonspeech activity. The duration of a single expiration may be extended to as much as 40 seconds by using the reserve air capacity and by husbanding air (Meader and Muyskens, 1962). The average rate of breathing may decrease to 8 expiratory-inspiratory cycles per minute, and inspiration may occur in a far shorter interval of time relative to the time taken up in expiration. Lenneberg (1964) notes that inspiration may be reduced to 0.15 of the total breath cycle. In Figure 2.8 the volume of air in the lungs and the subglottal air pressure have been plotted for a male talker who was reading the sentence "Joe ate his soup." [7] Note that the subglottal air pressure curve does not gradually fall. The subglottal air pressure instead remains relatively steady until the end of the expiration, where it abruptly falls. The inspiratory muscles are innervated to oppose the elastic recoil force when the lungs are full of air, and they gradually lessen their activity as the volume of air in the lungs decreases so that a relatively constant subglottal air pressure is maintained (Bouhuys, Procter, and Mead, 1966). The expiratory muscles are brought into play when the volume of air in

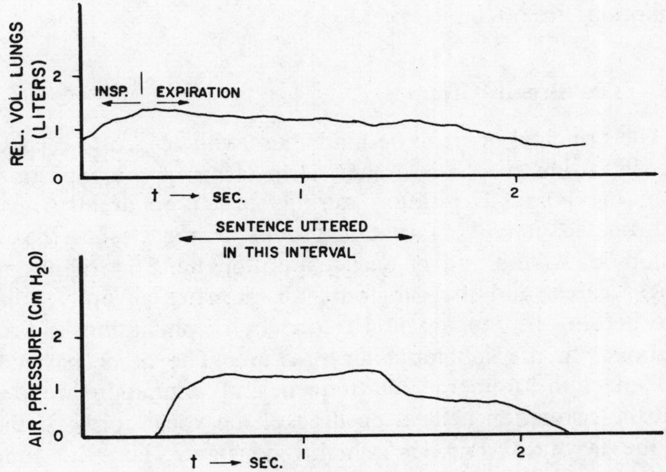

Figure 2.8 Relative volume of air in the lungs in liters and subglottal air pressure in cm H_2O during the production of speech.
The same speaker uttered a short declarative sentence soon after he registered the activity plotted in Figure 2.7. Note that the duration of the inspiratory phase is relatively short compared to the duration of the expiratory phase.

the lungs falls to the point where the elastic recoil force alone is insufficient to maintain the desired subglottal air pressure. A relatively constant subglottal air pressure can thus be maintained by bringing different muscles into play as the volume of air in the lungs decreases. During singing and when unemphatic, short declarative sentences are spoken, a steady subglottal air pressure is usually maintained until the end of the expiration, when the subglottal air pressure abruptly drops. The subglottal air pressure has to fall abruptly at the end of the expiration since the air pressure in the lungs must be below atmospheric pressure during inspiration.

[7] The procedure used to obtain these data is discussed in Chapter 4.

Momentary peaks in the subglottal air pressure occur during speech, and it is possible to associate these peaks with phonetic prominence.[8] It is, however, impossible to attribute these peaks to the activity of specific respiratory muscles without knowing the volume of air in the speaker's lungs. Stetson (1951) formulated a simple model of respiratory activity in which he assumed that the mean subglottal air pressure that is maintained throughout expiration is due to the activity of the abdominal muscles while the internal intercostal muscles produced additional separate pulses of air for each syllable. Stetson's model is, however, misleading, and its detailed assumptions are often incorrect.[9]

2.9 The Breath-Group

The principal point to be made here with regard to respiration and speech is that speech is organized in terms of the expiratory airflow from the lungs. Expiration during speech apparently involves the coordinated activity of several groups of muscles in the chest and abdomen. At the end of each expiration the flow of air out of the lungs ceases, and the subglottal air pressure abruptly falls. As we said before, the fundamental frequency of phonation is directly proportional to the subglottal air pressure. The other parameters that can affect the fundamental frequency of phonation are the tension and the phonation neutral position of the vocal cords. If the tension of the laryngeal muscles remains constant, then the fundamental frequency of phonation will fall at the end of the expiration.

It is a universal of human speech that, except for certain predictable cases, the fundamental frequency of phonation and the acoustic amplitude fall at the end of a sentence. The physiological basis of this phenomenon may be a condition of least articulatory control. If the tension of the laryngeal muscles is not deliberately increased at the end of expiration when the subglottal air pressure falls, the fundamental frequency of phonation will also fall. One can see that, in some sense, less "effort" is expended in the articulatory control problem if the laryngeal tension is not deliberately increased precisely when the subglottal air pressure falls. The speaker simply maintains about the same laryngeal tension throughout the entire expiration. He does not bother to increase the laryngeal tension to counter the

[8] The analysis of phonetic prominence and linguistic stress will be presented, in detail, in later chapters.

[9] See Chapter 9 for a discussion of Stetson's *Motor Phonetics*.

falling subglottal air pressure. This pattern of articulatory activity thus produces a prosodic pattern that is characteristic of the ones that are used to delimit the boundaries of unemphatic, declarative sentences in normal speech. We shall term this pattern of articulatory activity the "archetypal normal breath-group."

We shall show in Chapter 4 that other articulatory maneuvers are used by adult speakers to produce breath-groups that are acoustically or perceptually similar to the prosodic patterns that result from the archetypal articulatory maneuvers. Adult speakers, for example, can produce a breath-group where the subglottal air pressure function is similar to the archetypal pattern, though the speaker does not actually pause for inspiration at the end of the breath-group. Our data, however, indicate that the adult speakers generally do produce breath-groups on a single expiration (about 90 percent of the time). The data in Chapter 4, moreover, show that adult listeners perceive intonational signals[10] as though they had been produced by means of the primary or archetypal articulatory gestures. We shall use the term "breath-group" to encompass all the intonational signals that are acoustically or perceptually equivalent to the archetypal breath-groups.

Individual languages are undoubtedly characterized by specific coordinated patterns of activity involving the laryngeal and chest muscles in the production of "typical" breath-groups. In American English, for example, the tension of the laryngeal muscles in the basic, "least effort," normal breath-group appears to be constant throughout the entire breath-group. There is a fairly general agreement among most American linguists (e.g., Pike, 1945; Trager and Smith, 1951; Stockwell, 1962) that the basic intonation contour of American English should be transcribed as [231#] in the "phonemic" notation developed by these linguists. The fundamental frequency of the vibrating vocal cords appears to be a function of the subglottal air pressure and rises from a medium pitch to a higher pitch at the stress peak (which occurs at the peak subglottal air pressure) and then falls as the subglottal air pressure falls at the end of the utterance.[11]

On the other hand, these American linguists transcribed the basic British English (received pronunciation) intonation contour as

[10] We shall discuss some of the perceptual constraints that may motivate the perceptual recognition routine in Section 2.10.

[11] Detailed data on American English breath-groups will be presented in Chapter 4.

[331#]. This is said to be one of the reasons why these linguists feel that pitch and stress are completely independent.[12] What seems to be happening in British English is that at the start of each breath-group the laryngeal muscles are tensioned and then gradually relaxed in the course of the breath-group. The initial high pitch of the British English breath-group may be due to laryngeal muscle tension that is relaxed as the subglottal pressure builds up so that the high pitch is maintained through the middle of the breath-group. At the end of the breath-group both the laryngeal muscle tension and the subglottal air pressure have diminished, which results in a low pitch. Daniel Jones (1932) and most of the British phoneticians who recognize that stress and pitch are interrelated transcribe the American English contour as a monotone modulated by stress and British contour as a falling pitch contour modulated by stress.[13] This transcription seems to correspond to the lay opinion, which regards British English as having more inflection. The lay opinion has always bothered instrumental investigators who have correctly noted that the pitch range of British and American English is about the same. However, in terms of the necessary laryngeal muscular control American English may have less variation.[14]

We are, in essence, hypothesizing the existence of a normal synchronized pattern of activity involving the respiratory and laryngeal muscles which forms a basic breath-group that characterizes the intonation of a language.[15] This hypothesis is supported by the experimental evidence that has so far been obtained for the activity of the laryngeal and respiratory muscles. It is also supported by virtually all linguistic analyses of British English and American English (and to a lesser degree French, Thai, German, and Swedish). These analyses (cf. Chapter 9) invariably note that particular intonation patterns constantly recur and form the main part of the experimental corpus. The Tune I–Tune II system of Jones and Armstrong and

[12] Most of these linguists, however, admit that intonation and stress interact. Martin Joos (1962), for example, has noted that during World War II he was able to get satisfactory intonation from a Vocoder synthesizer about 90 percent of the time by having the pitch generator follow the amplitude of the acoustic signal. Where the amplitude increased, the pitch went up.

[13] The English "tune" analyses of intonation are discussed in Chapter 9.

[14] The normal breath-group of Russian may also be similar to the American English breath-group. According to Revtova (1965), the intonation of declarative sentences is similar in these languages.

[15] This pattern of activity obviously must be synchronized with the activity of the supraglottal vocal tract. The speaker, for example, must manipulate his lips to produce the sound /p/ when air is flowing out of the lungs. The breath-group must be coordinated with the segmental phonemes. Different languages may also differ with respect to the details of this coordination.

Ward, in particular, supports this hypothesis. We shall see how intonation can have certain linguistic functions that are realized acoustically by the use of this basic breath-group and simple modifications of it.

The presence of a basic synchronization between the laryngeal muscles and the chest muscles[16] to form a basic intonation contour for a language, of course, explains how children acquire a "native accent" so quickly. In the next chapter we shall take up the question of the early development of speech in infants, which illustrates both the relation of the prosodic features to emotion and the acquisition and function of the normal breath-group.

2.10 The Effects of the Supraglottal Respiratory System and Perception

The output of the larynx is, of course, filtered by the upper respiratory system. The final speech signal is thus determined, in part, by the transfer function of the upper respiratory system. This means that changes in the glottal volume velocity waveform may be drastically modified so that they are not directly apparent in the speech waveform. The amplitude of the volume velocity waveform, may, for example, momentarily increase because the subglottal air pressure suddenly increased. However, the amplitude of the speech waveform may *not* increase because the vocal tract configuration has changed from the vowel /a/ to the glide /y/. The transfer function of the compact vowel /a/ (cf. Jakobson, Fant, and Halle, 1952) results in a higher amplitude in the speech waveform even though the volume velocity waveform that excited the /a/ had a lower amplitude than the volume velocity waveform that excited the /y/. The listener must consider the transfer functions of the /a/ and the /y/ in order to assess the relative amplitudes of the volume velocity function.

We have observed that an increase in the subglottal air pressure can result in a glottal output that has a higher fundamental frequency. The perception of fundamental frequency is not adversely affected by the effects of the supraglottal respiratory system. When listeners are asked to match the pitch of a sustained vowel to the fundamental frequency of a sinusoid, they are capable of making very fine frequency discriminations. Flanagan and Saslow (1958) found that the

[16] On the neurological level there is evidence of a direct pathway between the laryngeal and chest muscles which perhaps facilitates this synchronization (Lenneberg, 1964). However, the absence of such a pathway would not mean that synchronization was not possible.

dl, or difference limen, for fundamental frequency was actually finer for synthesized vowels than it was for pure tones. Fundamental frequency may thus be a more consistent acoustic correlate than amplitude for changes in the subglottal air pressure.

Acoustical analyses directed at isolating the acoustic correlates of stressed syllables that have phonetic prominence in American English (Lieberman, 1960) and Swedish (Hadding-Koch, 1961) show that increases in amplitude, fundamental frequency, and duration are all cues to the perception of stressed syllables. The positive correlation between fundamental frequency and acoustic amplitude follows directly from the functional relationship between increases in the subglottal air pressure and the frequency at which the vocal cords vibrate.

Perceptual studies of phonetic prominence by Fry (1955, 1958) and Bolinger (1958), in which listeners heard synthesized vowel-like sounds, show that duration, amplitude, and fundamental frequency are all acoustic correlates of perceived phonetic prominence in English. However, in languages like Czech or Estonian, where length is an operant phonologic feature, duration is not an acoustic correlate of prominence.[17]

The increase in the durations of stressed syllables in languages where length is not a phonologic feature may follow from a match to the limitations of auditory perception.[18] A number of psychoacoustic experimenters, such as Lifshitz (1933, 1935) and Creelman (1963), have noted that under some conditions a listener's judgments regarding the loudness of clicks or short sinusoidal signals may depend on the durations of the signals as well as the intensity of the signals. If a listener hears two signals that have the same intensity, he will judge the longer signal to be the louder one. Integral relationships hold for sinusoidal signals that are shorter than 700 msec. If a listener hears two signals that have different intensities and durations, he will judge the signal having the smaller intensity to be louder if its duration is sufficiently longer.

Stevens, Sandel, and House (1962) also reported similar effects when using two component noise bursts. The results of this last ex-

[17] Personal communication from Professor Roman Jakobson.

[18] Traditional phonetic analyses make a distinction between stress-timed and rhythm-timed languages (e.g., *Principles of International Phonetic Alphabet,* 1949). In English, which is a stressed-timed language, stressed syllables are not supposed to occur faster than a certain maximum rate. An acoustic "refractory period" perhaps exists. After a heavy stress a certain minimum time would have to elapse before the next heavy stress. This might result in stressed syllables being longer in order to allow the air pressure to build up again. However, no quantitative experimental evidence has been as yet presented which would support this speculation.

periment, moreover, indicate that the context of a stimulus strongly affects its perception. The presence of a second signal in close proximity to a first signal strongly influences the perception of the first signal, and vice versa. The point is that one cannot analyze the intonational signal in terms of "simple" components of amplitude, duration, and fundamental frequency and expect to find that these "simple" components can always be independently perceived.[19]

The relationship of specific articulatory gestures to specific "simple" parameters of the speech signal is quite complex. As we have said before, changes in the subglottal air pressure can change the fundamental frequency, amplitude, and opening quotient of the glottal volume velocity waveform. Changes in the tension of the laryngeal muscles can also modify the opening quotient, amplitude, and fundamental frequency of the glottal volume velocity waveform. Thus it is often impossible to ascertain whether an increase in the fundamental frequency or the amplitude of the acoustic waveform radiated from the speaker's lips was caused by an increase in the subglottal air pressure or by a change in the tension of the speaker's laryngeal muscles. The acoustic correlates of these two articulatory gestures overlap. In Chapter 4 we shall present experimental data indicating that intonation patterns are "decoded" by listeners in terms of an archetypal pattern. The listener "decodes" the intonation pattern as though it had been produced by means of either a "normal breath-group" or a "marked breath-group" and an additional segmental distinctive feature,[20] prominence $[+P_s]$, which corresponds on the articulatory level to a momentary increase in subglottal air pressure on a vowel.[21] The marked breath-group $[+BG]$ is differentiated from the normal, unmarked breath-group $[-BG]$ at the articulatory level by the presence of an increase in the tension of the laryngeal muscles at only one point in the breath-group, its end where the subglottal air pressure falls. The marked breath-group $[+BG]$ in a sense represents

[19] Jakobson and Halle (1956) point out that "Languages where both length and stress appear as distinctive features are quite exceptional. . . ." This constraint may reflect the integrating properties of the auditory system which relate intensity and duration at the perceptual level (though both can obviously be independently perceived outside of the range of the integrating effects). In Estonian, for example, where the length of a consonant or vowel is significant, the distribution of stress is quite restricted. The first syllable of a word is always stressed. The listener could thus interpret all other perceived durations (which might sometimes reflect the intensity of the speech signal as well as the duration of the segment) as manifestations of the feature *length*.

[20] For a discussion of distinctive features see Jakobson, Fant, and Halle (1952).

[21] These comments, of course, are relevant only for languages where these features occur. Different languages have different recognition routines.

the simplest contrast that can be consistently made in terms of the unmarked, normal breath-group.

Particular languages are characterized, in part, by modifications of the laryngeal tension function in the nonterminal parts of the breath-group, for example, whether the laryngeal tension is relatively constant or whether it falls throughout the breath-group. Additional phonologic features that interact with the breath-group at the acoustic and articulatory levels may also occur in different languages. In American English our data show that fundamental frequency prominences that occur in the nonterminal parts of the breath-group are interpreted as though they were produced by the segmental feature [$+P_s$]. In Chinese some of the fundamental frequency variations apparently seem to be interpreted as the acoustic manifestations of segmental "tone" features. The presence of these segmental features may affect the fundamental frequency function of the entire breath-group. However, the terminal fundamental frequency contour of the breath-group always is the acoustic correlate of the suprasegmental breath-group. Though the listener must consider the fundamental frequency contour in the nonterminal parts of the breath-group to deduce whether the breath-group is marked (+) or unmarked (−), the articulatory maneuvers that take place in the terminal part of the breath-group determine whether it is marked or unmarked.

The main point to be emphasized here is that the recognition routine based on a fixed archetypal articulatory pattern results in a unique "analysis by synthesis," [22] that is, an analysis in terms of the articulatory gestures that are permissible in a language, even though the acoustic signal being analyzed could have been produced by several different patterns of articulatory activity.

2.11 Secondary Effects

In the preceding discussion of the activity of the larynx we have tacitly assumed that its output can be determined without reference to the rest of the respiratory system if the subglottal air pressure is

[22] "Analysis by synthesis" is discussed by Halle and Stevens (1959), and by Stevens (1960) and Stevens and Halle (1964) with regard to speech perception in general. Liberman and his colleagues at Haskins Laboratories (Liberman, Cooper, Harris, and MacNeilage, 1963) have explicitly formulated a "motor theory of perception" for the segmental phonemes in which phonemes are perceived or "computed," in part, by reference to the motor features of speech. We shall discuss models for speech production and perception in more detail in Chapter 8.

specified. This assumption is, for a first approximation, correct. However, the larynx is coupled to the rest of the respiratory system through both aerodynamic and mechanical effects.

2.11.1 Interactions with the Subglottal System. We have noted that the aerostatic and aerodynamic forces that act on the vocal cords ($\mathbf{F}_{as}$ and $\mathbf{F}_{ab}$ in Figure 2.5) are functions of the subglottal air pressure. Under most conditions the subglottal air pressure varies less than 5 percent of its mean value within the duration of each glottal vibratory cycle (van den Berg, 1956). The subglottal system has certain resonant frequencies. Van den Berg has noted that the subglottal air pressure fluctuates rather markedly during each glottal cycle when a resonance at approximately 300 cps is excited (van den Berg, 1957, 1960*b*).

In Figure 2.9 the cumulative distribution of the durations of the fundamental period has been plotted for several normal male speakers reading the sentence "Joe took father's shoe bench out" as a statement, a question, and a confidential communication. The abscissa is a scale of fundamental periods in milliseconds, and the ordinate shows the percentage of fundamental periods that are less than the abscissa value. Thus 30 percent of speaker 2's fundamental periods had durations less than or equal to 6.6 msec. Note that the plateau in this distribution centered at 7.5 msec. Phonation seldom occurred at fundamental periods of 7.0 to 7.5 msec in this sample.

Speakers 4, 1, and 2 all had plateaus in their cumulative distribution at about 7 msec. Speaker 3's distribution is typical of most speakers with high-pitched voices. The lowest fundamental frequency that his larynx produced is about 150 cps. Speaker 4's distribution is typical of many speakers with low-pitched voices. Note that his highest fundamental frequency is also 150 cps. All of this information is for phonation in the subjects' normal speaking voices. They did not use their falsetto registers when they read the test material. This discontinuity at approximately 150 cps has been noted to a greater or lesser degree for more than 60 speakers, who often read the test sentences with different intonations (Lieberman, 1963*b*). The speakers apparently avoided phonation at fundamental frequencies that would excite the 300-cps subglottal resonance. It is probably difficult to produce a normal glottal output when the subglottal pressure varies during each vibratory cycle. Johannes Müller, for example, performed experiments in which he coupled a "subglottal" resonator to the vibrating excised larynx. He noted that at certain fundamental frequencies, "the note was not so perfect" (Müller, 1848, p. 1020). Trendelenburg

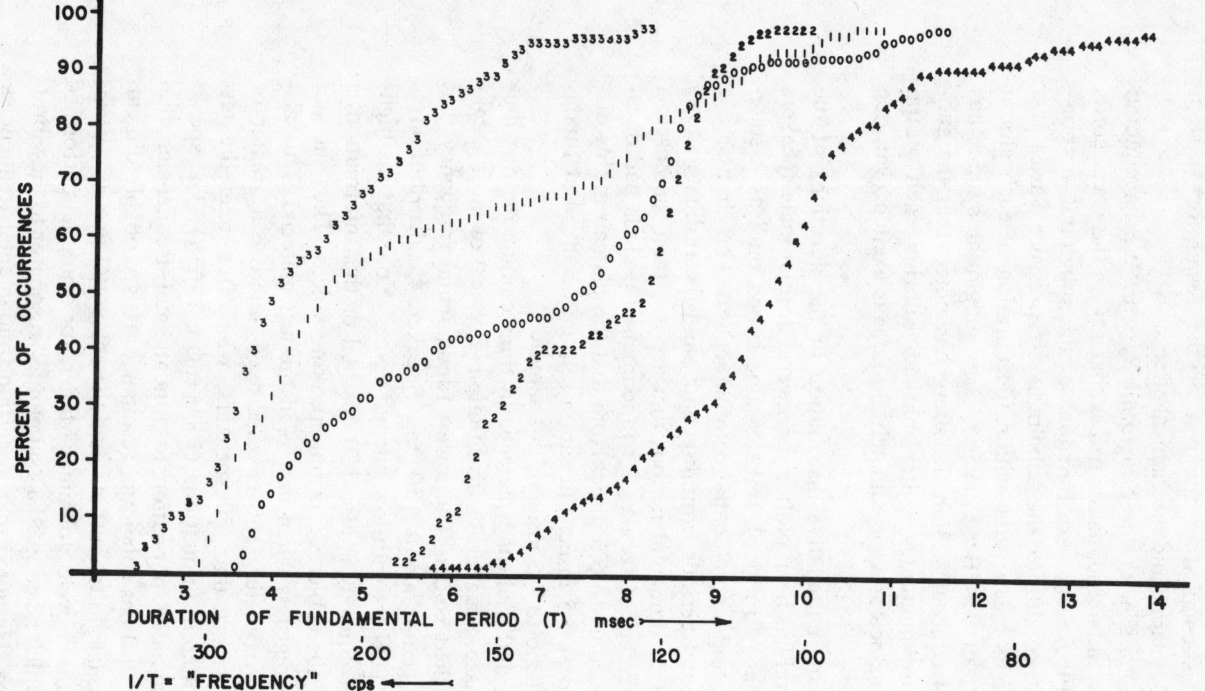

Figure 2.9 Cumulative distributions of fundamental periods for five adult male talkers.
The durations of the periods are plotted on the abscissa in milliseconds. The percentage of each talker's fundamental periods that is less than or equal to a particular value is plotted on the ordinate. Thus 30 percent of speaker 2's periods had durations of less than or equal to 6.6 msec. Note that phonation seldom occurred at fundamental periods of 7.0 to 7.5 msec duration (the plateau in the curves). This effect is probably due to the interaction of the 150-cps resonance of the subglottal respiratory system with the vibration of the vocal cords.

(1942) observed similar effects when he coupled long resonators to the mouth during normal phonation, which caused the pharyngeal pressure to fluctuate during each glottal cycle. The excited sound "broke" when the fundamental frequency excited the modified superglottal resonance.

Risberg (1961) and Hadding-Koch (1961) have noted similar effects for spoken Swedish. Normal speakers tend to avoid phonation at certain fundamental frequencies that seem to correspond to the resonances of the subglottal system. The so-called "phonemic" pitch levels described by Pike, Wells, Trager and Smith, and others (cf. Chapter 8) may merely reflect the phonetic effect of the discontinuities caused by the coupling of the subglottal system to the larynx. Hadding-Koch's results[23] are particularly suggestive, as she was trying to find acoustic correlates of these "phonemic" pitch levels.

2.11.2 Interactions with the Supraglottal System. Let us again return to Figure 2.7 and consider the energy relationships of the airflow. If the velocity of the air in the pharynx is relatively small compared with its velocity in the glottal constriction, the kinetic energy of the air in the pharynx and the trachea may be neglected. If we again assume that the distribution of velocity over the glottal oriface is uniform and that there is no viscous dissipation, the kinetic energy of the air in the glottis per unit volume is developed by the pressure difference $(P_s - P_o)$, and is

$$\rho \frac{V^2}{2} = P_s - P_o$$

(cf. Flanagan, 1958).

The pharyngeal air pressure P_o is atmospheric for open articulations, such as vowels, liquids, and some voiced continuant consonants. The pharyngeal air pressure, however, rises when the vocal tract is obstructed (Stetson, 1951; Jakobson, Fant, and Halle, 1952). In the limiting case the pharyngeal air pressure is equal to the subglottal

[23] Hadding-Koch measured the extreme fundamental frequencies of sentences that she had transcribed with the Trager-Smith system. She found that these frequencies clustered into two groups (which usually centered about 150 cps) that corresponded to the pitch levels. Pitch levels 1 and 2 might fall into the low group for a particular speaker. A different speaker might have only pitch level 1 in the low group and levels 2, 3, and 4 in the high group. The groups were also more distinct for heavily stressed vowels. This follows from the subglottal interaction theory because the glottal waveform would have more energy with increased vocal effort at 300 cps when the fundamental frequency was at 150 cps. The subglottal resonance would therefore tend to be excited to a greater degree with increased vocal effort, and phonation at 150 cps would not occur very often. The plot of the speaker's fundamental frequencies would therefore show two peaks.

air pressure when the vocal tract is completely closed.[24] The airflow under these limiting conditions, of course, ceases. For less extreme, momentary closures or for partial obstructions the pressure difference $(P_s - P_o)$ decreases, and thus the velocity of the airflow also decreases. The pressure in the glottis increases since $\frac{1}{2}\rho V^2 + P =$ Constant. The Bernoulli force that sucks the vocal cords together therefore decreases.

Measurements of the fundamental frequency of speech show that "pitch perturbations," or sudden fluctuations in the fundamental periodicity of the signal, occur quite frequently (Lieberman, 1961). The pitch perturbations are not randomly determined, and they usually are concommitant with the production of voiced stops and the onset and end of phonation (where the subglottal air pressure and the accelerating masses are changing). High-speed motion pictures (Soron and Lieberman, 1963) of the vocal cords, for example, show that large variations in fundamental periodicity occur at the end of phonation, as the arytenoid cartilages, which support the vocal cords, swing open.

Pitch perturbations are apparently essential cues for natural speech quality. When speech is synthesized electronically, these pitch perturbations must be preserved. If the pitch perturbations are removed, leaving only smooth pitch contours, listeners report that the synthesized speech has a "mechanical" quality (Cooper, Peterson, and Fahringer, 1957; Kersta, Bricker, and David, 1960). They also appear to play some role in transmitting the "emotional" quality of the talker's voice (Lieberman, 1961; Lieberman and Michaels, 1962). The hoarse vocal quality associated with certain types of pathologic larynges in which tumors or polyps occur on the vocal cords results, in part, from larger pitch perturbations. The pathologic masses on the vocal cords lower the mechanical damping factor of the larynx, making its acoustic output more sensitive to air pressure transients (Lieberman, 1963*a*). The pitch perturbations are superimposed upon the fundamental frequency contour of the utterance. Though the pitch perturbations thus seem to be relevant in communications systems for the preservation of natural vocal quality, speaker identification, and emotion, they do not appear to be the primary acoustic correlates of any linguistic information, and we shall, for the most part, tacitly ignore their presence in our discussion of intonation.

2.11.3 Mechanical Coupling. The larynx is, of course, connected

[24] In the absence of compensating articulatory gestures that increase the air volume of the supraglottal system. The larynx may, for example, descend (Trubetzkoy, 1939) or the pharynx may distend (Perkell, 1965).

to the rest of the human body. There exists the possibility that movements of other parts of the body will mechanically interact with the larynx to change the tension and the rest position of the vocal cords. Sonninen (1956), for example, believes that phonation can be influenced by a great number of extralaryngeal muscles, such as the pharyngeal muscles, the palatal muscles, the suprahyoids, and sternohyoids. As Proctor (1964) points out, this is undoubtedly true to a certain extent. However, the primary control of the larynx rests in the laryngeal muscles. A trained singer can, for example, control the quality of his phonation in virtually any posture.

Some of the movements of the larynx that are effected by means of the extralaryngeal muscles may, however, have a linguistic function. The larynx can move about 2 or 3 cm vertically in relation to the jaw. Of course, when it moves upward, it reduces the length of the supraglottal respiratory system. The formant frequencies that characterize specific vowels and consonants will therefore transpose to higher frequencies since the formant resonances are functions of the length and configuration of supraglottal vocal tract.

The larynx typically rises at the onset of phonation and descends at the end of phonation. These vertical laryngeal movements may be distinctive features in some languages, for example, the "imploded" and "exploded" stops cited by Trubetzkoy (1939). The mechanism that effects these adjustments is still a matter for speculation. The vertical movement may be caused by the static subglottal air pressure pushing against the larynx, or it may be the result of a deliberate muscular adjustment that pulls up on the hangers from the hyoid bone. The descent of the larynx can maintain a transglottal air pressure drop ($P_s - P_o$) when the upper respiratory system is obstructed and therefore may be a way of maintaining voicing during some stop sounds. However, there is relatively little information available that is relevant to these gestures, and, as with most aspects of laryngeal activity, further study is necessary.

3 Intonation in Infant Speech

In this chapter we shall examine some aspects of intonation in relation to the early development of speech in children. We shall present two main hypotheses: first, that there is an innate physiologic basis for the "shape" of the normal breath-group that seems to occur in so many languages; and second, that the chief function of the normal breath-group is to segment the speech signal into sentences. We shall make several assumptions in connection with these hypotheses which seem reasonable, and we shall present observations that support both these assumptions and the main hypotheses. The data and discussion that are presented in the following chapters are also relevant to these hypotheses; we are not merely resting our case on the observations that we shall discuss in this chapter. We want to demonstrate that the linguistic use of intonation reflects an innately determined and highly organized system rather than a set of unrelated facts that are fortuitously similar in many languages. We shall also briefly review some other aspects of the acquisition of language by children insofar as they explicate the line of reasoning that we wish to follow.

3.1 Some Observations of Adult Intonation

Although relevant phonetic or instrumental analyses are not available at present for most languages, it is possible to generalize about intonation to the extent of stating that short declarative sentences usually end with a falling fundamental frequency contour. Detailed instrumental analyses by Jones (1909), Chiba (1935), Fonagy (1958), Hadding-Koch (1961), and Abramson (1962), for example, show that this is the case for English, Spanish, French, Finnish, Hungarian, Italian, Thai, Japanese, Swedish, and German. Perceptual phonetic studies, when they note the intonation pattern of a language, also indicate that the intonation pattern associated with normal declarative sentences is characterized by a falling intonation contour at the end of the sentence. For the most part, phonetic studies rarely make any comments about the falling fundamental frequency contour that occurs at the end of a sentence, perhaps because the effect is so commonplace an occurrence that it does not warrant any special attention.

The normal breath-group, as we noted in Chapter 2, is a synchronized standard pattern of activity wherein the respiratory and laryngeal muscles act to produce phonation on the flow of expiratory air. The normal breath-groups of all languages are similar in that they end with a falling fundamental frequency contour.

Languages differ, in part, in that they have different normal breath-groups and allow different admissible modifications of their normal breath-groups. The normal breath-group of Swedish is, for example, different from the normal breath-group of American English. Different deviations from the normal breath-group are admissible in Swedish and American English. In Chapter 4 we shall present experimental evidence indicating that an identical signal may be interpreted differently by native speakers of Swedish and American English because both groups interpret the signal in terms of the different patterns of muscular activity that are admissible in their native languages. For the moment, however, let us return to the central issue of this chapter, which is the common element of all these normal breath-groups. We shall try to show that our first hypothesis accounts for the fall in fundamental frequency that always occurs at the end of the normal breath-group.

3.2 The Acquisition of Language by Children

We shall begin by discussing some other aspects of the acquisition of language by children which demonstrate the argument that we want to follow. Jakobson (1942) pointed out that the acquisition of speech by children is of interest to linguistics and psychology since it may reflect the structure of their innate linguistic competence.[1] Jakobson identified two phases of speech development. The "babbling" stage, in which the infant simply exercises his vocal apparatus and makes sounds for the sake of making sounds, occurs first. The infant probably makes every sound that he possibly can in this stage whether or not it occurs in the adult speech that he hears. The adult speech that he hears may even have little to do with the form of his babbling. Deaf children, for example, babble quite normally for the first six or seven months of their life. The second stage in the development of speech often begins with a period of comparative silence when the child is from one to two years old. The child then begins to use speech sounds in a meaningful way, and he employs the distinctions that are operant in the adult speech that he hears.

Jakobson points out that the distinctions most frequently occurring for all the languages of the world are the distinctions that the child first learns to use meaningfully. The order in which children learn to make meaningful speech distinctions thus mirrors the hierarchy of these features. The first distinctions are the most basic ones. Jakobson and Halle (1956) describe the process as follows:

> Ordinarily child language begins . . . with . . . the "labial stage." In this phase speakers are capable of only one type of utterance, which is usually transcribed as /pa/. From the articulatory point of view the two constituents of this utterance represent polar configurations of the vocal tract; in /p/ the tract is closed at its very end while in /a/ it is opened as widely as possible at the front and narrowed toward the back. . . . This combination of two extremes is also present at the acoustic level: the labial stop represents a momentary burst of sound without any great concentration of energy in a particular frequency band, whereas for the vowel /a/ there is no strict limitation of time, and the energy is concentrated in a relatively narrow region of maximum aural sensitivity [p. 37]. . . . the infant preserves for a time a constant syllable scheme and splits both constituents of this syllable, first the consonant and later the vowel, into distinctive alternatives.
>
> Most frequently, the oral stop, utilizing a single closed tract, obtains a counterpart in the nasal consonant. . . .

[1] Occasionally one finds statements that seem to imply that language is some accidental phenomenon—that it has no innate basis. The usual "evidence" is the statement that no part of the speech-generating apparatus is adapted exclusively for the production of speech as the heart, for example, is adapted to pumping blood. Therefore, so goes the argument, language is an "accidental" acquired facility. Quite aside from the preoccupation of this argument with the output devices—no one discusses the brain—the supposed data are erroneous. The results of studies in the comparative anatomy of the respiratory system, for example, of Negus (1949), demonstrate that in man the glottis has developed "for purposes of phonation . . ." (p. 40).

The opposition of nasal and oral consonant, which belongs to the earliest acquisitions of the child, is ordinarily the most resistant consonantal opposition in aphasia and it occurs in all the languages of the world except for some Amercan Indian languages [p. 38].

Although every child develops differently, Jakobson's observations appear to reflect the general trend of speech development in children. Leopold (1953), for example, states that "the speed and time of sound acquisition varies enormously between different children; but the sequence in categories and the relative chronology are always and everywhere the same, at least in great outlines."

Now the first "meaningful" element of speech behavior that can be observed in children actually occurs much earlier than from one to two years of age. In the very first months of life, during the babbling stage, and indeed during the very first minutes of life children employ "meaningful" intonational signals. The cries are at first meaningful only in that they have a physiological reference. We believe that these signals, which appear to be innately determined, provide the basis for the linguistic function of intonation in adult speech.

3.3 Infant Cries

Although human infants are speechless, they communicate by means of sound from the moment of birth onward. While other sounds, such as flatulence, coughs, sneezes, and squeaks, occur, the most characteristic sound of the newborn is the cry (Kurtz, 1963). The infant cry has a characteristic pattern. The pattern is apparently innately determined and is a characteristic human attribute. Mongoloid infants, for example, often lack these characteristic cries (Karelitz), and deviations from the normal pattern often signal other neurological abnormalities (Rubinstein, 1964). The infant cry has a rising-falling fundamental frequency contour. The duration of the cry is usually from one to two seconds, and the fundamental frequency initially rises. The fundamental frequency then remains relatively steady or gradually falls until the end of the cry, when it typically falls at a faster rate (Ostwald, 1963).

As Ostwald [2] points out, the infant cry is an attention-getting device. He notes that "One can now appreciate why a parent must interfere with the baby's crying: this sound is too annoying to be tolerated beyond a short period of time . . . a cry cries to be turned off!" As the infant matures, the vocalizations differentiate, and various types

[2] Ostwald reported that the peak sound pressure level at a distance of 10 inches ranged from 83 to 85 db. Peak energy occurred at 1400 cps.

of cries occur. Two types of cries can even be differentiated at birth: the "normal" cry and the "scream." The "scream," which occurs when the infant is excited, has been described as an extremely loud cry in which the vocalization becomes atonal as it rises to its peak fundamental frequency (Kurtz, *op. cit.*)

In contrast to the cry, infants produce other sounds, such as the gurgle noted by Kurtz, which do not induce adults to minister to them. Infants soon begin to babble. Irwin (1947) noted the start of babbling as the infant uttered /ae/-like sounds during the first few days of its life. The playful sounds of infants in general are quieter, they are not as shrill, and the perceived pitch often does not abruptly fall at the end of phonation[3] (Kurtz, *op. cit.;* Ostwald, *op. cit.;* Rubinstein, *op. cit.*). There thus seems to be a dichotomy between vocalizations that have an immediate physiologic reference—that can be satisfied by the attention of an adult—and the vocalizations that do not seek immediate attention.

The child, from the moment of birth, thus seems to have a referential cry that represents, in Darwin's[4] terms (1872, p. 348), "the direct action of the excited nervous system on the body, independently of will, and independently in large part, of habit." We shall try to show that the infant's hypothetical innate referential breath-group furnishes the basis for the universal acoustic properties of the normal breath-group that is used to segment speech into sentences in so many languages.

3.4 A Hypothetical Innate Referential Breath-Group

Let us first consider the articulatory gestures that might characterize the hypothetical innate referential breath-group. We must make certain assumptions about the control of the laryngeal and respiratory muscles during the production of this hypothetical referential breath-group. We shall try to avoid making any assumptions that do not seem warranted by the available physiologic and acoustic evidence. Where physiologic evidence is lacking, we shall assume that the infant

[3] Wolff (1966) in a recent functional study of infant vocalizations has collected spectrograms of these sounds. He differentiates three cry patterns at birth, a "basic" or hunger cry, an "angry" cry, and a pain cry as well as noncry vocalizations, which, he notes, are heard for the first time during the third week of life. Wolff observes that the cries all end with a falling fundamental frequency but that, in contrast, the noncry vocalizations often end with a level or a rising fundamental frequency contour.

[4] Hughlings Jackson (1915) in his studies of aphasia in 1866 also stated that the expression of emotion is innately determined, as did Sir Charles Bell (1848).

uses the simplest pattern of articulatory activity when more than one pattern of articulatory activity could have been used to produce the same acoustic output.

The infant, like the adult, must initiate phonation by bringing the vocal cords inward from their open breathing position and expelling air from his lungs. No other articulatory gestures can produce phonation. We shall assume that the infant does not precisely control the tension of his laryngeal muscles once phonation starts. He merely maintains the tension of the laryngeal muscles at or near the tension that they had as phonation started. This assumption is not particularly crucial, and the only pattern of laryngeal activity that we really must assume does *not* take place is a consistent, controlled increase in the tension of the laryngeal muscles at the end of the breath-group. Our assumption is, however, consistent with the available physiologic data. Bosma, Lind, and Truby (1964) in a study of 30 newborn normal infants combined cineradiography, sound recording, and esophageal pressure recording during pinch-elicited cries. It is impossible to determine quantitatively the subglottal air pressure from esophageal recordings without knowing the lung volume that corresponded to each pressure measurement as a function of time.[5] However, the esophageal pressure function does indicate when the subglottal air pressure is rising and when it is falling. The measured esophageal pressure functions for the cries all had a similar shape. The esophageal pressure gradually rose from the start of phonation to either a level or a slightly falling "plateau." The esophageal pressure then abruptly fell prior to inspiration. The infant cries observed by Bosma *et al.* were quite protracted and "commonly . . . continued longer than expiration,[6] so that the vocalization is carried over into the succeeding inspiration." The "shape" of the fundamental frequency contours of the cries was similar to the shape of the typical esophageal pressure contour. Qualitatively speaking, the gross variations of the fundamental frequency contour thus seem to be a function of the subglottal air pressure during infant cries.[7] The fundamental frequency, which rises initially as the subglottal air pressure builds up, remains level or slowly falls until the end of expiration, when it abruptly falls. The respiratory muscles can maintain the subglottal air pressure at a

[5] The reasons for this will be discussed in Chapter 4.

[6] The referential cry is probably prolonged as much as possible to effect the greatest response on the part of the hearer.

[7] The average tension of the expiratory muscles is probably a function of the "excited nervous system." The greater the excitement of the infant, the greater the subglottal air pressure and tension will be. Infant "screams" therefore have a higher fundamental frequency and amplitude than infant cries.

relatively high level as the lungs gradually collapse during expiration. However, at the end of expiration, when the lungs collapse to a certain critical point, a set of overriding respiratory reflexes automatically induce inspiration. The deflation or Hering-Breuer reflex,[8] for example, induces inspiration when the lungs collapse (Widdicombe, 1964; Hering and Breuer, 1868). The subglottal air pressure must fall at a rapid rate as expiration ceases, because the subglottal air pressure assumes a negative value during inspiration. If phonation is protracted until the last possible moment, the breath-group will therefore terminate with a falling fundamental frequency contour.

3.5 The Use of Intonation as a Meaningful Signal by Infants

In Chapter 4 we shall present experimental evidence indicating that the normal breath-group of American English which has a linguistic reference is quite similar to our hypothetical innate referential breath-group. The reference for the innate breath-group is, of course, at first egocentric and is the state of the efferent nervous system. It seems likely that children gradually learn to associate other, more social, references to intonational signals. Löwenfeld (1927) and Bühler and Hetzer (1928), for example, reported that infants from the age of two months onward responded positively to the human voice, while infants from the age of three months onward responded positively to friendly tones and negatively to angry tones of voice. The observed responses in these studies were eye and head movements.

The shift to intonation as a meaningful speech signal that has a reference to specific social situations is comparatively rapid. Schafer (1922) reported that a nine-month-old infant who responded to the intonation of the phrase *wo ist die Tick-tock?* by looking at the clock also looked at the clock when similar phrases like *wo ist die lala?* were spoken with the same intonation. The same child played hand-clapping games when the phrase *mache bitte bitte* was spoken in "Ammenton," the exaggerated intonation of the nursery. The child would not respond when the phrase was spoken with a normal intonation. At ten months of age the child would respond when *mache bitte bitte* was spoken with normal intonation. Lewis (1936) cites many ex-

[8] Other reflexes that are directly triggered by the oxygen level in the lungs or blood stream also induce inspiration (Widdicombe, 1964). The relevant point is that inspiration is automatically induced by primary respiratory reflexes.

amples where children first responded only to the intonation of a phrase and responded only to the words as they grew older.

It has often been noted that children soon mimic adult intonation. Lewis (*op. cit.*), for example, often refers to this phenomenon. An experiment aimed at confirming Lewis's subjective comments by quantitative acoustic measurements that are related to the imitation of intonation signals showed that mimicry of the average fundamental frequency range occurs at this age. A ten-month-old boy and a thirteen-month-old girl were recorded under several different conditions. The boy was recorded while he babbled alone in his crib and while he cried alone in his crib. He was also recorded while he babbled in an identical play situation with his father and his mother respectively. The child sat on his father's lap, and the parent spoke to him while he played with his dog. After fifteen minutes he sat instead on his mother's lap while she talked to him. Four interchanges took place. The average fundamental frequency of the child's babbling under these conditions was measured. About twenty minutes of "conversation" occurred under each condition. The same experiment was then repeated with the thirteen-month-old girl, who was beginning to speak. The girl was not recorded while she cried or spoke alone, and she played with her cat while she sat on her parents' laps. The average fundamental frequencies are presented in Table 3.1. Note that the average fundamental frequency of the boy's babbling while he "spoke" to his father was 340 cps, while his average fundamental frequency was 390 cps when he was with his mother. (The children's fathers used lower average fundamental frequencies than their mothers.) Both of these fundamental frequencies are lower than that of his solitary babbling or crying. The boy apparently lowered his fundamental frequency when he was with either parent, and he lowered his fundamental frequency more when he was with the parent having the lower fundamental frequency. The girl also apparently attempted to mimic the fundamental frequencies of her parents.

Lewis (1936), Leopold (1953), Bullowa *et al.* (1964), and others have noted that the first utterances of children must be regarded as one-word sentences rather than as isolated words in the sense that the child later uses a more fully specified phonetic output to express similar thoughts. When a one-year-old child says *mama,* he often wants to convey a complete request, like "mama, pick me up," "mama, feed me," "mama, hold me." The phonetic output *mama* is usually associated with other body movements. The child may lift his hands up so that he can be lifted, etc. The child only gradually uses the linguistic output as the primary cue to his underlying thought.[9] As Leopold (1953) suggests, "Most children begin with sentences of one word. . . . The word may be a noun, an adjective, a verb of the adult sentences, but it serves for the child as the vehicle of a complete statement." Lewis and Leopold also note that intonation is also one of the first speech signals that has a linguistic reference.

TABLE 3.1 Average Fundamental Frequency of Children's Babbling and Speech versus Average Fundamental Frequency of Children's Crying

		Utterance	
Subject	Condition	Speech	Crying
10-month-old boy	Alone in crib	430 cps	550 cps
	Playing with father	340 cps	500 cps
	Playing with mother	390 cps	420 cps
13-month-old girl	Playing with father	290 cps	450 cps
	Playing with mother	390 cps	450 cps

Note that the children's fundamental frequencies transposed toward the fundamental frequency of the parent with whom they were talking but the crying fundamental frequency remained high. The mimicry in speech perhaps represents a social use of speech, while the crying is egocentric since it still has an emotional reference.

Leopold, for example, states that "The only syntactic device used early in my case was the interrogative intonation, it was employed to ask for information or, much more commonly, to request a permission, rarely to ask for the name of the thing." Of course, the child must first be consistently using the falling fundamental frequency contour associated with statements in order to make this contrast possible.

At some point in the development of speech, intonation takes on a linguistic reference. This occurs quite early, before the child has acquired many of the distinctive features of his linguistic environment.

[9] The gradual separation of the linguistic from the nonlinguistic outputs is clearly shown in the study reported by Bullowa *et al.* (1964).

Lewis (1936, p. 115), for example, notes three stages in the development of language:

> (1) At an early stage, the child shows discrimination in a broad way, between different patterns of expression in intonation. (2) When the total pattern—the phonetic form together with the intonational form—is made effective by training, at first the intonational rather than the phonetic form dominates the child's response. (3) Then the phonetic pattern becomes the dominant feature in evoking the specific response; but while the function of the intonational pattern may be considerably subordinated, it certainly does not vanish.

Our second principal hypothesis is consistent with these observations. Children come to use the innate referential breath-group as the phonetic marker of complete sentences. It becomes the basis of the normal or "unmarked" breath-group of the language, and it is used to mark the phonetic output of complete sentences, which at first consist of single words or long babbled sound patterns accompanied by various body movements, such as pointing or hand waving. The child then learns the permissible variation on the unmarked breath-group, for example, the "interrogative" intonation.

We shall state the form that this variation on the unmarked breath-group may take in the next chapter, where we shall present the results of physiologic and perceptual experiments that indicate that intonation is both produced and perceived in terms of the articulatory patterns of the unmarked breath-group, the "marked breath-group," and the other intonational features that are admissible in a particular language.

4 Perceptual, Physiologic, and Acoustic Data

We have stated that intonation is produced and perceived in terms of an unmarked and a marked breath-group ([$-$ *BG*] and [$+$ *BG*]) and certain segmental features that interact with the breath-group because of the inherent constraints imposed by the human speech production apparatus and auditory system. In this chapter we shall precisely specify some of the physiologic and acoustic correlates of the unmarked and the marked breath-group as well as the segmental feature [$+ P_s$], and we shall present experimental evidence that supports our hypotheses.

4.1 Perceptual Data for Swedish and American English

We shall start by considering the results of an independent psychoacoustic experiment that was performed by Hadding-Koch and Studdert-Kennedy (1964). The experimenters were investigating the perception of the fundamental frequency contours that are usually associated with "yes-no" interrogative sentences and statements. They noted that "In both Swedish and American English the fundamental frequency (f_o) of so-called yes-no questions tends to show a final rising contour, while the f_o of statements tends to show a final fall." The object of the experiment was to see whether the earlier portions of the fundamental frequency contour would influence the perception of the final portion of a contour.

The experimenters recorded the words *For Jane* on magnetic tape. These words were found to be acceptable to both Swedish and American listeners, so they served as the "carrier" phase. The magnetic tape was attached to an acetate loop, on which the contours of a systematically varied sequence of intonation contours were also painted. The signal on the tape was then processed with a Vocoder (Dudley, 1939), and the intonation was controlled by the painted contours on the acetate loop (cf. Borst and Cooper, 1957). The net effect of the processing was a set of 42 intonation contours that occurred with identical words. The amplitude of the speech signal was kept fairly level throughout each intonation contour. A schematic illustration of one of the contours is presented in Figure 4.1.

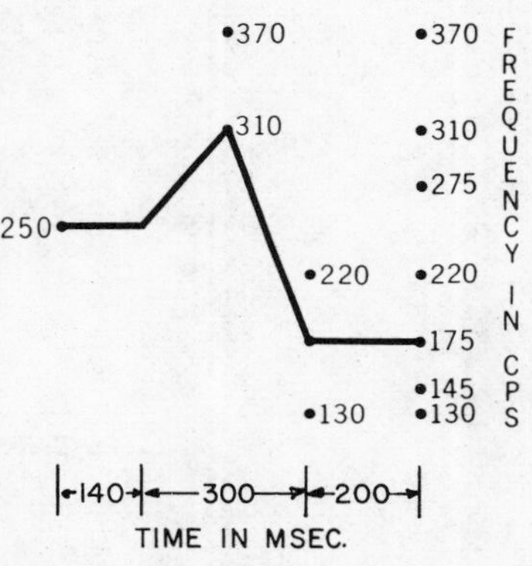

Figure 4.1 Schematic illustration of fundamental frequency contours employed by Hadding-Koch and Studdert-Kennedy (1964).
The words *For Jane* were processed by means of a Vocoder, whose pitch channel was controlled to obtain these fundamental frequency contours. The contours all started at 250 cps. This frequency was maintained for 140 msec over the word *For*. The contours then rose to 370 or 310 cps in approximately 100 msec. They then fell to one of three "turning points" at 130, 175, or 220 cps in approximately 200 cps. The contours then proceeded to one of seven "end points" between 130 and 370 cps in 200 msec. The total duration of each contour was 640 msec. (After Hadding-Koch and Studdert-Kennedy, 1964.)

The shape of the contours was based on Hadding-Koch's analysis of Swedish intonation (1961, pp. 85 ff.). The stimuli were presented to 25 Swedish and 24 American undergraduates, who, in two separate sessions, were asked to indicate for each stimulus: (1) whether it would be best categorized as a statement or a question; (2) whether it ended with a rising or a falling pitch.

In Figure 4.2 the percentage of response in each of the indicated classes versus the fundamental frequency of the end point minus the turning point is plotted for the responses of the American listeners to the stimuli that rose to 310 cps and fell to the 130 cps "turning point." The value of the terminal rise or fall is equal to the end point minus the turning point and is plotted on the abscissa, while the percentages of question and statement and of rising and falling terminal pitch contour responses are plotted on the ordinate. Hadding-Koch and Studdert-Kennedy noted that the "semantic" and "psychophysical" judgments agreed particularly well for this series of stimuli. They stated that "Insofar as semantic and psychophysical judgments agree, it would seem that listeners may have been using the *perceived* direc-

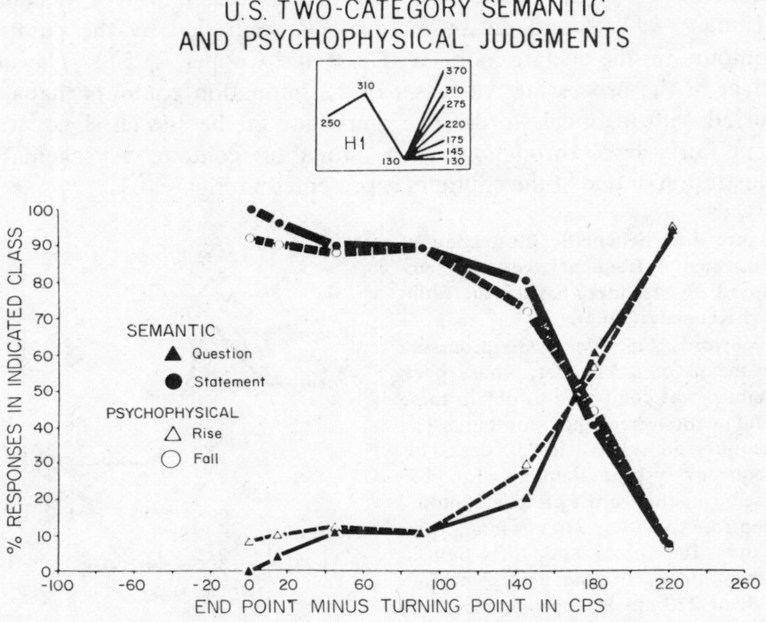

Figure 4.2 Percentage of statement and question responses (semantic: solid line) and of rise and fall responses (psychophysical: hatched line) as a function of terminal rise (positive) or fall (negative) in cycles per second.
The data are from the responses of the American listeners to the stimuli that rose to 310 cps and fell to the 130 cps "turning point." The value of the terminal rise or fall is equal to the end point minus the turning point and is plotted on the abscissa. (After Hadding-Koch and Studdert-Kennedy, 1964.)

tion of the terminal glide rather than its physically measured direction to make their semantic decisions."

In Figures 4.3 and 4.4 the "semantic" responses of the Swedish and American listeners are presented. The experimenters concluded from this information that "listeners may make use of the entire f_o contour in identifying questions and statements. Not only terminal rise or fall, but also preceding peak and turning point are relevant. These three variables interact in a manner that cannot be easily described. But, in general, for a given f_o at the other two points, an increase in f_o at

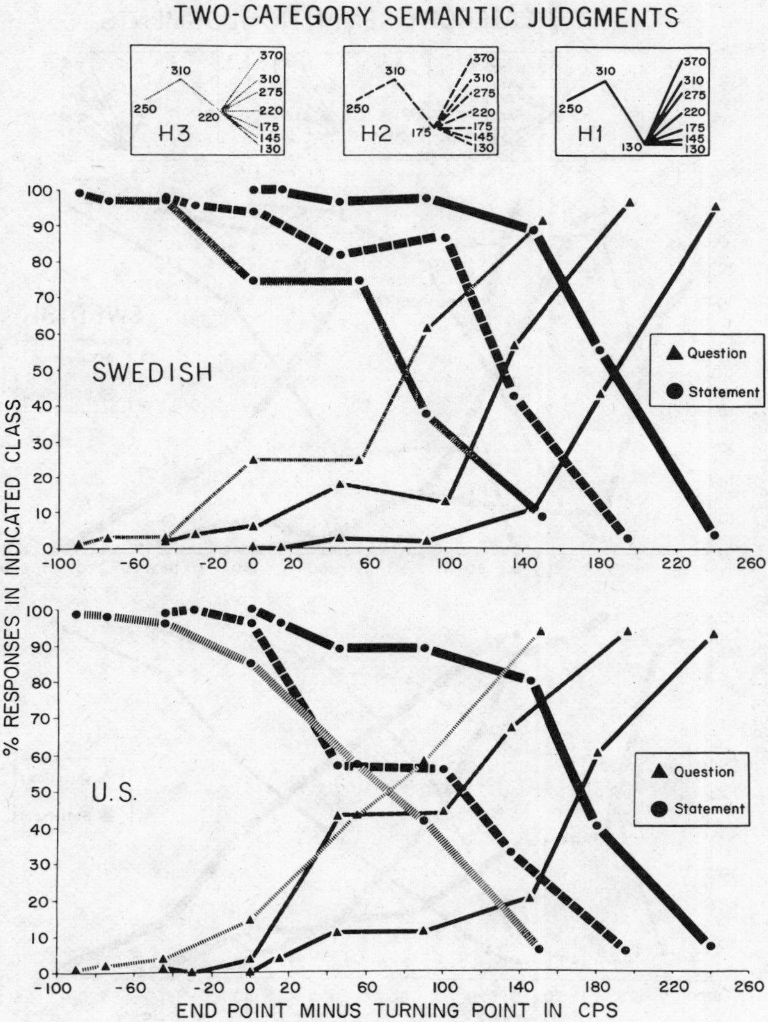

Figure 4.3 Peak f_o at 310 cps: percentage of statement and question responses as a function of the terminal rise (positive) or fall (negative) in cps (end point f_o minus turning point f_o).

Parameters of the curves are the turning point f_o: 130 cps (H1), 175 cps (H2), and 220 cps (H3). The Swedish data are plotted above, the United States data below. (After Hadding-Koch and Studdert-Kennedy, 1964.)

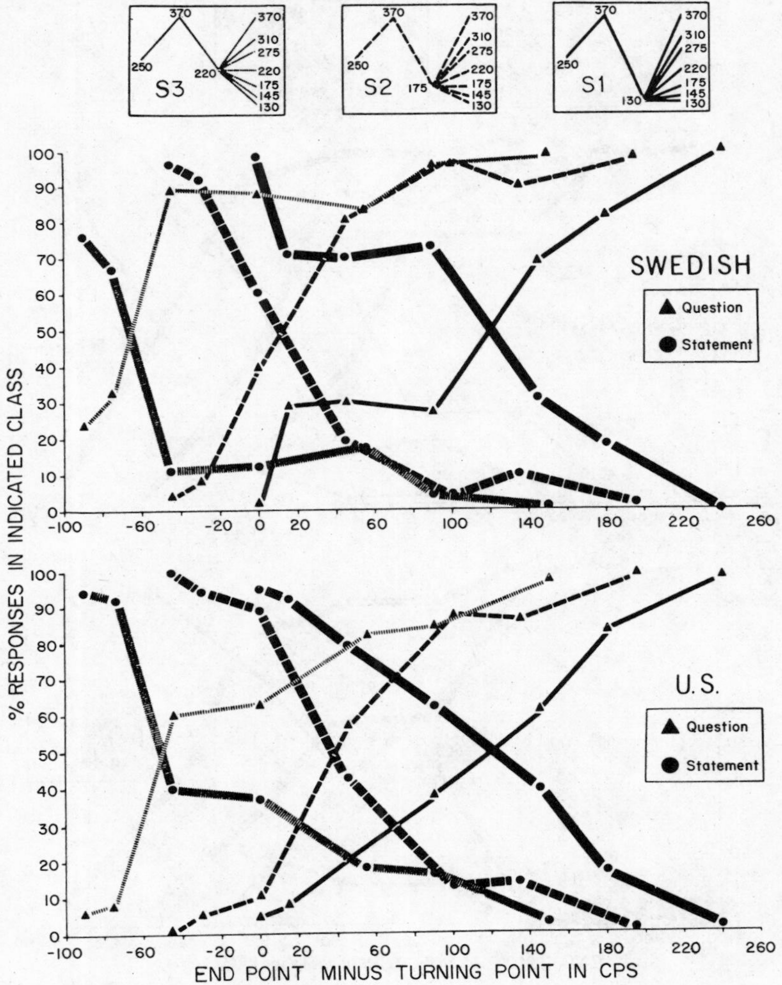

Figure 4.4 Peak f_o at 370 cps: percentage of statement and question responses as a function of the terminal rise (positive) or fall (negative) in cps (end point f_o minus turning point f_o).

Parameters of the curves are turning point f_o: 130 cps (S1), 175 cps (S2), and 220 cps (S3). The Swedish data are plotted above, the United States data below. (After Hadding-Koch and Studdert-Kennedy, 1964.)

the third point leads to an increase in the number of questions heard."

We have presented the data of this experiment because the listeners' responses seem to indicate that they were interpreting the intonational signals in terms of an archetypal pattern of articulatory gestures. The interactions between the several variables in this experiment, which are otherwise rather complex, can be simply interpreted in terms of this hypothesis. Let us first consider the responses of the American listeners.

We shall begin by repeating one of the hypotheses that was presented in Chapter 3. Let us suppose that the innate referential breath-group is the archetype or basis of the normal (that is, unmarked) breath-group of American English and that it is the phonetic output of a complete declarative sentence. The tension of the laryngeal muscles is constant during the production of the normal breath-group, and the fundamental frequency contour is a function of the subglottal air pressure. The fundamental frequency will therefore fall at the end (the last 150–200 msec of phonation) of the breath-group as the subglottal air pressure decreases.

Let us suppose that a permitted modification of the normal breath-group is an increase in the tension of the laryngeal muscles at the end of the breath-group where the air pressure falls. One of the principal acoustic effects of an increase in the tension of the laryngeal muscles, the vocalis, cricothyroid, cricoarytenoid, etc., is an increase in the fundamental frequency of phonation. We shall use the notation [+ *BG*] to represent the marked breath-group whose archetypal articulatory correlate is this increase in tension of the laryngeal muscles at the end of the breath-group. If the subglottal air pressure were constant, the acoustic correlate of the marked breath-group would always be a rising fundamental frequency contour. However, the subglottal air pressure generally falls at the end of the normal unmarked breath-group, which tends to counteract the rising fundamental frequency contour that would occur with a constant subglottal air pressure. The two effects interact, and the acoustic correlate of [+ *BG*] may be a level terminal fundamental frequency contour, a rising fundamental frequency contour, or a falling fundamental frequency contour that, however, falls less than it would have in the absence of the terminal increase in laryngeal tension.

We shall use the notation [+ P_s] to represent the segmental phonologic feature *prominence*. The archetypal articulatory correlate of [+ P_s] is a momentary increase in the subglottal air pressure that is superimposed on the breath-group by the activity of the respiratory muscles. This momentary increase in subglottal air pressure can occur at any part of the breath-group except at the very end of the breath-group. Let us for the moment also suppose that the presence of this momentary overpressure in the early part of the breath-group results in a lower air pressure at the end of the breath-group. This constraint could have a reasonable physiologic basis if we assumed that the main force involved in the production of the archetypal normal breath-group was provided by the elastic recoil of the lungs while the segmental feature [+ P_s] was executed by the added ac-

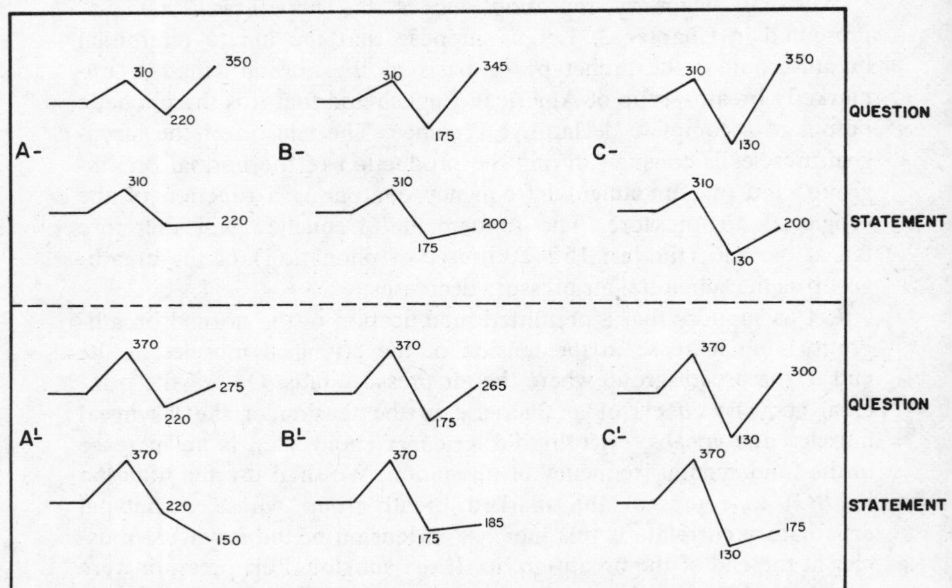

Figure 4.5 Six pairs of intonation contours.
The American listeners categorized one member of each pair as a question 80 percent of the time and the other member of each pair as a statement 80 percent of the time.

tivity of some expiratory muscle or group of expiratory muscles. In any event, let us assume that this constraint on [+ P_s] exists, whatever its causes may be.[1]

Let us now reexamine the data of the Hadding-Koch and Studdert-Kennedy experiment in the light of these hypotheses. In Figure 4.5 six pairs of intonation contours are sketched. The American listeners categorized one member of each pair as a question 80 percent of the time

[1] This effect might be a compensatory reaction that offsets a greater volume flow early in the breath-group. We shall discuss this effect in Sections 4.2.3 and 4.3.3.

time and one member of each pair as a statement 80 percent of the time. Note that the end points of all the question contours that had a high point of 310 cps are all approximately 350 cps while the end points of all the contours that had a high point of 370 cps range from 265 to 305 cps. Also note that the statement end points of all the 310-cps high-point contours range from 200 to 220 cps. The statement end points of the 370-cps high-point contours range from 150 to 185 cps. The question contours that had *lower* high points all had higher end points. The statement contours that had *lower* high points also had higher end points.

In Figure 4.6 we present two of these contours to make our point clearer. The two contours were identified as questions 80 percent of the time by the American listeners. Note that the end point of the 370-cps high-point contour is only 265 cps while the end point of 310-cps high-point contour is 335 cps. Why do the listeners perceive the two contours as though they had identical terminal rises? [2] The actual physical rise is obviously not the factor to which the listeners are responding. The terminal rise of the 370-cps high-point contour is 90 cps, while the 310-cps high-point contour's terminal rise is 160 cps. The listeners do not seem to be making their judgments in terms of the relative frequency range of the contours. The contour that had the smaller initial fundamental frequency excursion (the 310-cps contour) has the greater terminal rise.

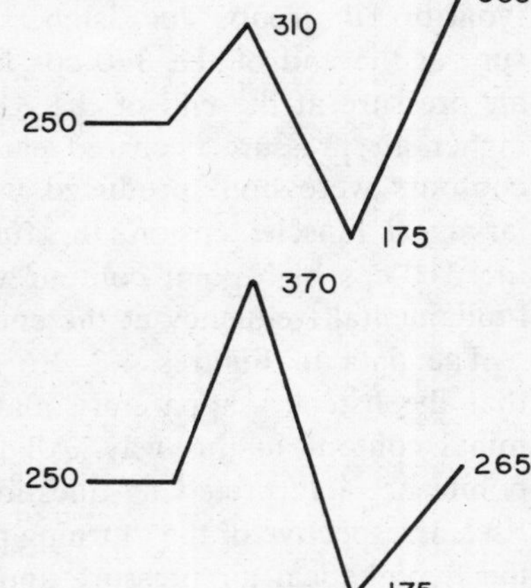

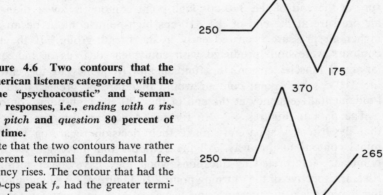

Figure 4.6 Two contours that the American listeners categorized with the same "psychoacoustic" and "semantic" responses, i.e., *ending with a rising pitch* and *question* 80 percent of the time.
Note that the two contours have rather different terminal fundamental frequency rises. The contour that had the 310-cps peak f_o had the greater terminal rise.

Let us consider our breath-group hypotheses. We should expect

[2] These two contours are ones where the "psychophysical" and "semantic" judgments were in very good agreement.

to find the constraints imposed by the speech production apparatus to be the factors that the listeners consider as they perceive the intonation contours by a process of "analysis by synthesis." The entire contour must be considered as an entity in this process because the listener "knows" that increases in the subglottal air pressure in the early part of the breath-group result in a lower air pressure at the end.[3] The listeners also "know" that not-falling terminal contours in English are due to increases in the tension of the laryngeal muscles which tend to raise the fundamental frequency.

The listeners deduce that the subglottal air pressure was higher at the midpoint of the 370-cps high-point contour because f_o is a function of the subglottal air pressure in the nonterminal part of the archetypal breath-group. The listeners therefore deduce that the air pressure at the end of the 370-cps high-point contour is lower than the air pressure at the end of the 310-cps high-point contour because a higher air pressure occurred early in the breath-group.[4] If the two contours were both produced with equivalent degrees of increased laryngeal muscle tension, the fundamental frequency at the end of the 310-cps high-point contour would therefore be greater than the fundamental frequency at the end of the 370-cps high-point contour.

The data in Figures 4.3–4.6 for the American listeners indicate that the listeners apparently make their decision regarding the terminal contour in this way. All the contours that have greater high points are interpreted as questions when they have lower terminal rises, irrespective of the "turning point." In Figure 4.7 we have plotted the hypothetical air pressure and laryngeal tension functions for the 310-cps and 370-cps high-point contours. Note that the same laryngeal tension results in a higher f_o at the end of the 310-cps high-point contour. The "high points" of all the contours were interpreted as though they were produced by means of a momentary increase in the subglottal air pressure over the subglottal air pressure that is typical of the breath-group. The fundamental frequency at the end of the contour then was interpreted as though it were the result of

[3] The listener "knows" this only if our premises are indeed correct. We are trying to state formally the linguistic competence of the listener with regard to the perception and production of intonation, and we are using this example, in effect, as a test of our hypotheses.

[4] Some additional constraints must be placed on the two intonation contours that the listener is analyzing. Both contours must have the same duration and the same average subglottal air pressure. We shall discuss these constraints in Section 4.3.3. The synthesized contours in this psychoacoustic experiment all had the same duration. They all started at the same fundamental frequency, so the listeners would have inferred that the same "average" subglottal air pressure was being used for each contour.

the subglottal air pressure of the now modified breath-group and of increases in the tension of the laryngeal muscles.

The perception of the listeners was keyed to their decisions regarding the possible articulatory gestures that could have produced these stimuli. They heard terminal rises only when they inferred the presence of an increase in the tension of the laryngeal muscles. The

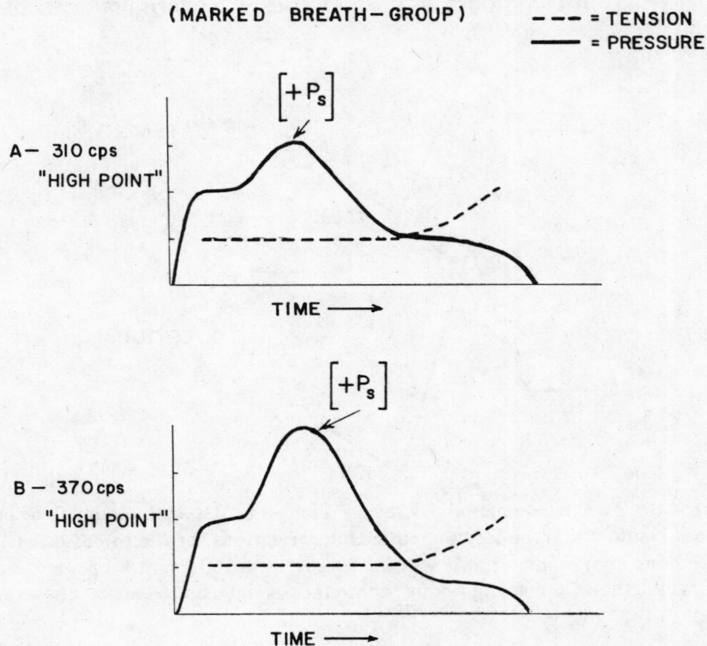

Figure 4.7 Hypothetical subglottal air pressure and laryngeal tension functions for the intonation contours of Figure 4.6.
Note that the same laryngeal tension function results in a higher terminal f_0 for the 310-cps high-point contour because the subglottal air pressure is higher at the end of this contour.

confidence of the listeners' responses reflected the calculated magnitude of the increased laryngeal tension. A greater degree of calculated laryngeal tension would be interpreted as a terminal rise more often than would a lower degree of increased tension.

In Figure 4.8 we have presented two contours abstracted from the Hadding-Koch and Studdert-Kennedy data that rather strikingly illustrate our point. The same terminal contour is interpreted as a rising contour 80 percent of the time when it is preceded by a 370-cps high-point and as a falling contour 80 percent of the time when it is preceded by a 310-cps high-point. These judgments were made by the Swedish listeners. Similar effects occurred for the American listeners. The Swedish listeners, in general, responded differently to the same contours. In Figure 4.9 we have abstracted a set of contours for the Swedish listeners from the data of Figures 4.3 and 4.4. Note that the Swedish listeners also behave in the same way as the American listeners for contours *b–b′*, and *c–c′*. The terminal rise of the

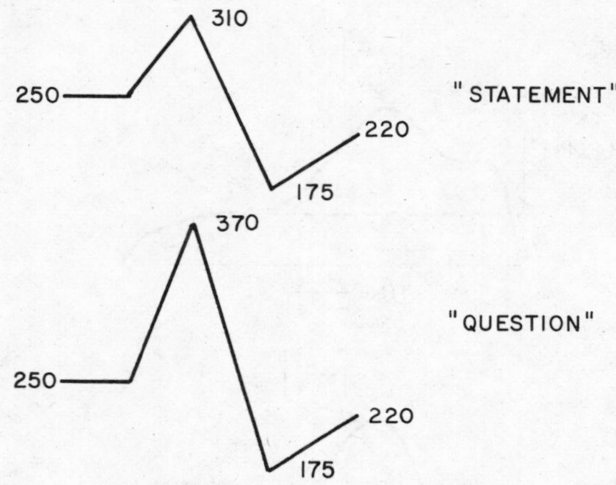

Figure 4.8 Two fundamental frequency contours that had identical terminal rises but resulted in opposite "semantic" interpretations for the Swedish listeners. The 310-cps high-point contour was interpreted as a statement 80 percent of the time, while the 370-cps high-point contour was interpreted as a question 80 percent of the time.

contour does not need to be as high for the utterance to be judged a question when the high point is higher. For both the Swedish responses to these contours and the American responses to the contours in Figure 4.5, a 60-cps high-point difference is approximately equivalent to a 75- to 40-cps end-point difference. The 370-cps high-point contours having an end point 40 to 75 cps lower than the end point of the corresponding 310-cps high-point contour are categorized as questions at the same level of confidence. The response of the Swedish listeners to contours *a* and *a′* is, however, rather different from the response of the American listeners to these same stimuli.

Now Hadding-Koch points out that traditional phonetic analyses say that Swedish yes-no ". . . questions may also be distinguished by a comparatively high f_0 throughout the utterance" (Hermann, 1942). The responses of the Swedish listeners to contours *a* and *a′*

support this view. They indicate that yes-no questions may have two distinct phonetic outputs in Swedish. The speaker may modify the basic breath-group by increasing the tension of the laryngeal muscles at the end of the breath-group as is the case for English. The Swedish listeners, like the American listeners, seem to interpret contours *b–b′* and *c–c′*, which have a fundamental frequency prominence at their midpoint, as contours modified by a subglottal pressure peak. The

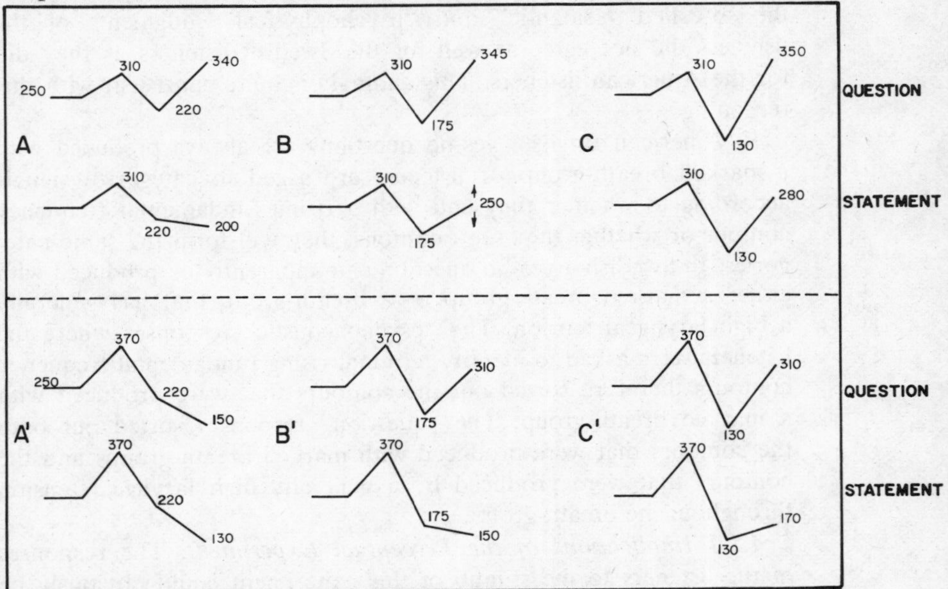

Figure 4.9 Six pairs of intonation contours.
The Swedish listeners categorized one member of each pair as a question 80 percent of the time and the other member of each pair as a statement 80 percent of the time.

terminal rises are then apparently ascribed to the effect of an increased laryngeal tension. The terminal fundamental frequency contour is a function of the interaction of the subglottal air pressure and the increased tension of the laryngeal muscles.

In Swedish a yes-no question may alternatively result in a phonetic output in which the laryngeal tension is raised throughout the entire breath-group. When a Swedish listener hears contour *a′*, he interprets it as a breath-group in which the tension of the laryngeal muscles throughout the entire utterance is higher than is the case for the normal breath-group. The listener notes that the fundamental frequency does not fall at the "turning point." The turning point of contour *a'* is 220 cps, while the other contours' turning points are 175 and 130 cps. The fundamental frequency rise at the high point is therefore interpreted as the acoustic output of a generally high laryngeal muscle tension rather than a transitory air pressure peak, as is the case for the other contours where the fundamental frequency abruptly falls after the high point. Hadding-Koch and Studdert-Kennedy noted that the so-called "semantic" and "psychophysical" judgments of the listeners did not agree as well for the Swedish listeners as they did for the American listeners. This anomaly is quite consistent with this reasoning.

In American English, yes-no questions are always produced with a marked breath-group. If listeners are asked to categorize signals according to whether they end with a rising fundamental frequency contour or whether they are questions, they will form the same categories. In Swedish a yes-no question can apparently be produced with either a marked breath-group or a breath-group that has generally a high laryngeal tension. The "psychoacoustic" responses where the listeners were asked to identify terminal rising fundamental frequency contours therefore sorted out the contours that were produced with a marked breath-group. The "question" responses sorted out both the contours that were produced with marked breath-groups and the contours that were produced by a generally high laryngeal tension throughout the breath-group.

4.1.1 Implications of the Perceptual Experiment. The responses of the listeners to the stimuli of this experiment could obviously be represented by means of a set of empirical functions that would fit the curves plotted in Figures 4.2, 4.3, and 4.4. What we have instead proposed is that the listeners perceive these signals by means of a feedback mechanism of the analysis-by-synthesis type, in which they use their knowledge of the phonologic features that produce intonational signals. We hypothesized that the listeners used the archetypal or primary articulatory correlates of these features, which we tried to motivate in terms of the physiologic and perceptual constraints of the speech production apparatus and the auditory system. These constraints obviously have an innate basis. In Chapter 3 we showed that the archetypal unmarked breath-group was manifested in the first utterances of neonates.

We are saying, in other words, that the intonational signal is perceived in terms of these archetypal patterns because they represent the most basic way in which intonational signals can be produced using the human vocal tract. The listeners respond to the intonation signals in this way precisely because the intonation contours are speech signals that are normally produced by the human vocal tract. The effects noted in the Hadding-Koch and Studdert-Kennedy experiment in fact tend to disappear when listeners hear nonspeech stimuli like pure tones. The perception of terminal rising fundamental frequency contours is, for example, almost independent of the initial "high point" of the contour.[5]

Our discussion of the articulatory activity that underlies Swedish intonation must, at present, rest on these perceptual experiments, which obviously are not definitive.[6] However, we have direct physiologic evidence available for American English which quantitatively supports our hypotheses regarding both the nature and the primacy of the archetypal correlates of the breath-group and the feature [P_s] as well as the alternative articulatory maneuvers that can produce equivalent acoustic or perceptual results.

4.2 Physiologic and Acoustic Data for American English

The following experiment was performed using special equipment, techniques, and facilities devised by Dr. Jere Mead of the Harvard School of Public Health, Dr. Donald F. Proctor of the Johns Hopkins University, and Dr. Arend Bouhuys of the John B. Pierce Foundation. These investigators have been pursuing an investigation of the activity of the respiratory system during phonation. Much of their work has involved the respiratory physiology of singing, and the experiment that we shall describe was conducted as part of a session in which singing was also studied.

4.2.1 Procedure. Four native male speakers of American English each recorded a list of sentences and words under several different conditions. Each speaker was recorded in a separate session. Two speakers were medical students. The other two were medical faculty members. The speaker sat in a sealed body plethysmograph, which allowed the volume events during phonation to be measured. The plethysomograph is essentially a sealed box in which the subject sits with his head projecting out through a rubber dam. Volume changes due to both the displacement of air from the respiratory system and the compression of gas can be accurately measured with this apparatus (Mead and Milic-Emili, 1964).

[5] Personal communication from Michael Studdert-Kennedy.

[6] The amplitude of the speech signal remained fairly constant for all the stimuli generated by Hadding-Koch and Studdert-Kennedy, which may have prevented the listeners from responding precisely as they would have if they were listening to natural speech stimuli.

The esophageal air pressure was measured by means of a 10-cm-long balloon that was attached through a flexible plastic tube to a manometer. The balloon was introduced through the subject's nose so that it did not interfere with normal phonation. The balloon was positioned by first bringing it up into the upper part of the esophagus until artifacts due to the motion of the neck were registered. The balloon was then lowered about one cm. Artifacts due to the motion of the neck are registered if the balloon is positioned too high.

The esophageal pressure was recorded with a Sanborn 268B transducer. The bandwidth of the pressure-recording system was in excess of 50 cps. The pressure recorded by the balloon is the pleural surface pressure relative to atmospheric. The lungs are isolated from the chest walls and the esophagus by the pleural membranes. The balloon therefore does not record the pressure in the lungs. However, it is comparatively simple to calculate the subglottal air pressure since the pleural surface pressure equals the pressure in the terminal air sacs (alveoli) of the lungs minus the static recoil pressure of the lung tissue. The static recoil pressure of the lungs P_{st} is a function of the volume of the lungs. As the lungs distend, the static recoil force increases. The static recoil pressure can be determined for any speaker as a function of the lung volume by instructing the speaker to hold his breath with his airways open for various lung volumes. Under these conditions, P_{pl} will be equal to $-P_{st}$. The alveolar pressure can then be determined for other conditions when the speaker does not hold his breath if the volume of the speaker's lungs is known.

During phonation most of the pressure drop in the respiratory system takes place at the glottis, so that alveolar pressure is approximately equal to the subglottal air pressure. The subglottal air pressure can thus be calculated from the esophageal balloon pressure for steady-state conditions if simultaneous recordings of the volume of the lungs and the balloon pressure are available. For transient conditions the calculated subglottal air pressure must be regarded as an approximation of the true subglottal air pressure. When we made quantitative measurements that involved the subglottal air pressure, we therefore tried to use only the quasi-steady-state portions of the calculated pressure functions where the subglottal pressure was relatively steady.[7] A detailed description of the techniques involved in the measurement of subglottal pressure may be found in Bouhuys, Proctor, and Mead (1966).

Each subject sang a series of sustained notes at low, medium, and

[7] The quasi-steady-state portions of the P_s function had variations of less than 0.2 cm H_2O over 100 msec.

high intensities. Then each read the list of sentences and words presented in Table 4.1 at a normal speaking level and at a loud speaking level. The subjects were unaware of the particular objectives of this experiment, and they had no knowledge either of formal linguistic theories or of acoustic phonetics. They were instructed to read the sentences in a natural way and were cautioned to avoid "acting." The subjects first read the material at a normal speaking level. They were asked to read the number of each sentence or word and then read the sentence or word twice. The acoustic signal was recorded by means of a Shure Brothers 98108 microphone that was placed 2 to 3 inches from the speaker's lips. The speech signal, balloon pressure, and lung volume were all recorded on a multichannel FM tape recorder. The speech signal was also simultaneously recorded on an Ampex 300 audio tape recorder, at 7½ inches per second.

The balloon pressure curves and volume data were then simultaneously plotted on a multichannel polygraph pen-and-ink recorder at a paper speed of 5 cm/sec. An additional channel was used to provide an approximate indication of the amplitude of the speech signal by driving one of the polygraph galvanometers with the speech signal. Normal sound spectrograms were made of some of the utterances on a Voiceprint Sound Spectrograph using the linear 3-kc display. Quantized spectrograms were made using the 7.5-kc logarithmic display. Both narrow-band (50 cps) and wide-band (300 cps) sound spectrograms were made.

The subglottal air pressure was derived by graphically subtracting the elastic recoil force from the pleural pressure recorded by the esophageal balloon. A pantograph was then used to retrace the calculated subglottal air pressure and the measured volume plots to the same time scale as the sound spectrograms. Synchronizing signals had been added at an earlier stage of the processing to both the sound spectrograms and the volumetric and pressure data, so it was possible to line up the spectrograms and the volume and pressure tracings with an accuracy of approximately $\pm$ 40 msec.

4.2.2 General Observations. The subjects, in general, followed their instructions. One speaker did not repeat each sentence or word when he read at his normal speaking level. Another speaker read the number of the sentence before he repeated the sentence. One of the speakers also tended to dramatize his readings. In all, the speakers read 462 sentences and 91 words. Each sentence in Table 4.1 was read 21 times, and each word was read at least 11 times.[8] The num-

[8] One of the speakers found it impossible to distinguish between word 6 and words 4 and 5 and refused to read word 6.

TABLE 4.1 List of Sentences and Isolated Words That Were Read by Each of the Four Native Male Speakers of American English

The speakers were asked to read the number of each sentence or word and then read the sentence or word twice.

Sentences

1. The life of a light house keeper formerly was very lonely.
2. The Pennsylvania Railroad still goes to New York City.
3. Did Joe eat his soup?
4. Our maid weighed 180 pounds but the Joneses had a light house keeper for more than twenty years.
5. Joe ate his soup, didn't he?
6. Did *Joe* eat his soup? (Joe doesn't usually eat soup.)
7. Grandfather was a rebel at heart because he was born in Alabama.
8. Joe ate his soup?
9. The peasants were induced to rebel from their masters.
10. Because so many electrical aids are available, the life of a light house keeper fortunately isn't very difficult these days.
11. Did Joe eat *his* soup? (He sometimes eats Bill's soup.)
12. Did Joe eat his *soup?* (He hardly ever eats soup.)
13. The number that you will hear is nine.
14. Joe ate his soup!
15. The number that you will hear is ten.
16. Joe ate his *soup!*
17. A stitch in time saves nine.
18. Joe ate his soup.
19. *Joe* ate his soup!
20. A stitch in time saves ten.
21. Joe didn't eat soup, did he?
22. You're going to drive down that rutted road?

Words

1. Pennsylvania Railroad
2. rebel (noun as in "grandfather was a rebel")
3. rebel (verb "to rebel")
4. light house keeper (someone who tends a light house)
5. light house keeper (a not-heavy house keeper)
6. light house keeper (a woman who dusts her house)
7. nine
8. ten

bers that identified the words or sentences were read a total of 402 times.

It was, of course, possible to determine the expiratory and inspiratory portions of the speakers' respiratory cycles by looking at the lung volume tracings. We found that 456 of the sentences and 85 of the words were produced on a single expiration regardless of the duration of the utterance. The speaker ended the expiration when he finished the sentence or word. The duration of these expirations ranged from 300 msec to 9 seconds. Two of the longer sentences were twice uttered using two expirations separated by a short inspiration. In two instances the two repetitions of the same sentence were uttered on one expiration. In three instances the two repetitions of the same word were uttered on one expiration. Thus 99.2 percent of the sentences or words were uttered on a single expiration. The length of the expiration was determined by the time that it took to utter the words that were part of the complete sentence. The length of the expiration was apparently linguistically conditioned.

Now it might be argued that each sentence or word was uttered on a single expiration because the utterances were in a list, which caused the subjects to pause between each utterance. This argument, however, does not explain why the subjects used separate expirations when they repeated each utterance. The treatment of the introductory numbers is also significant. The introductory numbers must be treated formally as one-word sentences.[9] The number that precedes each utterance is semantically and syntactically independent of the word or utterance that follows. Three of the subjects used a separate expiration for the introductory number 84 percent of the time. The fourth speaker used a separate expiration only 57 percent of the time. The striking fact about the subglottal air pressure plots for all the introductory numbers is that they all have the same "shape" whether or not the speaker ended the expiration after he uttered the introductory number. The speaker manipulated his respiratory muscles to produce a stereotyped subglottal air pressure curve whether he paused for an inspiration or not. The air pressure curves of the two sentences that were produced on the same expiration[10] also looked as though the speaker had paused for an inspiration, though in fact he did not. These data seem to indicate that the speakers in these cases used the air pressure contour that *would* have

[9] The single isolated words may be regarded as limiting cases or deleted metalinguistic sentences of the form "The word you will hear is ———."

[10] The long sentences that were produced with two breath-groups represent another phenomenon. The speaker used a marked breath-group [$+BG$] to indicate that the sentence was not yet over (cf. Chapter 5).

resulted from a single bounded expiration to segment the speech signal into complete sentences. The combined statistics for all of the introductory numbers and the test words and sentences show that a single expiration was used for each "sentence" 87 percent of the time. The air pressure contour that resulted from the activity of the respiratory muscles during a single expiration was used to segment the speech signal. In the other instances the speakers used alternate patterns of muscular activity to produce air pressure contours that were indistinguishable from the contours that occurred when expiration actually ended. *The subglottal air pressure contour that occurred during a single expiration thus seemed to serve as an archetypal pattern for segmenting the speech signal into sentences.*

The data that follow will be used to illustrate more precisely the articulatory and acoustic correlates of the marked and the unmarked breath-groups of American English and the segmental feature [+ P_s]. We shall also present data showing that speakers sometimes use alternate articulatory maneuvers that produce a speech signal acoustically or perceptually equivalent to the signal produced with the archetypal maneuver.

The speaker can obviously raise the fundamental frequency at the end of the sentence by means of a subglottal overpressure. He can also raise the fundamental frequency in the middle of the breath-group by increasing the tension of his laryngeal muscles. The acoustic correlates of increased subglottal air pressure and laryngeal tension tend to overlap, as we have seen in Chapter 2. However, the speaker "knows" that the listener will always perceive the acoustic signal as though it had been produced by the preferred archetypal pattern. The speaker can thus use equivalent articulatory gestures.

We shall examine representative utterances of three of our four speakers. The utterances of speaker 4, who produced exaggerated effects, will be omitted from this discussion. Speaker 4's air pressure data also show strong interference from his heartbeat, which makes it difficult to use his data.

4.2.3 Data on Individual Sentences—Speaker 1. In Figure 4.10 the subglottal air pressure, fundamental frequency, and the volume of air in the speaker's lungs are plotted as functions of time for speaker 1 when he read sentence 18, "Joe ate his soup," at a normal speaking level. A quantized wide-band (300-cps analyzing filter bandwidth) sound spectrogram is also presented.[11] Time is plotted with

[11] The sound spectrogram is quantized in 6-db steps. The plot is similar to a topographic map. Each contour represents a 6-db increment in amplitude.

respect to the abscissa. A logarithmic frequency scale that extends from 50 cps to 7.0 kc is plotted on the ordinate of the sound spectrogram. The synchronizing signals that were introduced to facilitate lining up the sound spectrogram with the other plots are all marked by means of vertical arrows placed below the abscissa of the sound spectrogram. In Figure 4.10 synchronizing signals are marked immedi-

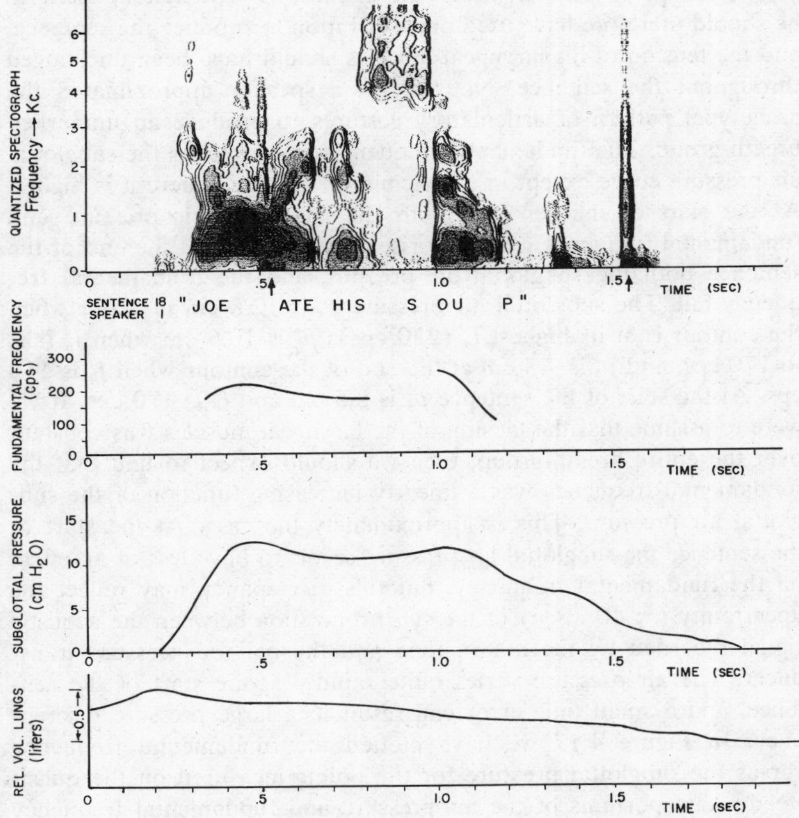

Figure 4.10 Acoustic and physiologic data for speaker 1 reading the declarative sentence "Joe ate his soup" (sentence 18).
A normal (that is, unmarked) breath-group [—BG] was used. The fundamental frequency, subglottal air pressure, and the volume of air in the speaker's lungs are plotted as functions of time. A quantized wide-band (300-cps analyzing filter bandwidth) sound spectrogram is also presented. Each contour line on the spectrogram represents a 6-db increment in amplitude. Two synchronizing pulses, which are marked by means of vertical arrows after 0.5 and 1.5 sec, are also indicated on the spectrogram.

ately after 0.5 sec and 1.5 sec. The fundamental frequency[12] is plotted in cycles per second in the graph below the spectrogram. The subglottal air pressure is plotted in centimeters of water, and the relative volume of air in the speaker's lungs is plotted in liters.

The speaker was uttering a short unemphatic declarative sentence. If our hypotheses are correct, he should have been using an unmarked breath-group. If he was using the archetypal articulatory pattern, he should therefore have used one expiration to produce the sentence, and the tension of his laryngeal muscles should have been unchanged throughout the sentence. Note that the speaker approximated the archetypal pattern of articulatory gestures to produce an unmarked breath-group. The fundamental frequency curve follows the subglottal air pressure curve except in the vicinity of 1.0 sec, where it is higher. At the start of the sentence both the subglottal air pressure and fundamental frequency gradually rise and then fall. At the end of the sentence both the subglottal air pressure and the fundamental frequency fall. The subglottal air pressure p_s is 12.8 cm of water when the contour is at its highest f_o (230 cps); p_s is 10.5 cm when f_o falls to 170 cps, and p_s is 7.8 cm at the end of the contour when f_o is 110 cps. At the start of the sentence p_s is 8.5 cm and f_o is 170 cps. If we were to assume that the tension of the laryngeal muscles was constant over the entire breath-group, then we should expect to find that the fundamental frequency was a linearly increasing function of the subglottal air pressure. This is approximately the case. At the start of the sentence the subglottal air pressure seems to have less of an effect on the fundamental frequency, but this discrepancy may reflect the uncertainty ($\pm$ 40 msec) of the synchronization between the acoustic signal recorded by the microphone and the balloon pressure transducer. The air pressure varies quite rapidly at the start of the sentence, and a small time error can result in a large pressure discrepancy. In Figure 4.17 we have plotted the fundamental frequency versus the subglottal pressure for the points measured on the quasi-steady-state portions of the air pressure and fundamental frequency functions of Figures 4.10–4.12.

Note that there is a time delay of approximately 130 msec[13] from the beginning of expiration when the subglottal pressure starts to rise (0 cm of water) to the point where phonation starts. In Chapter 2

[12] The fundamental frequency was derived by plotting the fifth harmonic of the fundamental frequency on a narrow-band spectrogram that was made using the linear 3.0-kc frequency display.

[13] We measured all time relationships on the unquantized wide-band spectrograms where it was easier to see the onset and end of speech.

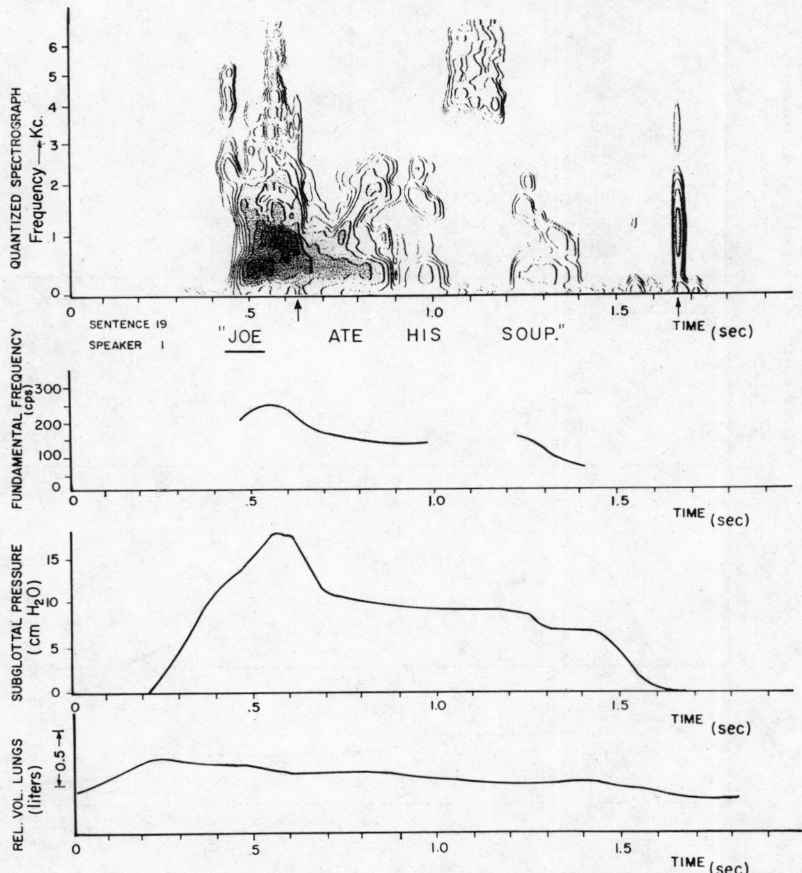

Figure 4.11 Acoustic and physiologic data for speaker 1 reading the declarative sentence "*Joe* ate his soup."
The speaker used a normal breath-group, but he placed prominence on the word *Joe* by means of a momentary increase in the subglottal air pressure. The fundamental frequency, subglottal air pressure, and the volume of air in the speaker's lungs are plotted as functions of time. A quantized wide-band spectrogram is also presented.

we noted that it takes approximately 100 msec for the vocal cords to move from their open inspiratory configuration into the proper configuration for phonation. The data presented in Figure 4.10 show that a similar delay occurs between the initiation of the expiratory airflow and the start of phonation. We have plotted this delay, which we shall call the "phonation delay," and the initial subglottal air pres-

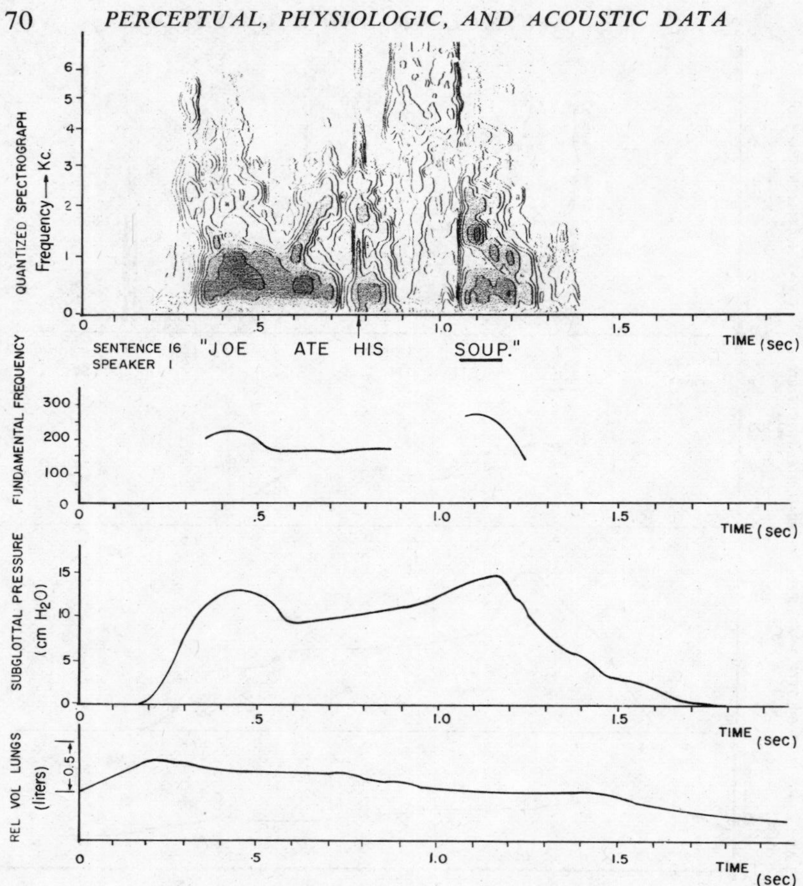

Figure 4.12 Acoustic and physiologic data for speaker 1 reading the declarative sentence "Joe ate his *soup*."
The speaker used a normal breath-group, but he placed prominence on the word *soup* by means of a momentary increase in the subglottal air pressure. Note that the subglottal air pressure and fundamental frequency both fall at the end of the sentence.

sure in Figure 4.34. We shall plot on this figure all the phonation delays and initial subglottal air pressure for all of the data that will follow.

In Figure 4.11 we have presented the data that were obtained when speaker 1 read sentence 19, "*Joe* ate his soup." All the data that follow will be for the sentences that were read at a normal speaking level. Note that there is a 180-msec delay between the start or the gradual rise of the subglottal pressure and the start of phonation.

Note that, in a qualitative sense, the fundamental frequency again seems to be an increasing function of the subglottal air pressure.

The subglottal air pressure is 17.5 cm on the word *Joe* and 9.0 cm at the beginning of the word *soup* in Figure 4.11. In Figure 4.10 the subglottal pressure is 12.5 cm for the word *Joe* and 11.7 cm at the beginning of the word *soup*. The speaker has emphasized the word *Joe* in Figure 4.11 by means of a momentary increase in the subglottal air pressure. When we discussed the results of the Hadding-Koch and Studdert-Kennedy psychoacoustic data, we hypothesized that a subglottal overpressure in one part of the breath-group would lower the subglottal air pressure elsewhere. We also said that the listeners would ascribe fundamental frequency prominences in the nonterminal portion of the breath-group to momentary increases in the subglottal air pressure.

The fundamental frequency contour of the sentence in Figure 4.11 has a high peak fundamental frequency early in its breath-group on the word *Joe*. We can see that the articulatory gesture that is responsible for this peak is, in fact, a momentary increase in the subglottal air pressure. The subglottal air pressure at the end of this breath-group is 2.7 cm lower than it is at the corresponding point in the breath-group of sentence 18 in Figure 4.10.

The physiologic evidence therefore supports our "air pressure perturbation" hypothesis since the presence of the subglottal air pressure prominence early in the breath-group lowers the air pressure at the end of the breath-group 2.7 cm. In Figure 4.17, where the fundamental frequency has been plotted with respect to subglottal air pressure for these sentences, we can see that the fundamental frequency varies at the rate of 16–20 cps per cm of water. If the tension of the laryngeal muscles followed the same pattern in both breath-groups, the fundamental frequency would thus be approximately 50 cps lower at the end of the contour that had the higher initial subglottal pressure peak.

In the psychoacoustic experiment that we discussed earlier, the American listeners needed a lower terminal fundamental frequency to "hear" a terminal rise when the contour had a higher initial fundamental frequency prominence. An intonation contour, for example, would be heard as a "question" 80 percent of the time when its terminal fundamental frequency was 40–80 cps lower than the terminal fundamental frequency of a similar contour that had a lower initial fundamental frequency prominence (cf. Figure 4.5). The 50-cps "terminal fundamental frequency adjustment" that we should expect from the subglottal air pressure contour of Figure 4.11 is thus within the range of the perceived fundamental frequency compensations that occurred in the independent psychoacoustic experiment. Note that the breath-groups in Figures 4.10 and 4.11 both have similar durations and similar "average" subglottal air pressures. We shall return to the constraints that must be placed upon the role of the "air pressure perturbation" hypothesis in Section 4.3.3.

In Figure 4.12 we have plotted the data for sentence 16. The phonation delay and the initial subglottal pressure, as well as the fundamental frequency versus subglottal pressure data, have been entered in Figures 4.34 and 4.17. The subglottal air pressure and fundamental frequency data fall into line with the data from Figures 4.10 and 4.11 on Figure 4.17. The phonation delay is again 130 msec. Note that the terminal fundamental frequency and subglottal pressure contours fall though the speaker has raised the subglottal air pressure at the start of the word *soup*.

The acoustic correlates of the subglottal pressure peaks in Figure 4.11 and Figure 4.12 were higher fundamental frequencies and greater envelope amplitudes. The duration of the words that received the peak subglottal air pressures was also longer in the utterances plotted in Figures 4.11 and 4.12 than it was in the unemphatic utterance plotted in Figure 4.10. The diphthong in *soup* has a duration of 220 msec in Figure 4.12, where it received the peak subglottal air pressure. It had a duration of 180 msec in Figures 4.10 and 4.11, where it did not receive the peak subglottal air pressure. The diphthong in *Joe* had a duration of 220 msec in Figure 4.10, where it was not emphasized. It had a duration of 270 msec in Figure 4.11, where it received the peak subglottal pressure. It had, however, a duration of 260 msec in Figure 4.12, where it did not receive the peak subglottal air pressure. The total duration of the utterance in Figure 4.10 was 900 msec. The total duration of the utterance plotted in Figure 4.11 was 980 msec, while the duration of the utterance in Figure 4.12 was 1000 msec. Longer durations thus seem to be associated with the words that received the peak subglottal air pressure. However, there may not be any causal relationship between the peak subglottal air pressure and the longer duration. The speaker may independently increase duration when he wants to emphasize a word. We shall present other data indicating that this seems to be what happens. The speaker can increase the duration of the vowel of an emphasized word without placing a momentary increase in subglottal air pressure on the vowel.

Figure 4.13 presents data derived from speaker 1 reading sentence

3, "Did Joe eat his soup?" The plot of the volume of air in his lungs is not presented in this figure. Note that the shape of the air pressure plot is quite similar to that of Figure 4.10 for the unemphasized declarative sentence "Joe ate his soup." However, the fundamental

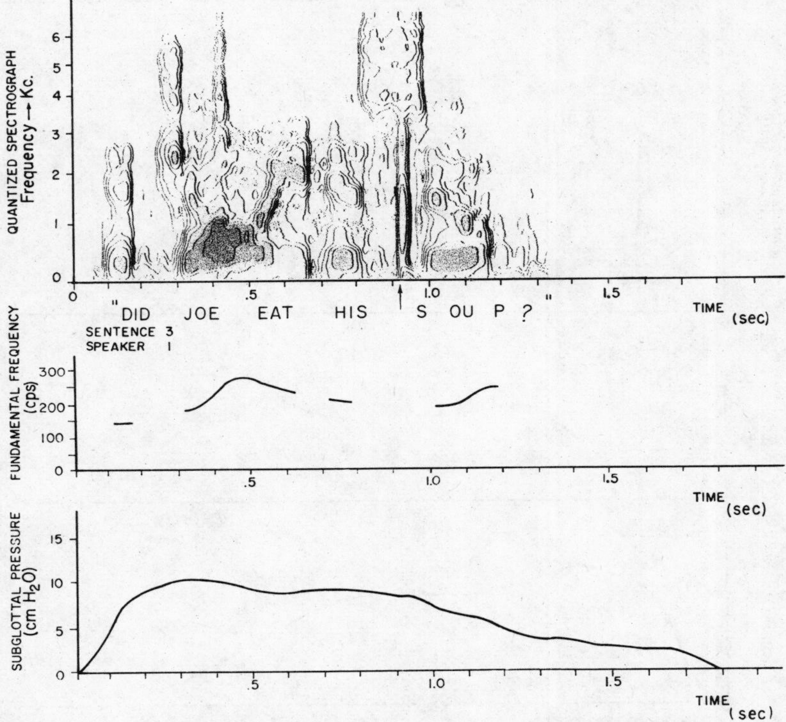

Figure 4.13 Acoustic and physiologic data for speaker 1 reading the interrogative sentence "Did Joe eat his soup?"
The speaker used a marked breath-group [+BG]. Fundamental frequency and subglottal air pressure are plotted as functions of time, and a wide-band spectrogram is also presented. Note that the fundamental frequency at the end of phonation rises though the subglottal air pressure is falling. The terminal rise in fundamental frequency thus is due to an increase in the tension of the laryngeal muscles.

frequency rises at the end of sentence 3, though the subglottal air pressure is falling. The subglottal air pressure at the beginning of the vocalic portion of the word *soup* is 6.8 cm. It falls by 4.6 cm at the end of phonation.

If the tension of the laryngeal muscles were held constant at the end of this utterance, we should expect the fundamental frequency to fall approximately 45 cps. The fundamental frequency instead rises 50 cps at the end of the breath-group. The speaker must therefore be tensioning his laryngeal muscles to produce a 100-cps rise in the fundamental frequency at the end of the breath-group to counteract the effects of the falling subglottal air pressure. The data in Figure

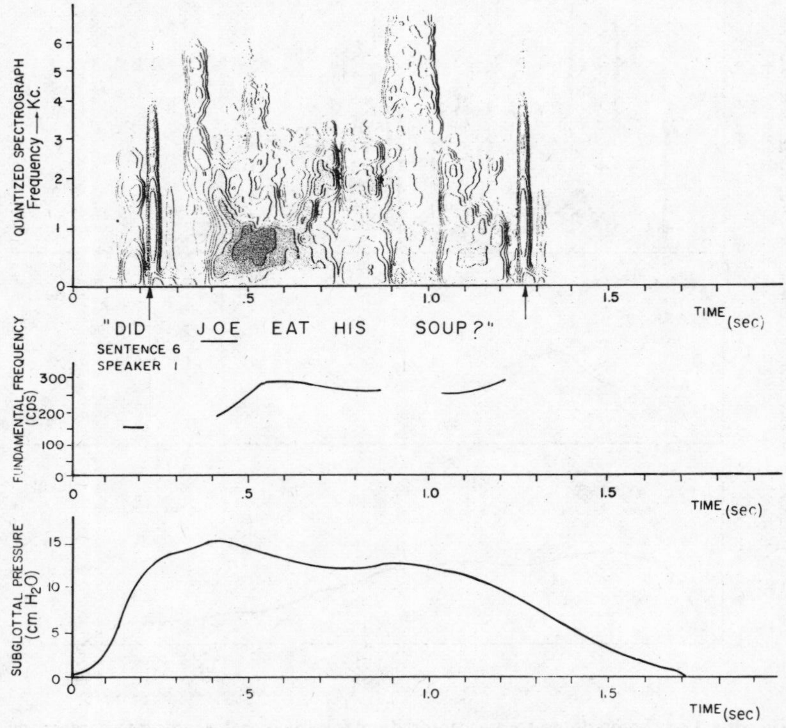

Figure 4.14 Acoustic and physiologic data for speaker 1 reading the interrogative sentence "Did *Joe* eat his soup?"
The speaker has used a marked breath-group. He has produced a terminal fundamental frequency rise by means of increased laryngeal tension. Prominence has also been placed on the word *Joe* by means of increased subglottal air pressure.

4.13 are therefore consistent with our hypothesis concerning the marked breath-group [+ *BG*]. The increase in the tension of the laryngeal muscles occurs at the end of the breath-group where the subglottal pressure falls. The acoustic correlate of this is a not-falling terminal fundamental frequency contour.

Figure 4.14 presents data for sentence 6, "Did *Joe* eat his soup?" The speaker placed extra prominence on *Joe* by placing the peak subglottal pressure on it. The subglottal pressure on *Joe* is 15.4 cm. In Figure 4.13 the subglottal pressure on *Joe* was 10.0 cm. The fundamental frequency and duration of the diphthong of *Joe* in Figure 4.14 are 290 cps and 240 msec, respectively. The fundamental frequency of Joe is 280 cps in Figure 4.13, where it was not supposed to be emphasized. However, the duration of the diphthong of *Joe* is 180 msec in Figure 4.13. The peak amplitude of the first formant of /o/ in *Joe* relative to the rest of the sentence is the same (to the nearest 6 db) in Figures 4.13 and 4.14. Perceptually, *Joe* is much more prominent[14] in Figure 4.14 than it is in Figure 4.13. Note that the fundamental frequency at the end of this sentence again rises though the subglottal air pressure falls.

Figure 4.15 gives the data for sentence 12, "Did Joe eat his *soup?*" The speaker has again emphasized *soup* by means of increased subglottal air pressure. In Figure 4.13, where the unemphasized question is displayed, the peak amplitude of the first formant of the vowel /u/ in *soup* was 6 db less than the peak amplitude of the first formant of the vowel /I/ in *his*. In Figure 4.15 where *soup* is emphasized the peak amplitude of the first formant of /u/ is 6 db greater than the first formant of /I/. Amplitude is thus a reasonably consistent acoustic correlate of [+ P_s] for speaker 1 though, in general, increases in the fundamental frequency and duration of the emphasized vowels are more consistent acoustic correlates of [+ P_s].

The pressure function of Figure 4.15 resembles that of Figure 4.12 (the sentence "Joe ate his *soup*"). The over-all magnitude of the pressure function is greater in Figure 4.15, but the shape is the same. Note, however, that Figure 4.15 ends with a rising fundamental frequency contour in contrast to Figure 4.12. In both utterances emphasis has been placed on *soup* by means of increased subglottal air pressures. The speaker, however, does not place the peak pressure at the end of phonation for the declarative sentence in Figure 4.12. If the peak air pressure were placed at the end of phonation, the declarative sentence would end with a not-falling fundamental frequency contour unless the speaker compensated by reducing the tension of his laryngeal muscles. The interrogative sentence in Figure 4.15, of course, ends with a rising fundamental frequency contour. The fundamental frequency rises 170 cps though the subglottal air pressure is falling during the last 70 msec of phonation. The fundamental frequency rise is actually steeper during the last 70 msec of

[14] We shall define the terms "prominence" and "emphasis" in Chapter 7. Briefly speaking, prominence is one of the perceptual manifestations of emphasis. Emphasis has sometimes been called "contrastive stress."

phonation. The speaker again increases the tension of his laryngeal muscles at the end of the breath-group. The two articulatory gestures —(1) the momentary increase in the subglottal air pressure associated with [+ P_s], and (2) the tensioning of the laryngeal muscles

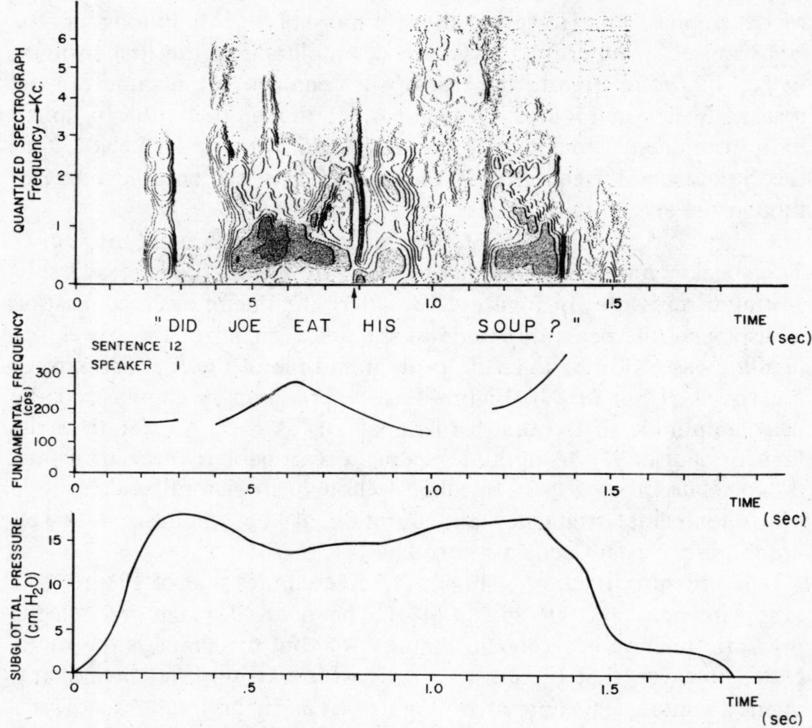

Figure 4.15 Acoustic and physiologic data for speaker 1 reading the interrogative sentence "Did Joe eat his *soup*?"
The speaker has used a marked breath-group. Prominence has been placed on the word *soup* by means of a relative increase in subglottal air pressure. However, the terminal fundamental frequency rise of the marked breath-group is again produced by means of an increase in the tension of the laryngeal muscles. Compare these data with Figure 4.12. Both breath-groups end with a falling subglottal air pressure, but the fundamental frequency does not fall at the end of the marked breath-group.

for the marked breath-group—are clearly independent for these data.

In two instances a speaker uttered the two repetitions of the same sentence on one expiration. In Figure 4.16 the subglottal pressure plots and fundamental frequency contours are presented for speaker

1 when he uttered sentence 15 twice on the same breath-group. The solid lines are the plots for the first utterance, 15*A*, and the dashed lines are the plots for the second utterance, 15*B*. Note that the general shape of the subglottal air pressure function is similar for both utterances. The speaker controlled his respiratory muscles and produced two similar pressure contours that are both similar to the pressure function of the normal breath-group that he used for his unemphatic sentences, for example, the pressure function in Figures

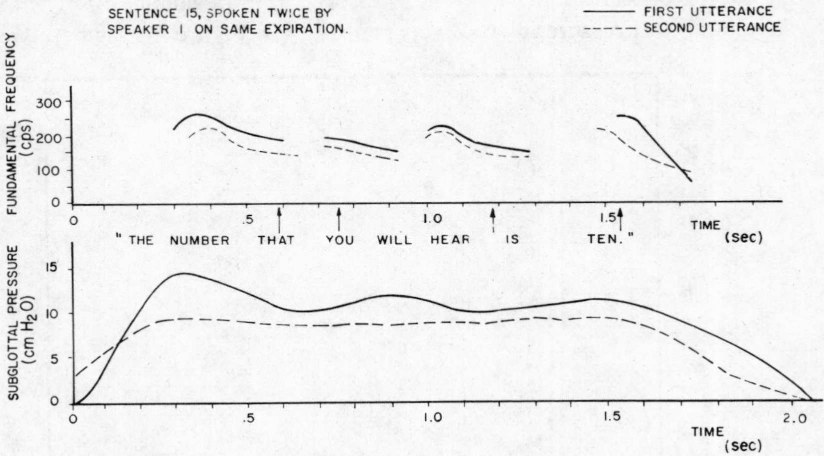

Figure 4.16 Fundamental frequency and subglottal air pressure are plotted as functions of time for speaker 1 reading the sentence "The number that you will hear is ten" twice on the same expiration.
Note that the subglottal air pressure and fundamental frequency contours of the repetition (dashed lines) have lower average values than the first rendition of the sentence (solid lines). Fundamental frequency and subglottal pressure were measured for both utterances at the four points marked by vertical arrows. The average fundamental frequency and subglottal pressure for these four points were 213 cps and 10.7 cm H_2O for utterance *A* and 175 cps and 8.9 cm H_2O for utterance *B*.

4.10 and 4.13. The magnitude of the pressure function of 15*B* is somewhat smaller than that of 15*A*.

The two fundamental frequency contours in this figure also have the same shape. The fundamental frequency contour for 15*B* again has a smaller magnitude than that of 15*A*. It seems evident that the speaker manipulated his laryngeal muscles in the same manner for both utterances. The lower fundamental frequency contour of utterance *B* would then follow from the lower subglottal air pressure of utterance *B*. This hypothesis was tested by determining the average fundamental frequency and subglottal air pressure of the slowly varying portions of both contours where we could be sure of lining up the corresponding points on the subglottal pressure and the fundamental frequency plots. The average fundamental frequency and subglottal pressure of the four points marked by arrows in Figure 4.16 was 213 cps and 10.7 cm H_2O for utterance *A* and 175 cps and 8.9 cm H_2O for utterance *B*. If the control of the laryngeal muscles was similar for both utterances, then the rate of change of f_o with subglottal air pressure is 21 cps/cm H_2O. The rate of change of f_o with subglottal air pressure is 16–20 cps/cm H_2O in Figure 4.17 where we

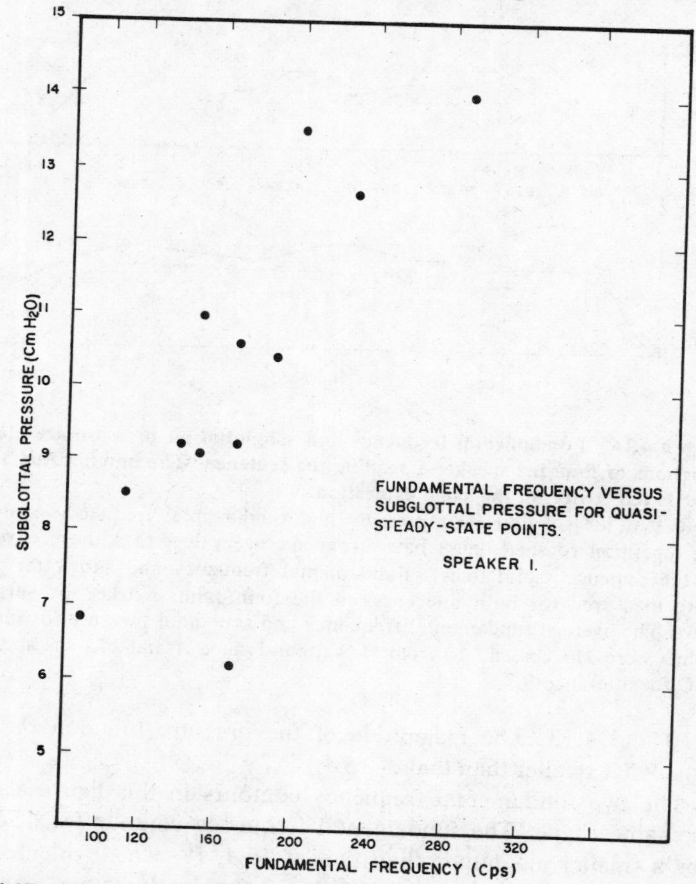

Figure 4.17 Fundamental frequency is plotted with respect to subglottal air pressure for the quasi-steady-state portions of the fundamental frequency and subglottal air pressure contours of Figures 4.10, 4.11, and 4.12 (speaker 1, normal breath-groups).

plotted f_o with respect to the subglottal air pressure for Figures 4.10, 4.11, and 4.12. We assumed that speaker 1 used unmarked breath-groups or unmarked breaths modified only by momentary increases in the subglottal air pressure to produce the utterances plotted in these figures.

Data on Individual Sentences—Speakers 2 and 3. In Figures 4.18,

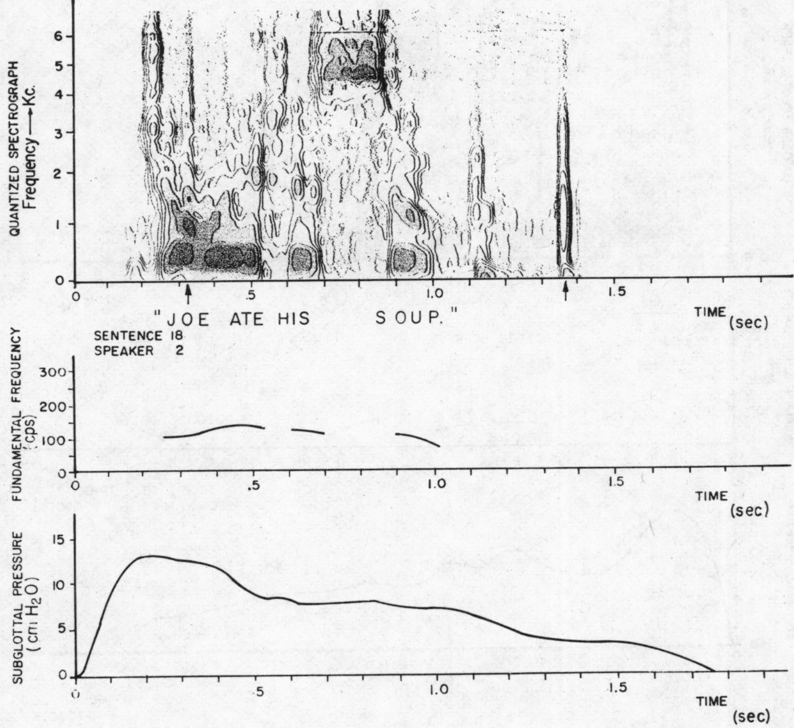

Figure 4.18 Acoustic and physiologic data for speaker 2 reading the declarative sentence "Joe ate his soup."
A normal breath-group that differed in detail from that employed by speaker 1 was used.

4.19, and 4.20 we have presented the fundamental frequency and subglottal air pressure plots for speaker 2 reading sentences 18, 19, and 16 in a normal speaking voice. Sound spectrograms of the utterances are presented, as was done for the previous data from speaker 1's utterances. The phonation delay and initial subglottal pressure is still plotted in Figure 4.34. If Figure 4.18 is compared to Figure 4.10, it is obvious that though speaker 2 starts his normal breath-group with a fairly large subglottal pressure peak (5.6 cm above the rest of the air pressure contour), he nonetheless starts phonation with a fundamental frequency that is lower than the fundamental frequency occurring later in the breath-group where the subglottal pressure is lower. Speaker 2 must therefore start his normal breath-

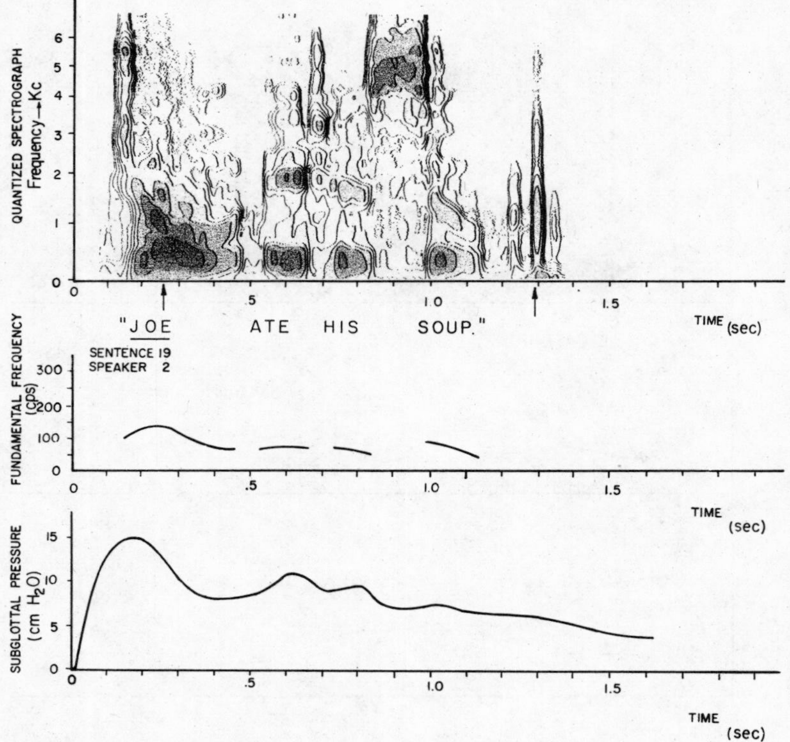

Figure 4.19 Acoustic and physiologic data for speaker 2 reading the sentence "*Joe* ate his soup."
A normal breath-group was used, and prominence was placed on the word *Joe*.

group with a lower tension on his laryngeal muscles. The lower tension tends to lower the fundamental frequency, and it thus counteracts the high initial subglottal air pressure that is typical for speaker 2's breath-groups. The fundamental frequency at the end of phonation also seems to drop faster (60 cps for 0.6 cm) than it would if the tension of his laryngeal muscles were not also relaxed. He produces a fundamental frequency contour whose gross characteristics are not very different from speaker 1's, but he uses a different pattern of articulatory activity.

In Figure 4.19 we see the presence of a momentary peak in the subglottal air pressure which has been placed on *Joe*. In Figure 4.20 a subglottal overpressure has been placed on *soup*. The fundamental frequency still falls at the end of the declarative sentence on Figure

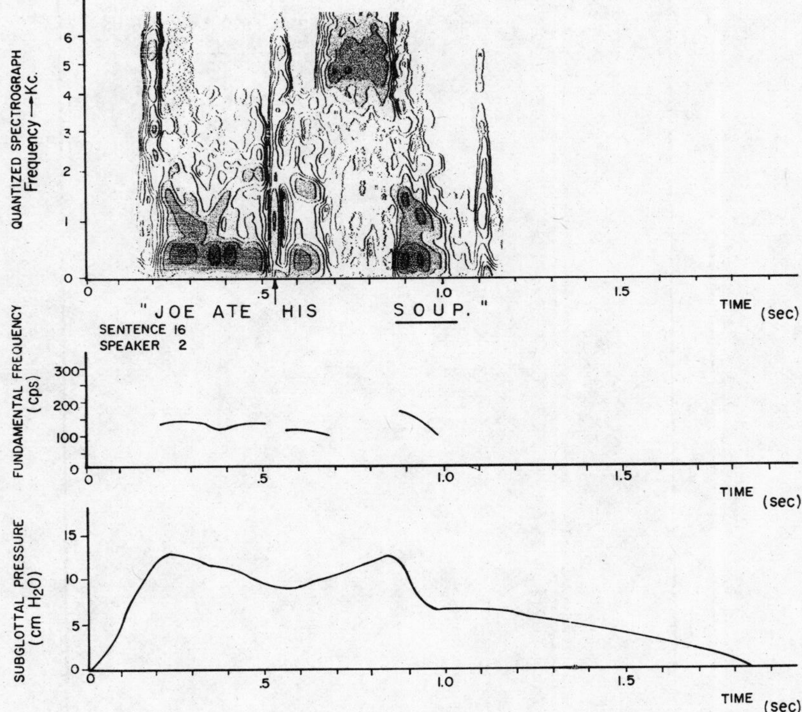

Figure 4.20 Acoustic and physiologic data for speaker 2 reading the sentence "Joe ate his *soup*."
A normal breath-group was used, and prominence was placed on the word *soup*.

4.20. However, the falling fundamental frequency in this case seems to be due to the falling subglottal air pressure. The terminal fall is 100 cps, and the subglottal air pressure falls 4.8 cm. In Figure 4.21 the fundamental frequency has been plotted with respect to the subglottal air pressure for quasi-steady-state intervals derived from the plots in Figures 4.18–4.20. The rate of change of f_o with respect to subglottal pressure is about 18 cps/cm H_2O for the data on

Figure 4.21. The data points in this plot are scattered more than those in Figure 4.17, where similar data points were plotted for speaker 1. This undoubtedly is the case because speaker 2 tends to vary the tension of his laryngeal muscles during his normal breath-group.

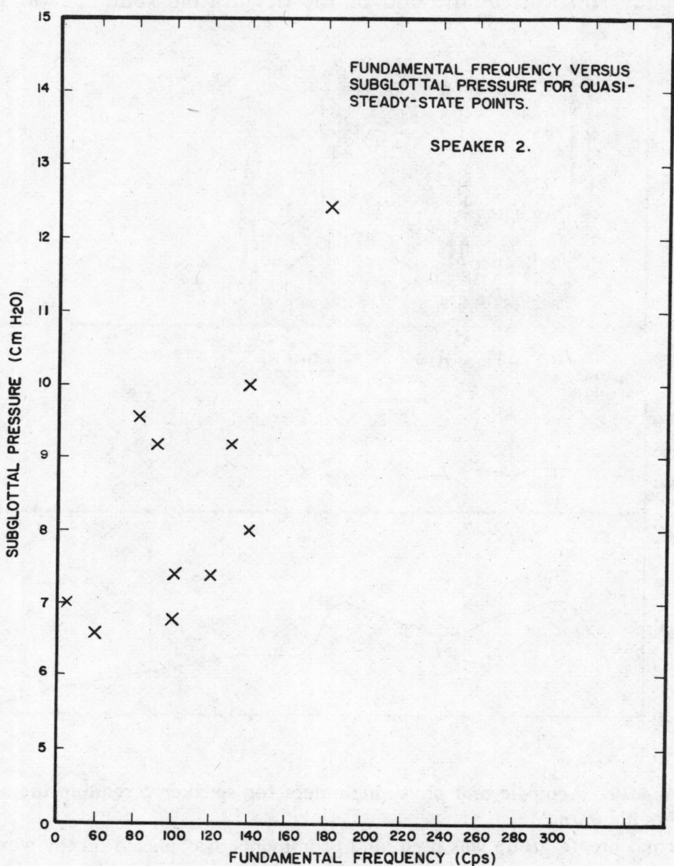

Figure 4.21 Fundamental frequency is plotted with respect to subglottal air pressure for the quasi-steady-state portions of the fundamental frequency and subglottal air pressure contours of Figures 4.18, 4.19, and 4.20 (speaker 2, normal breath-groups).

In Figures 4.22 and 4.23 we have presented data derived from speaker 2's utterances of sentences 3 and 8, "Did Joe eat his soup?" and "Joe ate his soup?" The fundamental frequency at the end of the two interrogative sentences of Figures 4.22 and 4.23 rises through the action of the laryngeal muscles, since the subglottal air pressure is relatively steady. Note that the subglottal air pressure contours are similar to that of Figure 4.18, where the data for the unemphasized declarative sentence are presented. All of the contours start with a comparatively high subglottal air pressure. However, the initial fundamental frequency for all of these sentences is slightly lower than

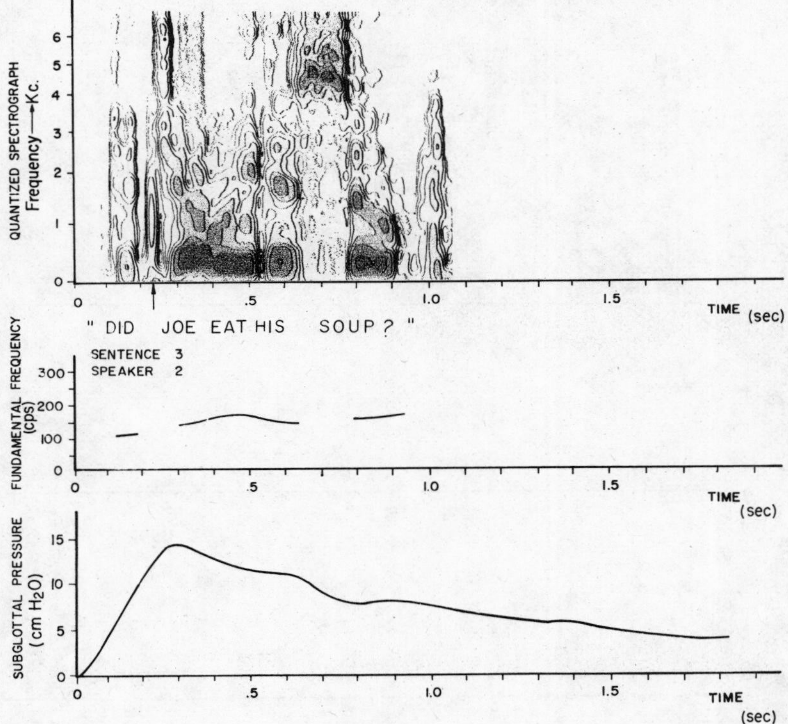

Figure 4.22 Acoustic and physiologic data for speaker 2 reading the sentence "Did Joe eat his soup?"
Marked breath-group.

the fundamental frequency that occurs in the middle of the breath-group where the subglottal air pressure is lower.

In Figure 4.24 the data points are plotted for sentence 6, "Did *Joe* eat his soup?" Emphasis is again placed on *Joe* by means of a momentary increase in the subglottal air pressure which perturbs the subglottal air pressure function that is usually associated with speaker 2's normal breath-group. However, f_o does not rise on *Joe,* perhaps because speaker 2 characteristically starts his breath-group with a lower laryngeal tension. The fundamental frequency again rises at the end of the breath-group through the activity of the laryngeal muscles. Note that the duration of the diphthong of the emphasized *Joe* is 300 msec, whereas its durations in Figures 4.22, 4.23, 4.20, and 4.18, where it is not emphasized, are respectively 150, 150, 150, and 130 msec. Its duration in Figure 4.19, where it was also empha-

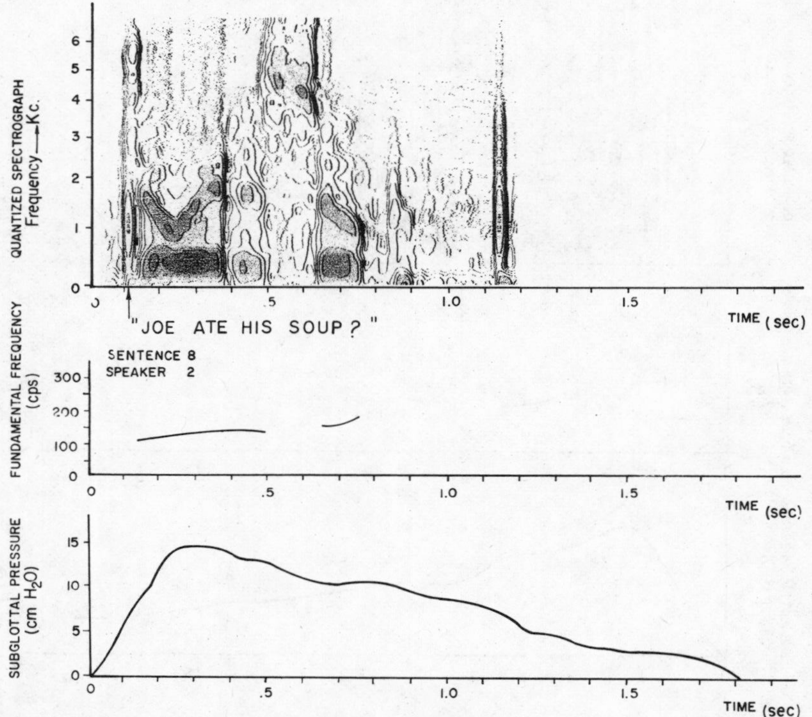

Figure 4.23 Acoustic and physiologic data for speaker 2 reading the sentence "Joe ate his soup?"
Marked breath-group.

sized, is 250 msec. The duration of the diphthong in *soup* is likewise 150 msec in Figure 4.20, where it receives emphasis. Its durations in Figures 4.18, 4.19, 4.22, 4.23, and 4.24, where it does not receive emphasis, are respectively 120, 130, 120, 110, and 130 msec. Duration thus seems to be an acoustic correlate of $[+P_s]$ for speaker 2.

The peak amplitude of F_1 of /o/ in *Joe* is the same vis-à-vis the amplitude of the vowels of *eat* and *his* in both the sentences where speaker 2 emphasized *Joe* and the sentences where he did not emphasize *Joe*. In Figure 4.24, where the peak subglottal air pressure occurred on /j/ of *Joe,* the amplitude /j/ at 5.5 kc is 6 db greater than it was in Figure 4.22, where *Joe* was not emphasized. The amplitude of F_1 and F_2 of /u/ in *soup* were 6 db higher in Figure 4.20 where *soup* was emphasized. Amplitude is thus not as consistent an acoustic correlate of $[+P_s]$ for speaker 2 as the fundamental frequency or the duration of the vowels.

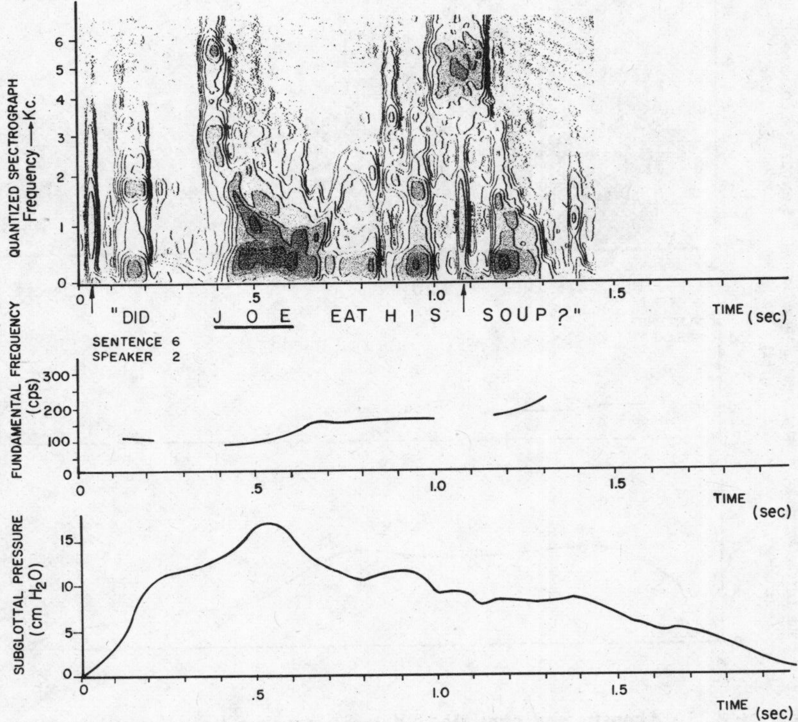

Figure 4.24 Acoustic and physiologic data for speaker 2 reading the sentence "Did *Joe* eat his soup?"
Marked breath-group, prominence on the word *Joe*.

In Figures 4.25, 4.26, and 4.27 the data for three of speaker 3's declarative sentences have been presented. In Figure 4.28 the fundamental frequency is plotted with respect to the subglottal air pressure for quasi-steady-state points derived from these figures. In Figures 4.29–4.32 the data for several of his interrogative sentences are plotted. Note that the subglottal pressure functions in Figures 4.25, 4.29, and 4.30, which are typical of this speaker's breath-groups when they are not perturbed by subglottal overpressures, are quite distinct from the corresponding curves for speakers 1 and 2. The subglottal pressure function of each speaker has a characteristic "shape."

The declarative sentences seem to make use of the archetypal articulatory gestures except that the fundamental frequency at the end of phonation in Figures 4.25 and 4.26 seems to fall through

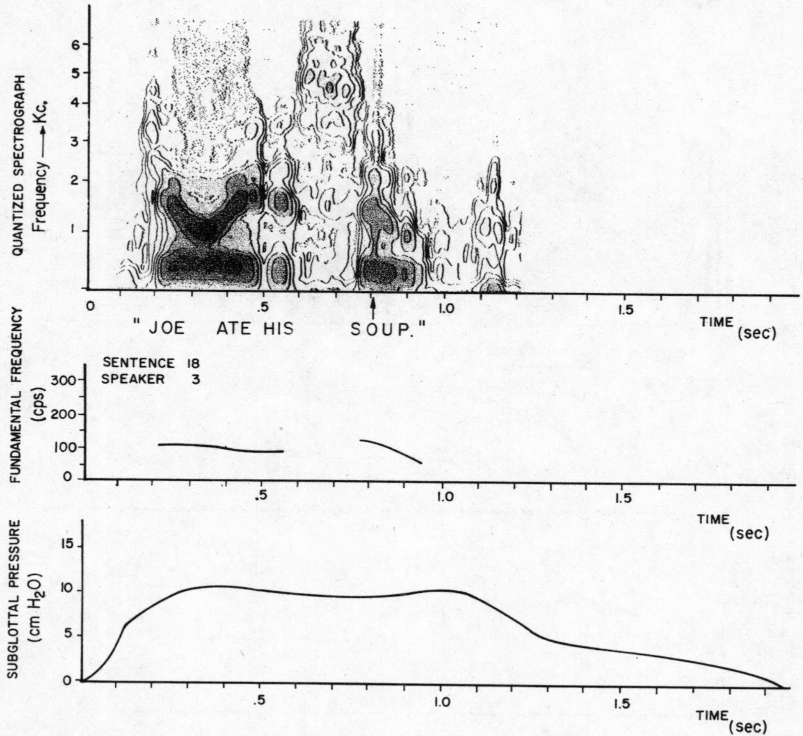

Figure 4.25 Acoustic and physiologic data for speaker 3 reading the sentence "Joe ate his soup."
Normal breath-group.

some laryngeal adjustment. The speaker is preserving the acoustic correlates of the normal breath-group though he does not produce the terminal fundamental frequency fall by reducing his subglottal air pressure.

In Figure 4.29 and 4.30 the data for two interrogative sentences are displayed. Both breath-groups obviously involve an increase in the tension of the laryngeal muscles at the end of phonation, since the fundamental frequency rises though the subglottal air pressure is either falling slightly or is steady. In Figure 4.31 emphasis has been placed on *soup* by means of a momentary increase in the subglottal air pressure. The archetypal articulatory correlate of the segmental feature [$+P_s$] has again been used by the speaker. The subglottal air pressure at the very end of phonation, however, is falling though the fundamental frequency rises 90 cps. The tension of the laryngeal

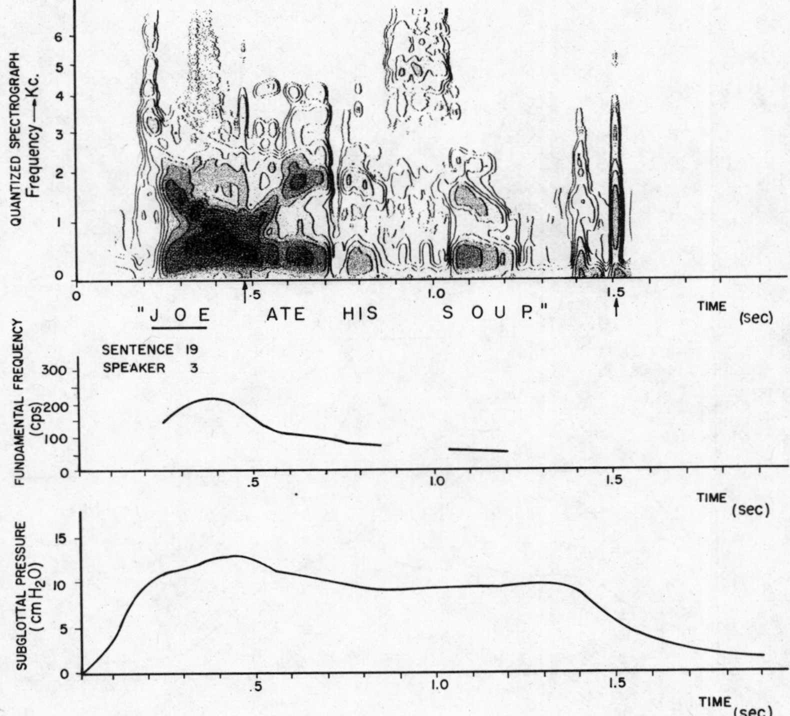

Figure 4.26 Acoustic and physiologic data for speaker 3 reading the sentence "*Joe* ate his soup."
Normal breath-group, prominence on the word *Joe*.

muscles must therefore have been increased at the end of phonation.

In Figure 4.32 the fundamental frequency again rises at the end of the sentence though the subglottal air pressure is falling. The marked breath-group has its usual articulatory correlates. Actually, there was no instance in the entire data sample, including the sentences that are not plotted here, in which the rising fundamental frequency contour typical of the interrogative sentences was not generated by means of an increase in the tension of the laryngeal muscles. In some instances the subglottal air pressure also increased at the very end of phonation. However, in no instance was the increase in the subglottal air pressure sufficient, in itself, to account for the magnitude of the terminal fundamental frequency rise. The segmental feature $[+P_s]$, however, often involved the use of articulatory gestures other than the archetypal increase in the subglottal air pressure. In Figure

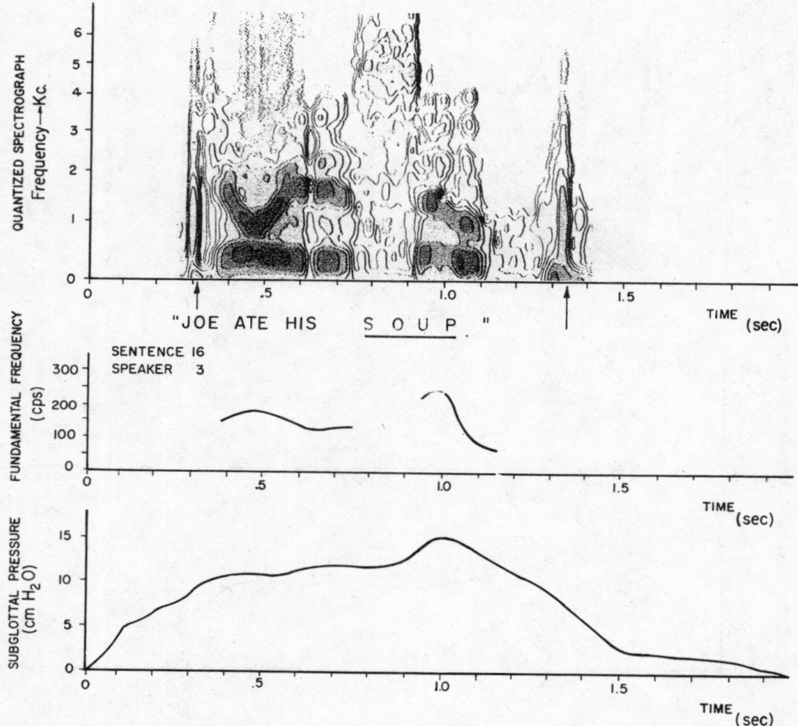

Figure 4.27 Acoustic and physiologic data for speaker 3 reading the sentence "Joe ate his *soup*."
Normal breath-group, prominence on the word *soup*.

4.32, for example, the speaker emphasized *Joe* by increasing its duration. The duration of the diphthong of *Joe* is 250 msec in Figure 4.32. Its average duration was 150 msec when speaker 3 did not emphasize *Joe*. It seems significant that its duration was also increased to 300 msec when it was emphasized in Figure 4.26 and also received a momentary increase in subglottal air pressure. The increased duration that seems to be one of the articulatory correlates of $[+P_s]$ therefore seems to be independent of the subglottal overpressure. Both the

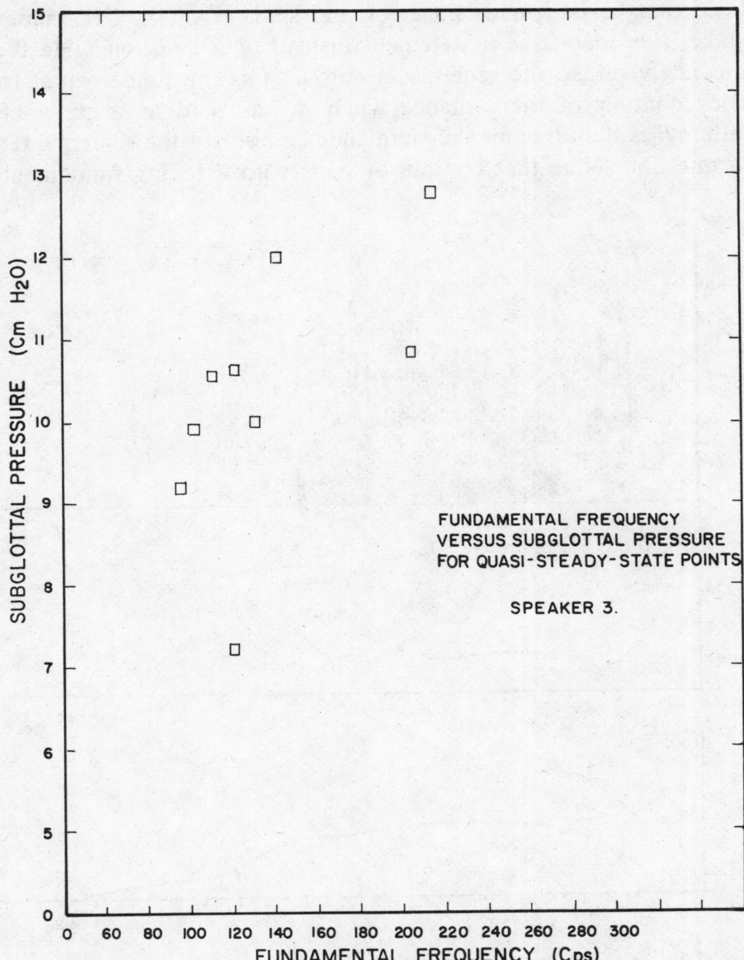

Figure 4.28 Fundamental frequency plotted with respect to subglottal air pressure for the quasi-steady-state portions of the fundamental frequency and subglottal pressure contours of Figures 4.25, 4.26, and 4.27 (speaker 3, normal breath-groups).

increased duration and the subglottal overpressure appear to be independent at the articulatory level. Perceptually, the increased duration probably is interpreted in terms of loudness because of the integrating properties of the auditory system (cf. Chapter 2).

In Figure 4.33 we have presented two fundamental frequency contours for sentence 22, "You're going to drive down that rutted road?" Speaker 3 first read the sentence as a statement. He suddenly noticed that he had made an error and said, "Drat it, I've made a mistake, I've read it as a statement instead of a question." He then immediately reread the sentence. Contour *A* is the fundamental frequency contour of the sentence when it was read as a statement. Contour *B* is the fundamental frequency contour of the sentence read as a question. Note that contour *A* ends with a falling fundamental

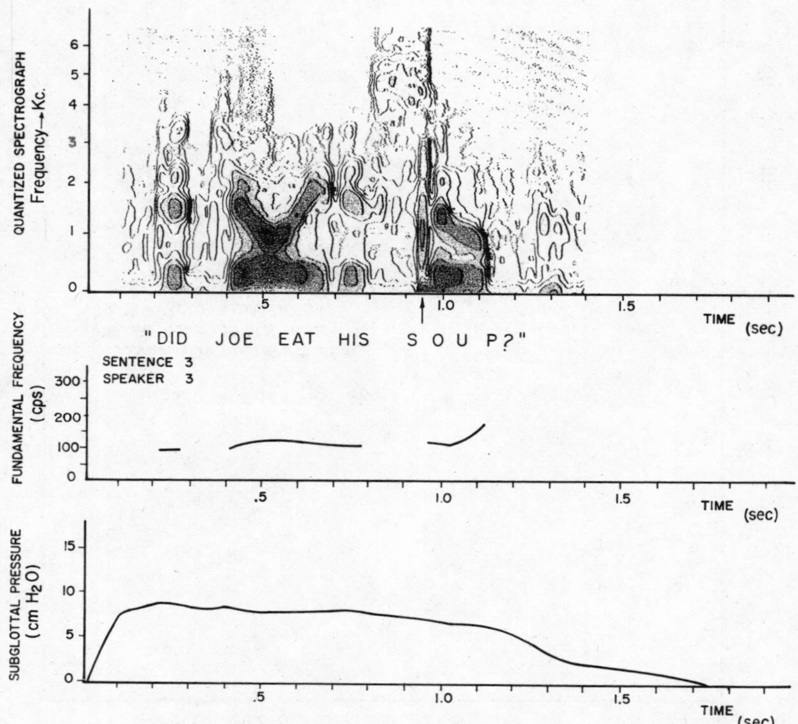

Figure 4.29 Acoustic and physiologic data for speaker 3 reading the sentence "Did Joe eat his soup?"
Marked breath-group.

frequency contour while contour *B* ends with a rising fundamental frequency contour. The subglottal pressure fell during the word *road* in both utterances. The minimal distinction between the question and the statement again is the presence of an increase in the tension of the laryngeal muscles at the end of phonation.

The quantized spectrograms show that the amplitude of the vowels that were emphasized were sometimes relatively greater than they were when they were not emphasized. In Figure 4.26 the amplitude of

F_1 of diphthong /ow/ of *Joe* is 6 db greater relative to the vowels of *ate* and *soup* than it is in Figure 4.25, where it was not emphasized. In all the other examples the relative amplitude of the emphasized vowels was unchanged or smaller. Amplitude is thus not a consistent acoustic correlate of $[+P_s]$ for speaker 3.

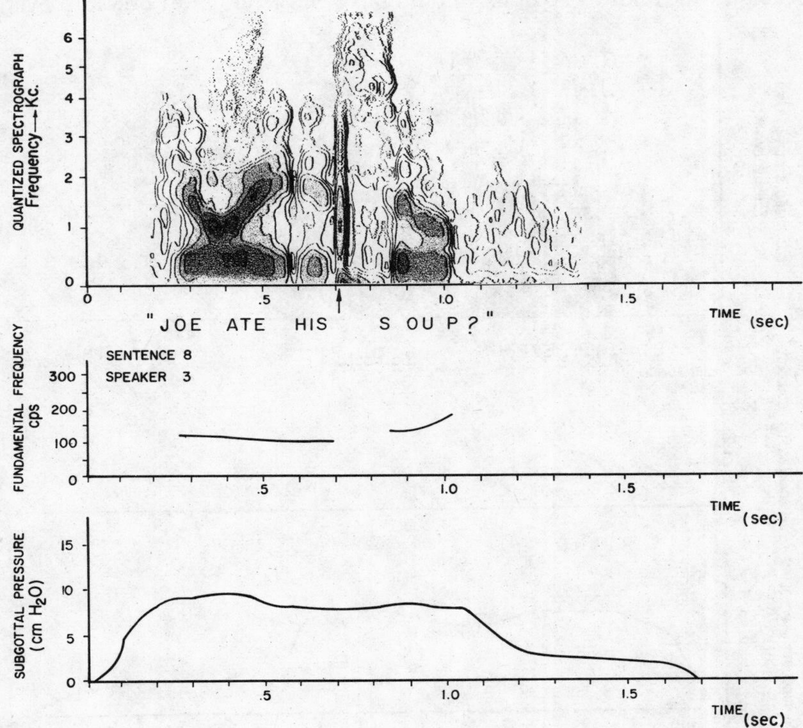

Figure 4.30 Acoustic and physiologic data for speaker 3 reading the sentence "Joe ate his soup?"
Marked breath-group.

4.3 Discussion of Data

4.3.1 The Start and End of the Breath-Group. In Figure 4.34 we have plotted the phonation delay versus the initial subglottal air pressure. The phonation delay is the interval between the beginning expiration and the start of phonation. The data points have been measured from the fundamental frequency and subglottal pressure functions that we have been discussing in this chapter. The data show that phonation starts most often at a pressure of approximately 8–9 cm of

H_2O after a delay of 120–200 msec. Two conditions must be met in order to develop a subglottal pressure. The subglottal respiratory system must be building up a positive alveolar pressure, and there must be some obstruction to the airflow at the glottis. We obviously would have zero subglottal pressure if there were no obstruction to the airflow, and we obviously could have zero subglottal pressure even

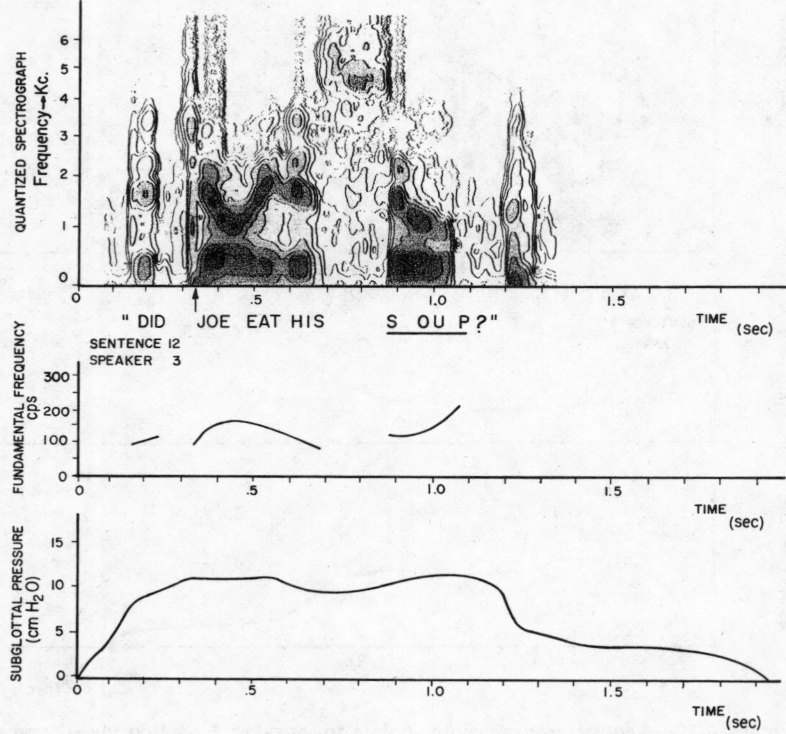

Figure 4.31 Acoustic and physiologic data for speaker 3 reading the sentence "Did Joe eat his *soup*?"

Marked breath-group, prominence on the word *soup*.

if the glottis were fully closed, if air was not forced out from the lungs. The data on Figure 4.34 show that the initial subglottal air pressure is due to the coordinated action of both the respiratory and the laryngeal muscles.

As we noted earlier, observations of the activity of the vocal cords that were obtained by high-speed cameras (cf. Chapter 2) show that it takes about 100–150 msec for the vocal cords to get into position for phonation after they have been in their open respiratory position.

Note that this duration approximately matches the average minimum phonation delay in Figure 4.34.

Figure 4.34 thus shows that expiration has already started as the vocal cords begin to close. The subglottal respiratory system must generate a positive alveolar pressure during expiration. The laryngeal

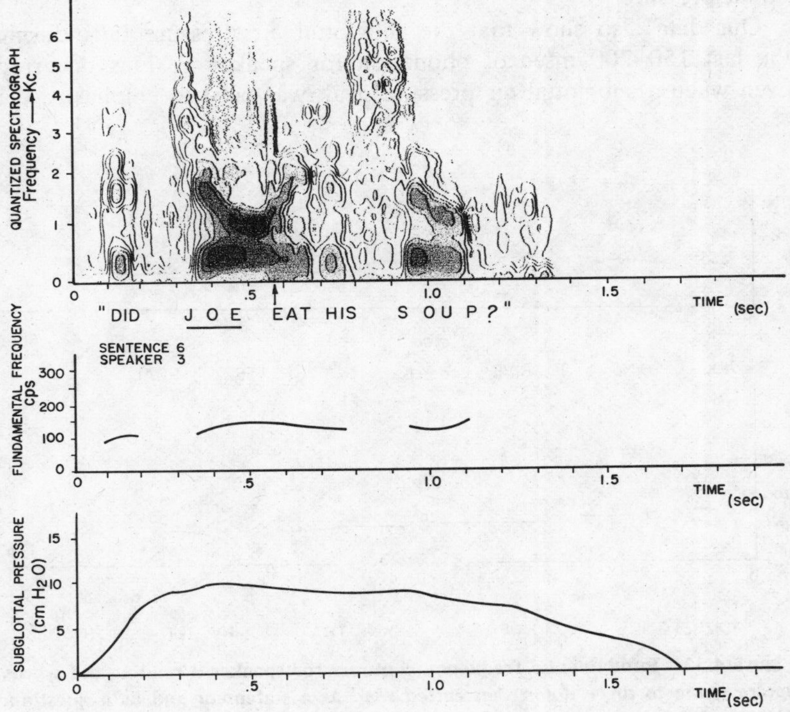

Figure 4.32 Acoustic and physiologic data for speaker 3 reading the sentence "Did *Joe* eat his soup?"

Marked breath-group, prominence on the word *Joe*. Note that the acoustic correlate of $[+P_s]$ is, in this instance, simply an increase in the duration of the vocalic portion of *Joe*. There is no momentary increase in the subglottal air pressure or the fundamental frequency of *Joe*.

muscles constrict the glottis, and the subglottal pressure builds up. However, the respiratory muscles[15] also continue gradually to build

[15] We are not stating that expiratory muscles build up the subglottal air pressure. The elastic recoil force provides most of the motive force for expelling air from the lungs. In order to maintain a low subglottal air pressure at a large lung volume, it is necessary to oppose the elastic recoil force by tensing the inspiratory muscles. A build-up in subglottal air pressure may therefore be effected by relaxing the inspiratory muscles.

up the subglottal pressure while the vocal cords move inward, since the subglottal pressure increases as the phonation delay becomes longer. In most of the breath-groups plotted in this chapter the subglottal pressure continues to rise after the start of phonation, which clearly shows that the respiratory system continues gradually to build up the pressure.

Our data also show that the subglottal air pressure falls during the last 150–200 msec of phonation for speaker 1. This occurred even when a subglottal air pressure peak was used to emphasize the

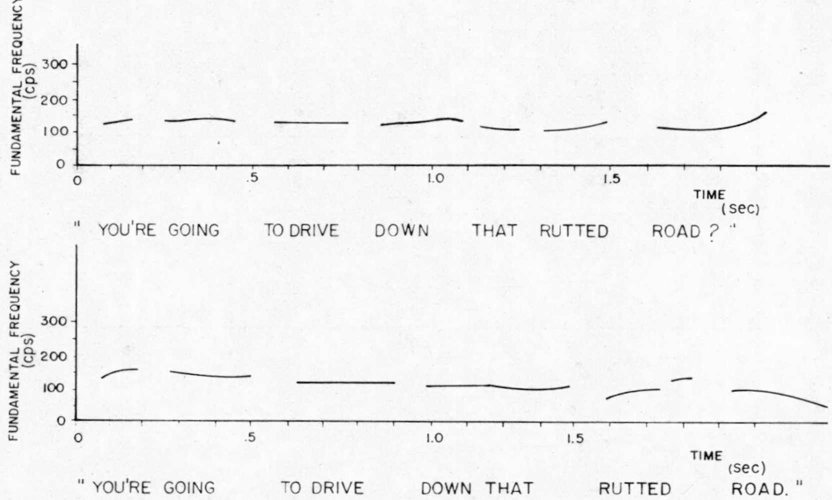

Figure 4.33 Fundamental frequency contours for speaker 3 reading the words *you're going to drive down that rutted road* as a statement and as a question. The speaker read these words as a statement in error and then immediately corrected himself. Note the terminal fundamental frequency contour of the question.

last word in the sentence (Figures 4.12 and 4.15). The subglottal air pressure also fell during the last 150–200 msec of phonation for speakers 2 and 3's breath-groups except for the instances where they departed from the archetypal pattern and maintained a high subglottal air pressure to the end of phonation. The increase in laryngeal tension of the marked breath-group [+*BG*] always occurred during the last 150–200 msec of phonation.

These plots also show that the subglottal pressure either begins to fall at a faster rate or has fallen to a low pressure (3 cm H_2O or less) approximately 100–200 msec after the end of phonation (e.g.,

Figures 4.15, 4.31, 4.32). These data seem to show that the subglottal pressure falls as the glottal obstruction is removed, since the high-speed motion pictures of the vocal cords also show that it takes about 100 msec for the vocal cords to open at the end of phonation. The subglottal respiratory muscles seem to operate more sluggishly than the laryngeal muscles. They often continue to maintain expiration after the end of phonation.

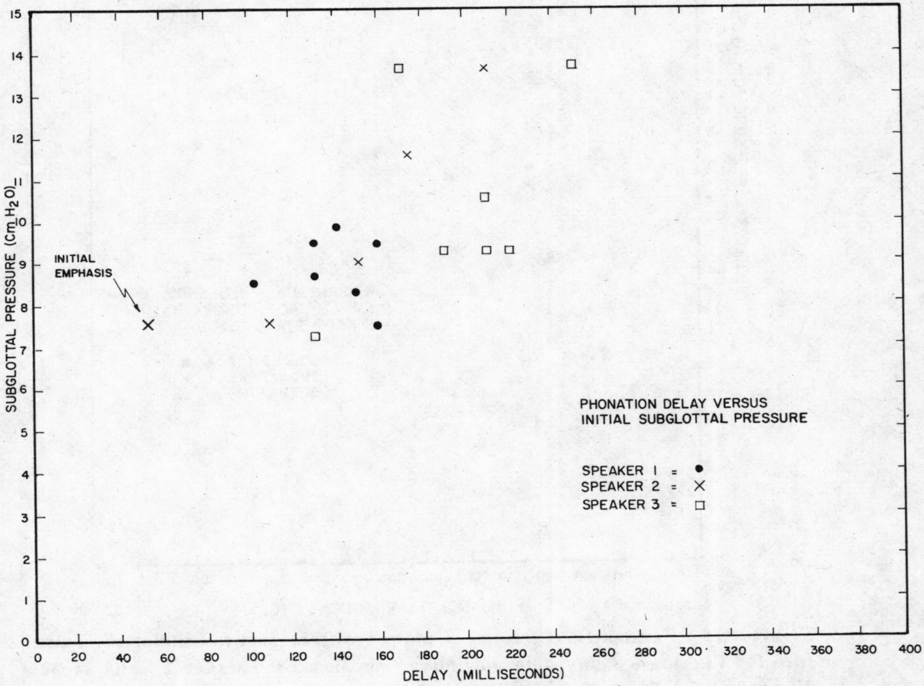

Figure 4.34 Duration of the interval between the beginning of expiration and the start of phonation versus the subglottal air pressure on the onset of phonation plotted for the displayed utterances of speakers 1, 2, and 3.

4.3.2 Fundamental Frequency and Subglottal Air Pressure. In Figure 4.35 we have combined all the data points that were plotted on Figures 4.17, 4.21, and 4.28 for each speaker. Fundamental frequency has been plotted on the abscissa and subglottal air pressure on the ordinate. The calculated correlation coefficient is 0.85, and the correlation is significant at the 0.0001 level. All these data points were measured from the fundamental frequency and subglottal pressure contours of declarative sentences at points where we assumed

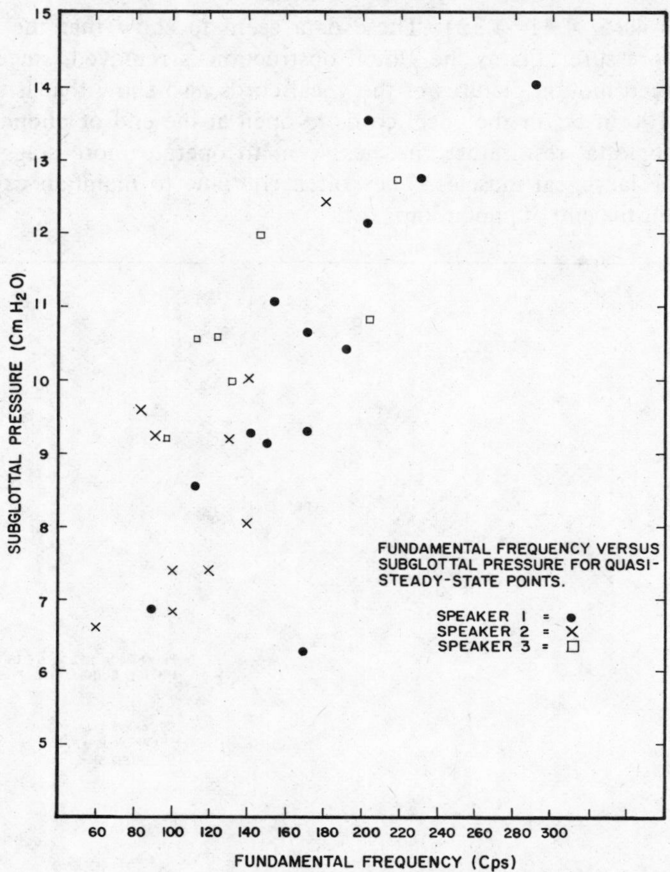

Figure 4.35 Fundamental frequency plotted with respect to subglottal air pressure for the quasi-steady-state portions of speaker 1's, speaker 2's and speaker 3's normal breath-groups.
The data on Figures 4.17, 4.21, and 4.28 are assembled here. The "linear" rate of change of f_o with respect to the subglottal air pressure is approximately 16 cps/cm H_2O for speaker 1, 18 cps/cm H_2O for speaker 2, and 22 cps/cm H_2O for speaker 3.

that the tension of the laryngeal muscles was unchanged,[16] so that the fundamental frequency was a function of the subglottal air pressure.

[16] It is important to note that we are not claiming that the normal breath-group always has a uniform laryngeal tension. Its *archetypal* articulatory correlate is a uniform laryngeal tension that results in an acoustic output where f_o is a function of the subglottal air pressure. The speaker may use alternate articulatory gestures to produce an acoustic output that is similar to the acoustic output of the archetypal articulatory correlate.

We assumed, in short, that these sentences had archetypal unmarked breath-groups. This assumption thus seems to be reasonably valid.

The "linear" rate of increase of fundamental frequency with respect to subglottal air pressure is about 20 cps/cm H_2O. The calculated linear rate of change of f_o with respect to p_s for each individual speaker is: 16 cps/cm H_2O for speaker 1, 18 cps/cm H_2O for speaker 2, and 22 cps/cm H_2O for speaker 3. Van den Berg (1960), in an experiment with an excised male larynx, measured f_o as a function of the subglottal pressure with tension as a parameter. Van den Berg applied tensions to the laryngeal muscles that he considered appropriate for phonation in the chest and falsetto registers. He excited the preparation with a mechanical source that supplied air at regulated pressures at the appropriate temperature and relative humidity. The rate of change of f_o with respect to air pressure varied from about 5 to 13 cps/cm H_2O for the chest register, depending on the tension of the laryngeal muscles and the average fundamental frequency. For the falsetto register the rate of change of f_o with respect to p_s varied from about 20 to 10 cps/cm H_2O. Phonation occurred at either 100 or 130 cps in the chest register at a subglottal air pressure of 10 cm of water in this experiment. These values may vary for different speakers.[17] As van den Berg (1960) points out, ". . . every larynx sang after its own fashion."

The rate of change of f_o with respect to p_s that was obtained through our indirect technique for normal speech is somewhat greater than that obtained by van den Berg. The range of air pressures over which phonation occurred according to our data is consistent with van den Berg's data as well as the range of pressures reported by

[17] The operating characteristics of the same larynx may differ according to whether pitch is being carefully controlled during singing or whether pitch is relatively uncontrolled during speech. Ladefoged and McKinney (1963) in a physiologic experiment, for example, noted that an increase in esophageal air pressure of 6 to 7 cm H_2O corresponded with an increase in fundamental frequency of one-half octave when a speaker uttered a group of vowels at different loudness levels without attempting to control pitch. When the speaker controlled pitch and sang the vowels, they found that ". . . it was difficult to find any quantifiable relationship between the three physiological parameters (subglottal pressure, volume velocity, and fundamental frequency). . . ." Öhman and Lindqvist (1966) in a measurement of the relationship between subglottal air pressure and fundamental frequency found that increases in subglottal air pressure had only a small effect on the fundamental frequency when a speaker sang a vowel. Ohman reports that an increase of 1 cm H_2O in the subglottal air pressure correlated with a reduction of 0.16 msec in the fundamental period (approximately 2.5 cps per cm H_2O in the range of fundamental frequencies explored). Thus a "tighter" control of fundamental frequency may function during singing.

other studies in which the subglottal air pressure was measured during phonation in tracheotomized subjects (Strenger, 1958) or by a needle inserted into the trachea (Isshiki, 1964).

4.3.3 Some Constraints on the "Air Pressure Perturbation" Hypothesis. The physiologic and acoustic data suggest that some obvious constraints must be placed on the "air pressure perturbation" hypothesis that we proposed to explain the data of the Hadding-Koch and Studdert-Kennedy psychoacoustic experiment. If two archetypal breath-groups have approximately the same durations and average subglottal air pressures, then a momentary increase in the subglottal air pressure in the initial part of one breath-group will lower the air pressure at its end vis-à-vis the corresponding unperturbed breath-group. For example, the air pressure at the end of the breath-group in Figure 4.11 is 2.7 cm H_2O lower than the air pressure at the end of the breath-group in Figure 4.10. Both of these breath-groups were produced by means of the archetypal articulatory gestures, and they both had similar durations and average subglottal air pressures. This effect was not apparent if the two breath-groups that were being compared had different average subglottal air pressures or different durations. For example, the air pressure is not lower at the end of the breath-group in Figure 4.14 vis-à-vis the breath-group in Figure 4.13. The average subglottal air pressure in Figure 4.14 is approximately 4 cm H_2O higher than the average subglottal air pressure in Figure 4.13. The durations of the breath-groups in Figures 4.22 and 4.24 are not similar, expiration is prolonged approximately 350 msec longer in the breath-group in Figure 4.22, and the air pressure perturbation effect is not present.

We examined our entire data sample and compared all the utterances of sentence 18, "Joe ate his soup," with all the utterances of sentence 19, "Joe *ate* his soup," for each speaker. We also compared sentence 3, "Did Joe eat his soup?" with sentence 6, "Did *Joe* eat his soup?" We found that the subglottal air pressure was lower at the end of the sentences where the speaker placed a momentary peak pressure on *Joe* when we compared these sentences with utterances that were produced with breath-groups that had similar durations (within 100 msec) and similar average subglottal air pressures (within 1 cm H_2O).

Sixteen sentences were examined for speaker 1. Two of these sentences were produced with different average subglottal air pressures (the sentences in Figures 4.13 and 4.14). The other 14 sentences were produced with breath-groups that had similar durations and average air pressures. The average difference between the subglottal air pressure at the end of the perturbed breath-group and the "similar" unperturbed breath-group was 2.8 cm H_2O, with a standard deviation of 0.8 cm H_2O for the unmarked breath-groups. The average terminal air pressure difference for the similar marked breath-groups was 1.8 cm H_2O, and the standard deviation was 0.75 cm H_2O. All the air pressures were measured at the end of phonation. Twelve sentences were examined for speaker 2. Four sentences were produced on breath-groups that had dissimilar average air pressures. One sentence was produced on an extremely long breath-group. The perturbation effect did not occur in these four sentences. One other sentence also could not be examined since an artifact was present in the subglottal air pressure recording. We were able to compare two pairs of unmarked breath-groups and one pair of unmarked breath-groups. The terminal pressure differentials between the perturbed and unperturbed unmarked breath-groups were 2.5 and 3.0 cm H_2O, while the terminal pressure differential for the pair of marked breath-groups was 2.0 cm H_2O. Twelve sentences were also examined for speaker 3. In one of the marked breath-groups he emphasized *Joe* by simply increasing its duration so that no air pressure perturbation effects were noted. The average air pressures and the durations of four of the other breath-groups were also dissimilar, and the perturbation effect could not be noted. The air pressure differential for two pairs of similar marked breath-groups was 1.0 cm H_2O. The air pressure differentials for two other pairs of marked breath-groups were 4.0 and 6.0 cm respectively, but these utterances were produced with very high subglottal air pressures that are not typical of the rest of the data sample. (The speaker was reading at a "loud" level for these four sentences.)

These data therefore support the "air pressure perturbation" hypothesis subject to these additional constraints. The average terminal pressure differential of the perturbed breath-groups was 2.3 cm H_2O.[18] Since the average rate of change of fundamental frequency with respect to subglottal air pressure is 20 cps/cm H_2O (Figure 4.34), the momentary increase in subglottal air pressure on *Joe* would have resulted, on the average, in a 46-cps fall in the terminal fundamental frequency. This frequency fall is within the range of fundamental frequency deviations (40–80 cps) for which we assumed the listeners in the psychoacoustic experiment compensated by means of the air pressure perturbation effect. However, we must point

[18] If we exclude the two "loud" sentences.

out that our air pressure calculations are only approximations, since the uncertainty imposed by the time synchronization between the acoustic signal and the subglottal air pressure recording may have been as high as ± 40 msec for some of the sentences. The subglottal air pressure recording system has, moreover, been calibrated only for quasi-steady-state conditions, and the transient balloon pressure values may not be related to the subglottal air pressure in exactly the same way as the quasi-steady-state values are.

In the psychoacoustic experiment all the intonation contours had the same duration, and they all started from the same steady-state fundamental frequency (250 cps), so that the listeners could reasonably infer that they had the same average air pressure. The additional constraints that we have imposed on the air pressure perturbation hypothesis were therefore satisfied.

As we mentioned earlier, the physiologic basis of this effect may perhaps be a consequence of the fact that the elastic recoil force of the lungs is the main force that acts to expel air out of the lungs during each breath-group. The elastic recoil force is a function of the instantaneous volume of the lungs. Now the average subglottal air pressure of each breath-group is determined by the extent to which the respiratory muscles oppose or aid the elastic recoil force. A speaker can maintain a given subglottal air pressure at virtually any lung volume by either opposing or supplementing the elastic recoil force by tensing the muscles of the chest and abdomen.

Let us suppose that the pattern of muscular activity that defines the breath-group is independent from the muscular activity that defines the segmental feature $[+P_s]$. The speaker, in other words, determines the pattern of muscular activity that complements the elastic recoil force without regard to whether any of the vowels in the breath-group's span are marked $[+P_s]$. This is a reasonable assumption since all distinctive features are essentially assumed to be independent at the articulatory level. (They constitute an "orthogonal" vector space.)

The presence of $[+P_s]$ in the early part of the breath-group results in a greater airflow out of the lungs, which, of course, lowers the volume of the lungs more than would have been the case if $[+P_s]$ had not occurred. The elastic recoil force, which is a function of the volume of the lungs, therefore decreases. The air pressure in the breath-group is thus lower than it would have been in the absence of $[+P_s]$ early in the breath-group. The air volume plots of our data unfortunately contain certain artifacts that make it impossible to verify this hypothesis quantitatively.

4.3.4 Other Segmental Intonational Features—Interactions between Features. In many languages like Chinese, Thai, etc., additional segmental "tone" features exist. The primary acoustic correlates of these tones seem to be different functions of fundamental frequency (Chang, 1958; Abramson, 1962), and the question of interactions between these tonal features and the suprasegmental intonational features arises. Although these tonal features are clearly segmental, their acoustic correlates may still interact with the suprasegmental features just as $[P_s]$ does. Fortunately, we do not have to speculate about this problem. Chang (*op. cit.*) in an acoustic and phonetic study of the tones and intonation of the Chengtu dialect (Szechwan, China) noted that this dialect had two sentence intonation patterns, a "falling tune" that is used for ordinary and emphatic statements, sentences expressing emphatic approval, awe, contempt, etc., and a "rising tune" that is used for questions. The rising pitch in the question occurs at the very end of the sentence on a special particle. As Chang observes,

> These particles are meaningless by themselves, but they play an important part in bringing out the intonation of the sentence and thus denote whether the sentence is a question or a statement. If the particle is pronounced on a high pitch level or with a rising tone, then the sentence is a question. If on the other hand the particle is pronounced with a falling tone, then the sentence is a statement. It may be asked whether it is these particles that fix the intonation of the sentence or whether they merely bring out the intonation more clearly to the listener by indicating whether the sentence has a rising or a falling tune. The latter explanation seems a more plausible one since the same particle can be used in different types of sentences and it is then pronounced with different tones [p. 78].

Chang notes that four tones exist in this dialect: I a high-rising, II a low-falling, III a high-falling, and IV a low falling-rising. When these tones occur on the final syllable of a sentence that has a falling tune, Tone I becomes mid-level, Tone II remains low-falling, Tone III remains high-falling, and Tone IV becomes low low-falling, checked by a glottal stop. When the tones occur on the final syllable of a sentence with a rising tune, Tone I remains high-rising and often ends higher than usual, Tone II becomes low-level, Tone III becomes high-level, and Tone IV becomes low-rising. Chang also discusses other perturbations of the tones that occur when they are concatenated in connected speech. Other perturbations occur when the speaker makes the syllable on which the tone occurs more prominent. Listeners apparently decode the fundamental frequency contour in terms of the suprasegmental intonation and the segmental tones.[19]

Abramson (*op. cit.*) in his acoustic and phonetic study of Thai also notes that the sentence intonation and the segmental tones interact. He states that the rising intonation used for yes-no questions in Thai ". . . may so affect the lexical tone of the final syllable [of a sentence] as to make it indistinguishable from /ˇ/ (a dynamic rising tone)."

Egerod (1956) in his study of the Lungtu dialect (of Chinese) adds the following:

> The sentence intonation is superimposed on the individual tones and determines the absolute pitch and general inflection of the utterance, whereas the tones determine the relative difference in pitch and inflection among the syllables. The sentence intonation modifies the pitch and inflection on the tones. Only at the end of an utterance may the tone be modified beyond recognition by the intonation.

The fact that the tones are segmental features whereas the intonation is a suprasegmental feature may make the perception recognition routine feasible for these languages. Note that for these languages, which are unrelated to English, the rising intonation that differentiates a question is restricted to the last syllable of the utterance, as is the case for our English data. The phonemic tones of these languages are probably effected at the articulatory level by changes in muscle tension since prominence by stress[20] is an independent factor in Chang's study.

Note that the fundamental frequency contours of the utterance plotted for the three speakers in Figures 4.10–4.33 all show variations in the fundamental frequency within the breath-group. To a degree these variations follow from the variations of the subglottal pressure functions. However, they often seem to be the result of variations in the tension of the laryngeal muscles during the nonterminal portion of the breath-group. The points in Figure 4.35, where fundamental frequency is plotted with respect to subglottal air pressure, have a fair amount of horizontal dispersion, which indicates that the laryngeal tension is not always constant throughout the nonterminal portion of each breath-group. Our initial hypothesis regarding the complete absence of variations in the tension of the laryngeal

[19] Other tone interactions may have different causes. The "sandhi" may not arise from interactions on the articulatory level.

[20] Stress is equivalent to force of utterance in Chang's study, which follows Daniel Jones's phonetic system (cf. Chapter 9).

muscles during the production of a declarative sentence in American English must therefore be considered a first approximation.

There is a great deal of variation from one speaker to the next regarding these nonterminal fundamental frequency variations. Speaker 3 tends to use fewer fundamental frequency variations than speaker 1 (compare Figures 4.25 and 4.10). The three speakers do not even produce similar relative variations for the same sentence (compare Figures 4.25, 4.18, and 4.10). These variations may represent chance variations in the tension of the laryngeal muscles which continually has to be set and reset as the vocal cords move in and out of the "phonation neutral position" to produce vowels and voiced consonants or unvoiced consonants. However, the data in Figure 4.16 (where two fundamental frequency contours that had similar "shapes" were produced for two repetitions of the same sentence that had different average subglottal air pressures) indicate that the speaker may sometimes be controlling the fundamental frequency contour through deliberate modifications of laryngeal tension. Successive productions of the same sentence by the same talker often had similar fundamental frequency contours. All three of the speakers appear to be producing normal utterances. Some listeners occasionally said that speaker 3's voice was "flat" compared with the other two speakers, but no linguistically relevant contrasts between the three speakers' utterances were noted.

Several studies of English speech (Berry, 1953; Lieberman, 1963*c*) have suggested that fundamental frequency, amplitude, and duration are all functions of the relative importance of the word in an utterance. Obviously, semantic and social factors as well as syntactic factors enter into the assessment of a word's relative "importance." These variations in fundamental frequency may manifest the importance or "functional load" of each word in the sentence. The mechanism whereby these fundamental frequency variations are produced is at present a matter for conjecture. The mechanism might consist of "tone" features similar to those of Chinese, which may involve variations in laryngeal tension superimposed on the breath-group laryngeal tension contour. Variations in subglottal air pressure may also be involved. Further study of these questions is obviously necessary.

4.4 Summary and Discussion of Hypotheses and Observations

Let us pause to review our hypotheses in the light of the data that we have already discussed before we turn to discuss some of the linguistic functions of the breath-group.

1. We presented data showing that the breath-group is a suprasegmental feature whose scope in the examples that we discussed was usually the constitutent sentence. In the examples that will follow in Chapter 5 we shall demonstrate that the scope of the breath-group may delimit any constituent in the derived phrase marker. The breath-group at the articulatory level involves a coordinated pattern of muscular activity that includes the subglottal, laryngeal, and the supraglottal muscles during an entire expiration. The data show that the subglottal respiratory muscles start to force air out of the lungs while the laryngeal muscles close the glottis to its "phonation neutral position" and adjust the tension of the vocal cords. The supraglottal vocal tract simultaneously begins to move into position and phonation commences at a specified fundamental frequency that the speaker can repeat at will. At the end of the sentence the subglottal respiratory muscles lower the subglottal air pressure during the last 150–200 msec of phonation. The tension of the laryngeal muscles for the unmarked American English breath-group appears to remain relatively steady throughout the sentence. The fundamental frequency of phonation is thus a function of the subglottal air pressure function, and it falls during the last 150–200 msec of phonation.

2. The falling terminal fundamental frequency contour that results from the absence of an increase in the laryngeal tension at the end of the unmarked breath-group apparently is a universal aspect of the unmarked breath-group. Data on the cries of newborn infants were reviewed in Chapter 3 which showed that these initial vocalizations have the general form of the unmarked breath-group insofar as the fundamental frequency falls at the end of phonation, because the subglottal pressure falls. This aspect of the breath-group, which is apparently innately determined, may be the result of a condition of minimum articulatory control. The speaker does not bother to increase the tension of his laryngeal muscles to maintain the fundamental frequency as the subglottal air pressure falls. Phonetic data were briefly reviewed which indicated that many related and unrelated languages apparently have an unmarked breath-group that is characterized, in part, by a falling terminal fundamental frequency contour.

3. Phonetic analyses were cited in Chapter 2 indicating that the breath-groups of individual languages might each be characterized by different patterns of laryngeal tension control in the nonterminal parts of the breath-group. In British English, for example, the tension of the laryngeal muscles may initially be high and may gradually fall

throughout the breath-group in contrast to American English, where the laryngeal tension apparently remains relatively constant throughout the breath-group. The developmental data reviewed in Chapter 3 indicated that children may acquire the idiosyncratic aspects of the breath-group of their native language during the first year of life. The scope of the breath-group in all of the languages reviewed can encompass the constitutent *sentence*.

4. The existence of a marked breath-group [+*BG*] was hypothesized. The marked breath-group contrasts with the unmarked breath-group during the last 150–200 msec of phonation where the tension of the laryngeal muscles increases in the marked breath-group. The increased tension of the laryngeal muscles counters the falling subglottal air pressure, and the marked breath-group thus has a terminal not-falling fundamental frequency contour. The marked breath-group is consequently in a sense the "simplest" alternative to the unmarked breath-group since the laryngeal tension is increased at only one point in the breath-group—when the subglottal air pressure falls.

The relatively steady laryngeal tension function that characterizes the nonterminal portions of the American English breath-group and the falling laryngeal tension function that probably characterizes the British English breath-groups (cf. Section 2.9) may perhaps be regarded as the "simplest" contrasts with the terminal fundamental frequency contour of the marked breath-group. They result in a level or a falling fundamental frequency contour that brings into relief the terminal not-falling fundamental frequency contour of the marked breath-group. The details of the nonterminal laryngeal tension functions of the breath-groups of other languages undoubtedly vary, but it is unlikely that any language has a laryngeal tension function that rises before the terminal part of the breath-groups, since this could lead to confusions between the marked and the unmarked breath-groups. The breath-groups of different languages may perhaps also be characterized, in part, by specific nonterminal subglottal air pressure functions and by different coordinations between the muscles that generate the breath-group and the supraglottal muscles that articulate the segmental phonemes. These hypotheses on the language-specific aspects of breath-groups are, of course, speculative in the absence of detailed physiologic data on many languages.

5. A segmental phonologic feature [P_s] was hypothesized. The "archetypal" articulatory correlate of [$+P_s$] is a momentary increase in the subglottal air pressure that can occur in any part of the breath-group except the last 150–200 msec of phonation. More than one instance of [$+P_s$] can occur in a single breath-group although there

probably are some constraints on how close momentary subglottal air pressure peaks can occur.

6. The archetypal articulatory correlates of the unmarked and marked breath-groups and [$+P_s$] are the most basic articulatory maneuvers that can map out these features. The archetypal unmarked breath-group, for example, is produced on a single bounded expiration. The innately determined cries of neonates were produced on archetypal unmarked breath-groups. The archetypal articulatory patterns perhaps may reflect the "optimal" use of the innate physiologic mechanism.

We noted that other alternate articulatory maneuvers could produce acoustic signals that were acoustically or perceptually equivalent to the signals that were produced by the archetypal maneuvers. A speaker can, for example, produce the subglottal air pressure function that is characteristic of the breath-group without pausing for inspiration between two adjacent breath-groups. However, we hypothesized that the listener perceives intonational signals in terms of the archetypal articulatory correlates of the marked and the unmarked breath-groups and the segmental feature [P_s]. We hypothesized that the listener uses a feedback mechanism of the analysis-by-synthesis type using his knowledge of these archetypal patterns.

7. We examined the data of an independently motivated psychoacoustic experiment. The data of this experiment were consistent with the notion of analysis by synthesis in terms of the archetypal patterns of the unmarked and the marked breath-groups and the segmental feature [P_s]. The data also showed that Swedish and American listeners perceived identical stimuli in different ways according to the phonologic features that may be operant in each language. The responses of the Swedish listeners showed that Swedish may have a feature that raises the tension of the laryngeal muscles throughout the breath-groups.

8. We then examined some of the data of an experiment in which relevant physiologic and acoustic data were measured for four speakers of American English. The data of this experiment show that these speakers indeed employed the archetypal articulatory gestures.

a. In a sample of 957 breath-groups 87 percent of the breath-groups were produced on a single expiration.

b. Quantitative calculations of the relationship between fundamental frequency and the subglottal air pressure were made for the utterances of three of the speakers. The fundamental frequency increased at a rate of 17–20 cps per cm H_2O. These calculations showed that the tension of the laryngeal muscles was relatively constant during the nonterminal portions of the breath-group.

c. The marked breath-group was always differentiated from the unmarked breath-group by an increase in the tension of the laryngeal muscles during the last 150–200 msec of phonation.

Detailed data for each of the three speakers were also examined. These data showed that speaker 1's breath-groups were most often produced by means of the achetypal patterns. He placed emphasis on vowels by means of a momentary increase in subglottal air pressure —the archetypal articulatory correlate of $[+P_s]$. The data for speaker 1 also showed that he occasionally used alternate articulatory maneuvers to produce signals that were acoustically or perceptually equivalent. Speakers 2 and 3 used alternate articulatory maneuvers more often than speaker 1. Many of the variations in laryngeal tension that occurred during the nonterminal portions of their breath-groups were consistent. These variations appeared to be idiosyncratic "personal" articulatory patterns that compensated for subglottal air pressure patterns that were also consistent for each speaker. The segmental feature $[+P_s]$ was most often manifested by means of alternate articulatory gestures. The acoustic correlates of $[+P_s]$ in these data (i.e., fundamental frequency, duration, and amplitude) are consistent with the results of the acoustic analysis of English that were noted in Chapter 2.

9. Other intonational features occur in "tone" languages like Chinese. While the scope of these features, like $[+P_s]$'s, is clearly segmental, they nevertheless may interact with the breath-group at the acoustic and the articulatory level. Phonetic and acoustic analyses were briefly reviewed which indicated that the tones can interact with the over-all suprasegmental intonation and $[+P_s]$, but the listener is able to deduce what the appropriate tone is, probably through a process of analysis by synthesis. Some of the variations in fundamental frequency that occur within the nonterminal portions of English sentences may perhaps be the acoustic correlates of similar features.

10. In the hierarchy of phonologic features the breath-group is more basic than the segmental feature $[P_s]$. The basic form of the archetypal unmarked breath-group is indeed manifested in the initial cries of newborn infants. The breath-group may be a feature of every language. It is doubtful whether $[P_s]$ is used in every language or whether it even occurs in a substantial number of unrelated languages. The distribution of $[P_s]$ is perhaps closer to the distribution of the segmental "phonemic tones" (e.g., the "tones" of Chinese).

5 The "Phonemic Phrase"

We shall show in this chapter that the suprasegmental breath-group is an explicit characterization of the "phonemic phrase." The breath-group can encompass different consitituents of the derived phrase marker. Though its scope is often the constituent *sentence,* it can also occur on smaller constituents, and a sentence can hence be divided into two or more breath-groups. We shall discuss some of the circumstances that may motivate a speaker to break up a sentence into more than one breath-group. The segmental Trager-Smith analysis (1951), which is, in part, concerned with the manifestations of the "phonemic phrase," will also be discussed, and the effects of emotion on intonation which are confused with the linguistic aspects of intonation in the Trager-Smith analysis will be briefly summarized.

5.1 The Division of a Sentence into Breath-Groups

5.1.1 Physiologic Reasons. In Chapter 4 we observed that sentences were usually uttered on a single marked or unmarked breath-group. Two of the long sentences were, however, uttered on two breath-groups. The duration of a breath-group can, of course, be extended to encompass the duration of a long sentence. Small children usually utter declarative sentences on one unmarked breath-group. They will do this even when the sentence is quite long, and they sometimes run out of breath before they come to the end of the sentence.

Children will, for example, often utter sentences like *I went to the zoo, where I saw the lions, the tigers, the elephants, the bears. . . .* The list of animals may be interminable, and the child runs out of breath before he completes the sentence.

It is often physiologically more convenient to divide a sentence into more than one breath-group. When an adult speaker divides a sentence into two breath-groups, the nonfinal breath-groups are marked. The presence of the terminal not-falling fundamental frequency contour of the marked breath-groups implies continuation; the sentence is not yet over. The breath-group here is analogous to the "phonemic phrase" or the "phonemic clause" in traditional terms.

This function of the breath-group is quite similar to the division of sentences proposed by the "Tune I and Tune II" analyses[1] of Armstrong and Ward (1926) and Jones (1932). Tune I on the acoustic level is equivalent to the unmarked breath-group, while Tune II is equivalent to the marked breath-group. The examples of the application of Tunes I and II that are cited in these studies are fundamentally correct. Jones (*op. cit.,* p. 254), for example, states that

> Pauses are continually being made in speaking. They are made (1) for the purpose of taking breath, (2) for the purpose of making the meaning of the words clearer.
>
> Pauses for breath are normally made at points where pauses are necessary or allowable from the point of meaning.

5.1.2 "Disambiguation" by Breath-Group Division. When a listener hears a sentence, he must derive its underlying phrase marker in order to arrive at a semantic interpretation. Many sentences are unambiguous. If a linguistically competent listener hears a sentence of this type, he will derive only one underlying deep phrase marker starting with the phonetic input. The sentence *I saw the boy who fell down the stairs* has, for example, only one deep phrase marker. Some sentences are, of course, ambiguous. The sentence *Flying planes can be dangerous* clearly has two distinct underlying phrase markers. The sentence can mean either that the act of flying a plane can be dangerous or that aircraft in flight are inherently dangerous. The two deep phrase markers have very similar derived phrase markers that result in identical phonetic outputs. When the sentence is part of an extended context, such as a discussion of the reactions of student pilots to emergencies, the sentence may appear to be unambiguous. The listener is able to use the information furnished by the context to

[1] These analyses are discussed in Chapter 9.

guide his syntactic recognition routine. However, it is impossible to use intonation to "disambiguate" this sentence when it is spoken in isolation.[2]

Some sentences are, however, ambiguous if only the string of words that results from the derived phrase marker is considered. More than one deep phrase marker could have resulted in the same phonetic string of words. However, each of the different deep phrase markers results in a derived phrase marker that has a different constituent structure. The derived phrase markers that resulted from the different underlying deep phrase markers thus have different constituent structures, though the phonologic component forms the same string of words from each derived phrase marker. If certain conditions are met, these sentences can be "disambiguated" when they are spoken by dividing the utterance into breath-groups. The breath-groups can divide the speech signal into segments that acoustically manifest "breaks" in the constituent structure of the derived phrase marker. A string of n words can thus be segmented into two contiguous strings of i and j words, where $i + j = n$, by producing the first i words on one breath-group and producing the second j words on a second breath-group. The first breath-group would be marked, which would indicate that the sentence was not yet complete.

An ambiguous sentence can thus be disambiguated when the constituent structures of the several derived phrase markers can each be identified by unique contiguous constituents. The following examples, some of which are drawn from the extensive literature connected with "phonemic" Trager-Smith pitch and stress transcriptions, will serve to illustrate this process. We shall return to the question of what these segmental "phonemic" transcriptions really mean. For the moment it will suffice to say that the "phonemic" pitch notation[3] 231# is equivalent to an American English unmarked breath-group while the notation 232/ or 232// is equivalent to a marked breath-group.

Our first example was noted by Stockwell (1962, p. 51), who comments that his "examples are real in the sense that they are caught on the fly, not constructed. . . ." The sentence *I'll move on Saturday* is ambiguous since it can mean either that the speaker is moving his household effects on Saturday, as in (A), or that he will continue his wanderings on Saturday, as in (A[1]). The point is whether the verb

[2] Verbal communication of experiment by Chomsky and Miller.

[3] Trager and Smith term these sequences "phonemic clauses." The "phonemic phrase" to Trager and Smith is the sequence of words that is the scope of the breath-group.

phrase in the sentence is *move* or *move on*. The underlying phrase markers are shown in (A) and (A^1). The derived phrase marker that

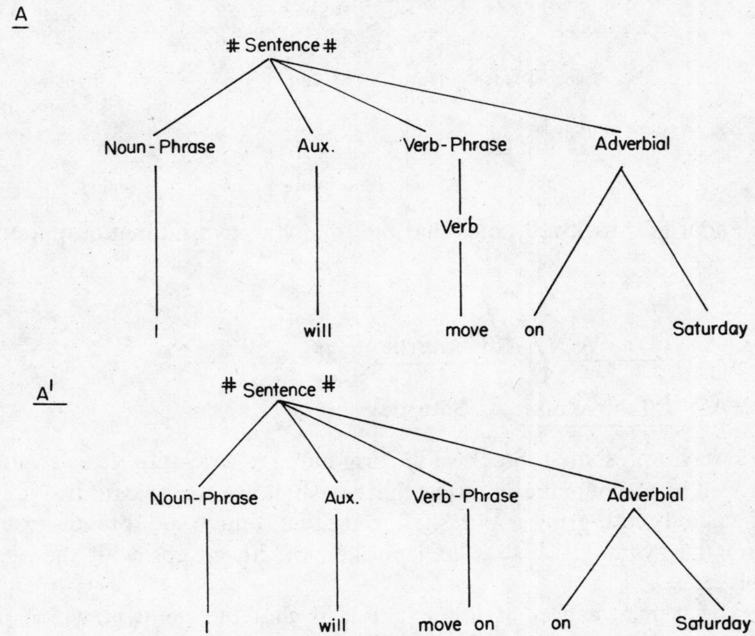

follows deep phrase marker A is shown in (A-d), which can also be written in the following form:

((I) (will) (move) ((on) (Saturday)))
S N N Aux Aux VP VP Adv P P N N Adv S

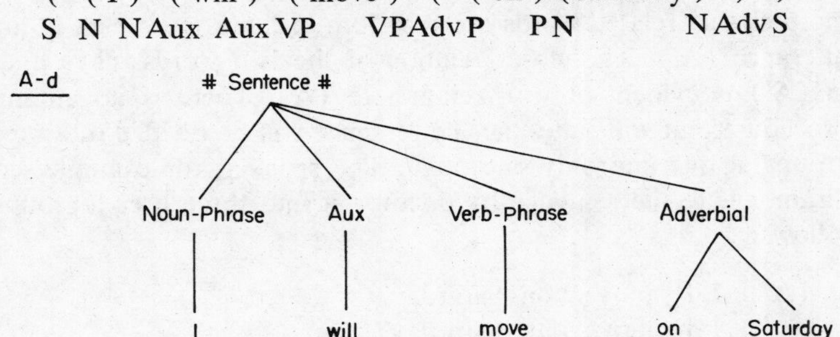

The derived phrase marker that follows from deep phrase marker (A^1) is illustrated in (A^1-d), which can again be written in the form

((I) (will) ((move) (on)) (Saturday))
S N N A A VP VP Adv Adv S

where the unlabeled parentheses on *move* and *on* represent word

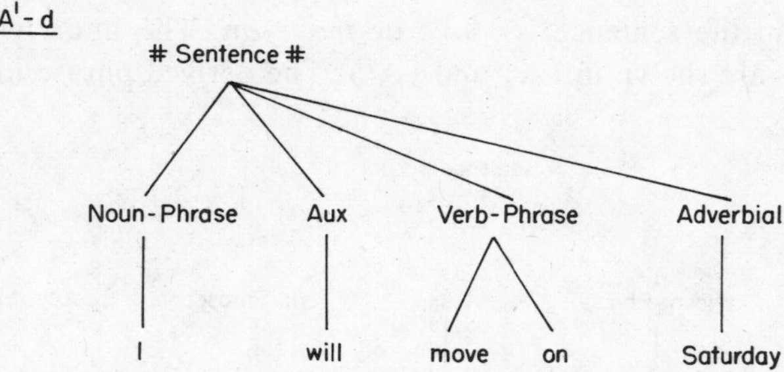

boundaries. Stockwell notes that the following two intonation patterns can occur:

2 3 2 2 3 1
(A) Ì'll móve / òn Sáturday #
2 3 2 4 1
(A′) Ì'll mòve ón / Sáturday #

We have presented Stockwell's original Trager-Smith transcription as well as a schematic notation that we shall use to indicate the scope of each breath-group. We shall represent unmarked breath-groups with the symbol ——\ and marked breath-groups with the symbol ——/

The crucial aspect of this example is that the point at which the two breath-groups segment the sentence indicates that the words *move* and *on* are more closely "linked" in (A′) than they are in (A). In this example these words are directly dominated by the constituent verb phrase in the derived phrase marker (A¹-d). The more closely related words are therefore in the same breath-group in utterance (A′). The closer relation of the two words *move* and *on* in (A′) is evident only in relation to (A). There is no automatic procedure that will state that the sentence will be divided into breath-groups at one and only one point. The speaker, for example, could disambiguate the sentence by dividing it into three breath-groups as follows:

(A*) I'll, move, on Saturday.
(A′*) I'll, move on, Saturday.

If these sentences occurred in the course of a normal conversation, the speaker would in all likelihood utter the entire sentence on one breath-group. If a listener was unable to resolve the ambiguity from the context of the conversation and asked the speaker what he meant, the speaker would again in all likelihood paraphrase the utterance. If he wished to convey utterance (A′), he might not delete the particle *on,* and he would say *I'll move on on Saturday*. The speaker need only consider the particular deep phrase marker that he wishes to convey when he disambiguates the sentence by paraphrasing it.

The process of disambiguating the sentence by means of breath-groups is by comparison fairly complex. The division of the sentence into several breath-groups can only indicate relative differences in the constituent structure of the ambiguous derived phrase markers. The scope of a breath-group can be any constituent of the derived phrase marker.

The sentence *The cat fell off the roof* could, for example, be slowly dictated. Each word could be produced on a single breath-group,[4] that is,

(B1) The, cat, fell, off, the, roof.

The same sentence could also be produced as follows:

(B2) The cat fell, off the roof

or

(B3) The cat, fell off the roof.

The breath-groups can delimit any constituent of the derived phrase marker:

(B-d) (((The) (cat)) ((fell) (off) ((the) (roof))))
SNP NPVP NP NPVPS

The sentence can, of course, be produced on one breath-group, as in

(B4) The cat fell off the roof.

The alternate intonation patterns (B1), (B2), (B3), and (B4) do not change the "meaning" of the sentence, because there are no alternative derived phrase markers that have similar formatives and different constituent structures. Only one deep phrase marker can underlie this sentence. Intonations (B1), (B2), (B3), and (B4) are all stylistic variants that are produced by placing breath-groups on some of the constituents of the derived phrase marker. The breath-groups that precede the sentence's final breath-group are all marked. For similar reasons intonation patterns (A′) and (A′*) had the same "meaning." The fact that the speaker chooses to say,

[4] The syllable is perhaps the smallest unit that can be produced on a single breath-group when polysyllabic words are considered.

(A′) I'll move on, Saturday

instead of

(A′*) I'll, move on, Saturday

is simply a matter of efficiency; it is simpler to produce the sentence on fewer breath-groups so long as the duration of any breath-group does not exceed some critical time, T_c, where ventilation becomes necessary. The fact that the words *I'll* and *move on* are in the same breath-group in utterance (A′) and in different breath-groups in utterance (A′*) has no linguistic significance. There are no deep phrase markers that could produce derived phrase markers in which these words[5] are more closely related in utterance (A′). Utterances (A′) and (A′*) are therefore interpreted as stylistic variants.

The speaker might produce utterances (A*) and (A′*) if he wished to dictate the sentences and preserve their "meanings." However, speakers usually avoid dividing a sentence into many small breath-groups, and intonation patterns (A) and (A′) are probably more typical than intonation patterns (A*) and (A′*). A "trading relationship" probably exits. It is physiologically more convenient to utter a sentence using fewer breath-groups so long as the length of any breath-group does not become too long. On the other hand, it may be important to manifest the derived constituent structure by dividing the sentence into breath-groups. The speaker apparently divides the sentence into the longest breath-groups that will still manifest the crucial aspects of the derived constituent structure.[6]

In order to disambiguate the sentence *I'll move on Saturday,* the speaker had to consider specifically wherein the derived phrase markers (A-d) and (A^1-d) differed. The speaker may have intended to communicate deep phrase marker (A^1), and he accordingly formed derived phrase marker (A^1-d). The sentence would normally be produced on one breath-group, and it would be ambiguous. The

[5] To be more precise, the string of formatives on which the phonologic component of the grammar acts to shape these words; cf. Katz and Postal (1964).

[6] Bierwisch (1965) in his recent study of German sentence intonation proposes some further restrictions on the division of the derived phrase marker into breath-groups. He proposes an algorithm that takes into account the derived constituent structure, the presence of accented vowels, and the rate at which the speaker is talking. Bierwisch's algorithm correctly predicts, for example, that speakers will not produce this utterance:

(A*) I will move on Saturday.

The rate at which an individual talks is, of course, determined in part by whether he thinks that the sentence might be ambiguous if he did not manifest the details of its constituent structure by dividing it into breath-groups.

speaker had to look at the string of words and derive deep phrase marker (A) in order to ascertain the constituent structure of derived phrase marker (A-d). The speaker may perhaps perform a syntactic analysis of the words of the sentence that he wants to disambiguate with intonation. He may first derive the other deep phrase markers that can underlie the string. He then computes the derived phrase markers of the alternative deep phrase markers. The speaker then can disambiguate the sentence if contiguous words have different constituent relationships in the derived phrase markers.

Let us consider a few more examples of this process. Stockwell (1961*b*, p. 48) noted the following two utterances in which "intonational morphemes" supposedly carry the meaning of the sentence:

```
      2   3       2    2                3    1
(C)   They décorated / the girl with the flówers  #
      2                3 2              3    1
(C′)  They decorated the gírl / with the flówers  #
```

Utterance (C) may be paraphrased as: *They decorated the girl who had the flowers.* Utterance (C′) may be paraphrased as: *They decorated the girl by giving her flowers.* The derived phrase marker of utterance (C) is shown in (C-d), and the derived phrase marker of

C-d

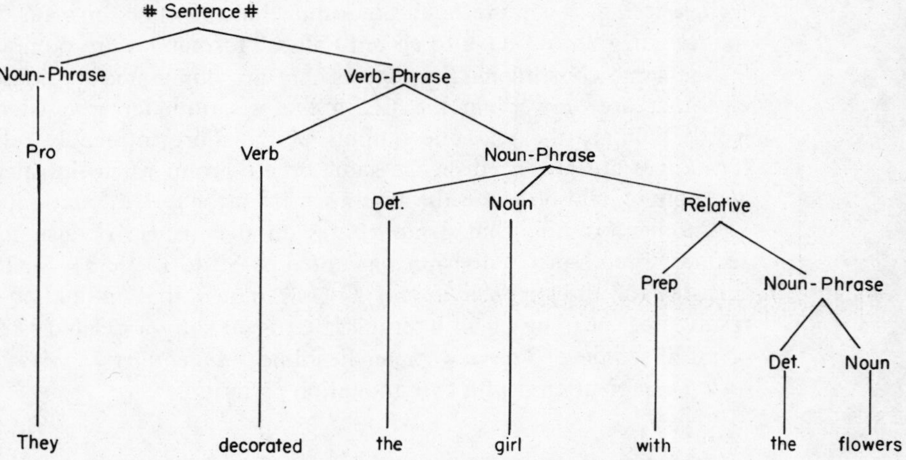

utterance (C′) is shown in (C′-d). The words *the girl with the flowers* are more intimately related in (C-d), and therefore they occur in the same breath-group in utterance (C). Note that if we adopt the number of constituents at which "branching" takes place as a measure of relatedness, one node separates the strings {the girl} and {with the flowers} in (C′-d), whereas no node separates them in (C-d). If all the constituents that dominated these words were counted in the "path" between all these words, then five nodes would intervene in (C′-d) and four nodes would intervene in (C-d). What

C′-d

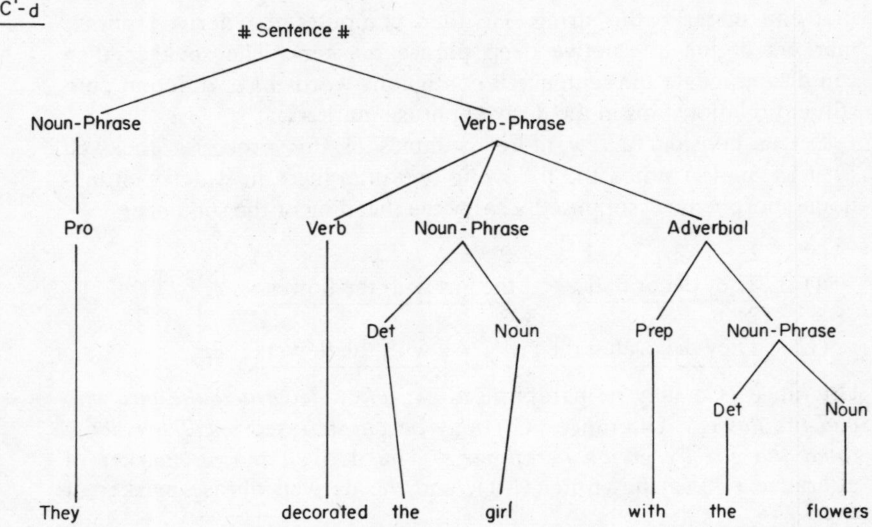

we are trying to capture is an algorithm that measures how far "up" the tree diagram we have to go until all the formatives are dominated by the same constituent. Formatives that are dominated by constituents that are "lower" in the tree are more intimately related. The words that are the phonetic outputs of the more intimately related formatives are produced on the same breath-group when the speaker attempts to disambiguate the utterance by means of intonation.

Another example that demonstrates another aspect of disambiguation by breath-group division was noted by Sledd (1955*b*). Sledd, in a review of Fries's *Structure of English,* noted that intonation can resolve the meaning of an utterance that is actually a deleted version of a full sentence. The newspaper headline *Vandenburg reports open forum* can be uttered with two intonation patterns:

3 2 2 3 1
(D) Vandenburg // reports open forum #

3 2 2 3 1
(D′) Vandenburg reports // open forum #

The derived phrase markers of these two utterances are shown in (D-d) and (D′-d). The division of the utterance into breath-groups

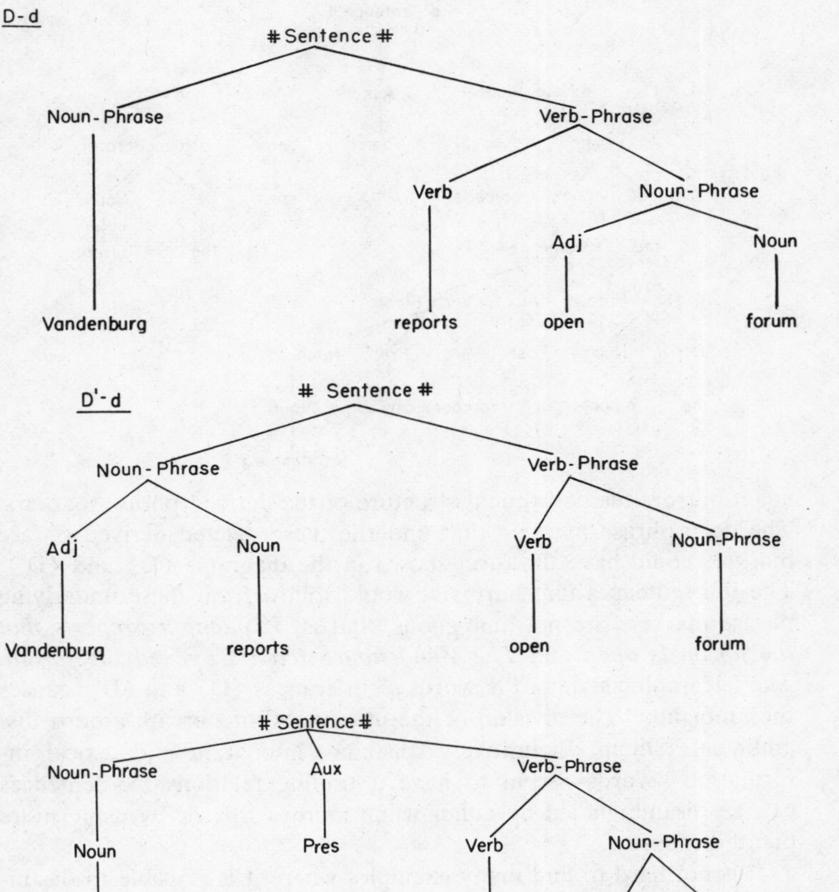
D-d
Sentence
Noun-Phrase
Verb-Phrase
Verb
Noun-Phrase
Adj
Noun
Vandenburg
reports
open
forum
D'-d
Sentence
Noun-Phrase
Verb-Phrase
Adj
Noun
Verb
Noun-Phrase
Vandenburg
reports
open
forum
D
Sentence
Noun-Phrase
Aux
Verb-Phrase
Noun
Pres
Verb
Noun-Phrase
Vandenburg
reports
Det
Noun
Def
Comp
forum
the
Sentence
Noun-Phrase
Aux
Verb-Phrase
Def
Noun
Pres
Verb
Noun-Phrase
def
Noun
wh
the
forum
be
open

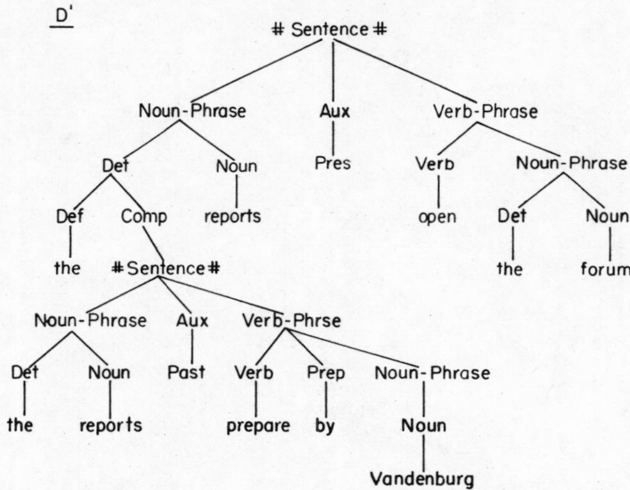

again mirrors the constituent structure of the derived phrase markers. The deep phrase markers that underlie these deleted derived phrase markers could have the form shown in the diagrams (D) and (D′). The full sentences that normally would follow from these underlying phrase markers are not ambiguous, that is, *Vandenburg reports that the forum is open* and *The Vandenburg reports opened the forum.* The telegraphic style of the words of utterances (D) and (D′) causes the ambiguity. The division of the utterances into breath-groups disambiguates them. Figuratively speaking, intonation and lexical information—words—seem to have a trading relationship. Sentences can be disambiguated by either using more words or by using more breath-groups.

It is not hard to find many examples where it is possible to disambiguate an ambiguous sentence by dividing it up into breath-groups. The sentence *They kept the car in the garage,* which has two underlying deep phrase markers (E) and (E′), may be divided into two breath-groups as follows:

(E) They kept, the car in the garage.
(E′) They kept the car, in the garage.

The deep phrase markers are shown in the diagrams (E) and (E′). Deep phrase marker (E) would result in the sentence *They kept the car which was in the garage,* and the sentence would not be ambiguous. However, the words *which was* do not appear in the phonetic output. Some optional transformations are probably applied in the syntactic processing of the deep phrase marker, and the words that

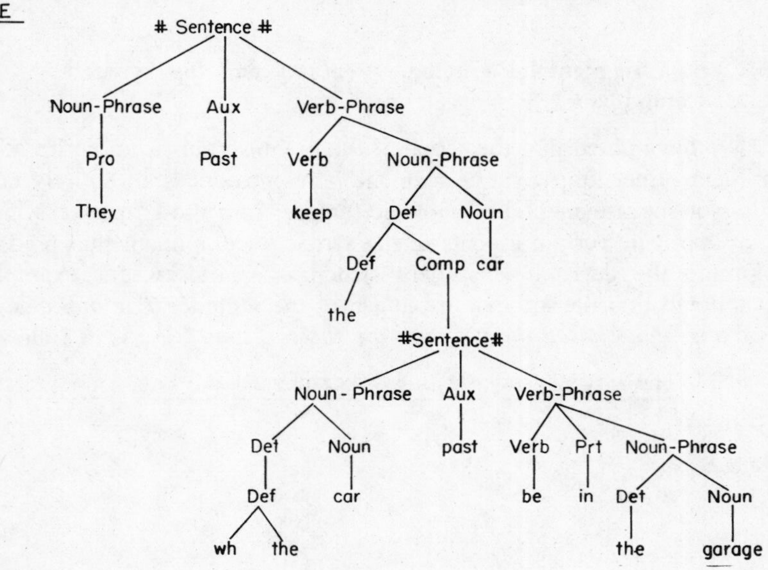

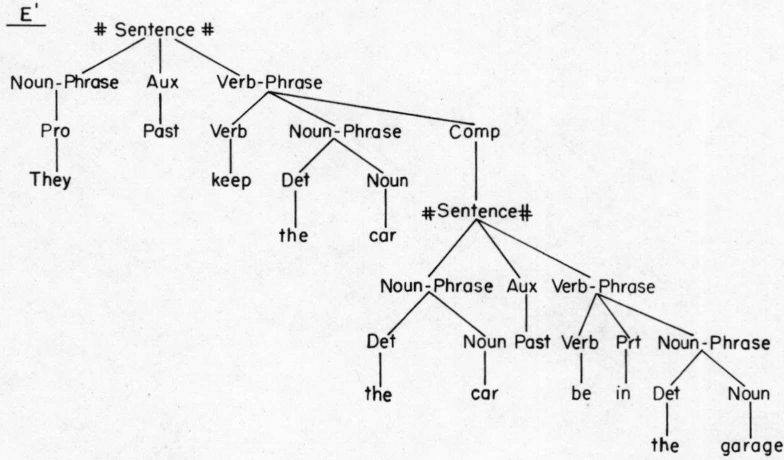

result from the derived phrase marker are ambiguous. The derived phrase markers that follow from (E) and (E′), however, have different constituent structures and the utterances are disambiguated by means of breath-group division. The sentence *I fed her dog biscuits* is another simple example of the potential use of breath-group division to disambiguate a sentence, that is,

(F) I fed her, dog biscuits.
(F′) I fed her dog, biscuits.

5.2 Suprasegmental Phonologic Features and the Syntactic Component

We have noted that the scope of the breath-group is an entire constituent rather than a single segment. This introduces an entirely new class of suprasegmental phonologic features into the grammar, which may motivate certain aspects of the syntactic component that tend to simplify the derived constituent structure. Chomsky, for example, has noted that the intonation pattern of the sentence *The boy chased the dog, that chased the cat, that ate the rat, that . . .* is as follows:

(G) The boy chased the dog, that chased the cat, that ate the rat, that . . .

G-d I

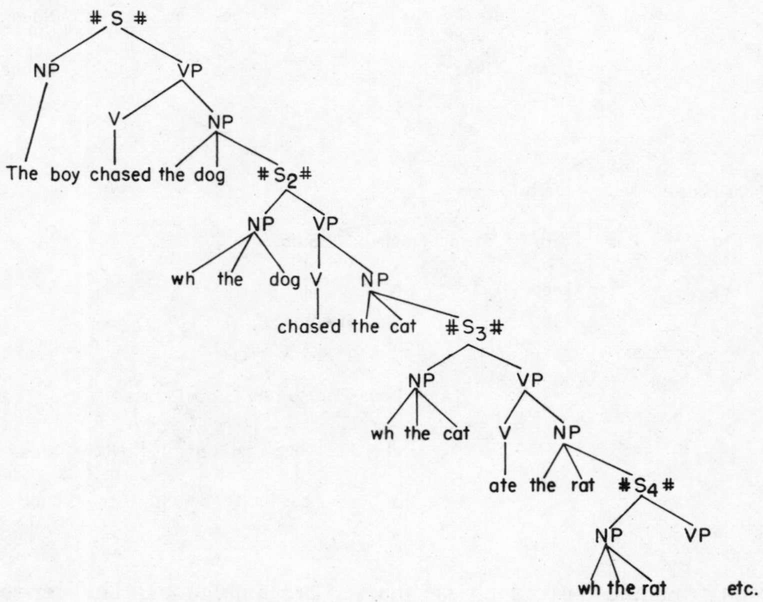

S
NP VP
V NP
The boy chased the dog #S₂#
NP VP
wh the dog V NP
chased the cat #S₃#
NP VP
wh the cat V NP
ate the rat #S₄#
NP VP
wh the rat etc.

The usual derived phrase marker for this sentence is indicated in (G-d1). We should like to say that the derived phrase marker of this sentence is still more simplified and has the structure shown in (G-d2). A single breath-group would then span each constituent *sentence* in the derived phrase marker. The simplication of the derived phrase marker might be viewed as an optimization procedure wherein the syntactic component produces a derived phrase marker that is

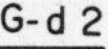

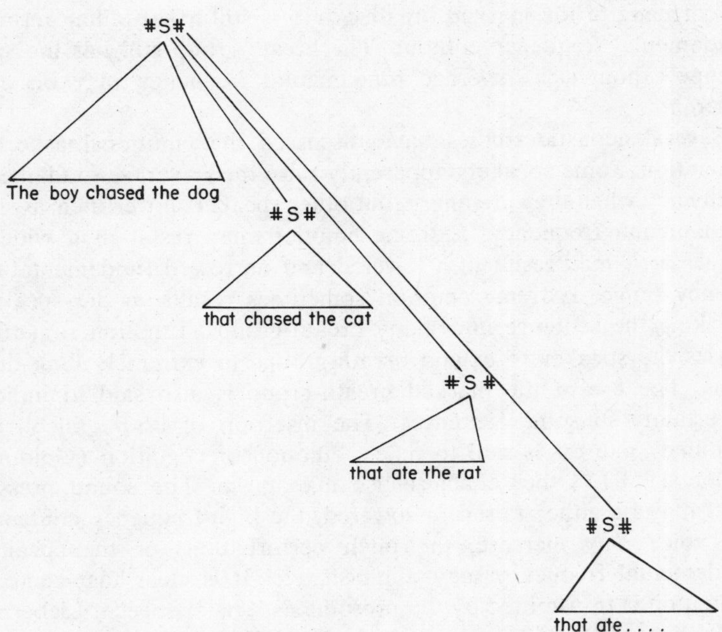

most easily mapped out by the available phonologic apparatus, in this case the suprasegmental feature breath-group.

5.3 Emotion

Note that the specific intonation pattern of a sentence that follows from its division into breath-groups has no "meaning" of its own. It specifically does *not* indicate the attitude or emotion of the speaker. The breath-group is a phonologic feature. It has no independent semantic status. The semantic interpretation of a sentence follows from the underlying deep phrase marker.

The emotion of the speaker can modify the intonation of an utterance just as it can modify other aspects of the speech signal like the preciseness of the speaker's articulation or the words that he may omit. However, these aspects of intonation are not primary linguistic phenomena. They are apparently superimposed on the linguistically predictable aspects of intonation, though it is, at present, not clear how they are manifested in the acoustic signal. However, the effects of emotion are independent of the linguistic aspects of the speech signal. One recognizes a yes-no question whether the speaker's voice expresses anger or not (Lieberman and Michaels, 1962). The acoustic correlate of the marked breath-group is still a not-falling terminal fundamental frequency contour. The breath-group still has the same "shape" though the average fundamental frequency may be quite different.

Several acoustic studies have discussed the emotional aspect of intonation. Some speakers apparently raise their average fundamental frequency when they are angry, but other speakers lower their average fundamental frequency. Extreme emotion may result in a wider f_0 range, or it may result in a lowered and narrowed fundamental frequency range. Extreme emotion sometimes results in the speaker's breaking the sentence into many breath-groups. Emotion sometimes causes the speaker to extend breath-groups to extremely long durations. The use of the marked breath-group is also said to indicate uncertainty in some sentences. The insertion of both "filled" and "unfilled" pauses[7] is said to reflect emotion or cognition (Goldman-Eisler, 1958). Other changes also take place. The sound pressure level may be either raised or lowered, the high-frequency content of the voice may increase, the pitch perturbations of the speaker's fundamental frequency may diminish, etc. It is clear that some information is transmitted by the prosodic aspects of speech. Lieberman and Michaels (1962), for example, in a forced-choice test showed that listeners could differentiate eight emotional states 50 percent of the time when the prosodic features of complete sentences were isolated from the words of the sentence. Denes (1959), however, found that he got almost random responses when he isolated the prosodic features of isolated words and asked listeners to associate these prosodic contours freely with emotional states. Uldall (1960) and Hadding-Koch (1961) both noted that the emotion that the listeners associated with a particular contour was very much dependent on what the sentence's words were. There probably are some general aspects of intonation and stress that relate to particular emotional states. However, all we can say at the present time, without knowing the idiosyncrasies of a particular speaker, is that emotion is marked by a departure from the normal speaking habits of the individual.

[7] These "pauses" must be differentiated from the pauses that occur at the end of breath-groups. Boomer and Dittmann (1962) show that pauses occurring at the ends of "phonemic clauses" (i.e., juncture pauses) have a higher perceptual threshold than the "hesitation pauses" occurring unexpectedly within phonemic clauses. The phonemic clauses that map out the derived constituent structure are syntactically determined. The "hesitation pauses" appear to manifest cognition or emotion.

5.4 Taxonomic Analyses of Intonation and the "Phonemic Phrase"

One of the most widely accepted analyses of intonation is the system proposed by Trager and Smith in their *Outline of English Structure* (1951). They attempt to apply the principles of taxonomic segmental analysis to intonation. In Chapter 9 we shall discuss this theory in detail. Briefly, this system makes use of four pitch levels, three terminal junctures,[8] and various vocal qualifiers to describe the pitch contour of an utterance. It also uses four levels of stress to describe the stress relationships of the speech signal. Stress and pitch are supposed to be completely independent. The linguist is, for example, supposed to be able to perceive the stress levels of an utterance independently of his perception of the pitch levels.

Stress and pitch are supposed to relate to rather distinct linguistic levels in this system. Stresses are supposed to distinguish certain morphemic classes from each other, while pitch levels and terminals are supposed to provide acoustic cues that tell a listener where the phrases of a sentence begin or end. In the words of the *Outline of English Structure,*

> The contribution of the phonological analysis of stress, juncture, and intonation patterns . . . is that it makes . . . the recognition of immediate constituents and part of speech syntax into solidly established objective procedures, removing once and for all the necessity of defending one's subjective judgments as to what goes with what [p. 77].

Trager and Smith isolated "pitch morphemes" by considering pairs of utterances like

```
       2    3    2     2                  3     1
(C)  They décorated  /  the girl with the flówers   #
       2              3 2        2        3     1
(C′) They decorated the gírl  /  with the flówers   #
```

[8] Trager and Smith use essentially these three terminal junctures to differentiate between the unmarked breath-group (contours that end with #), marked breath-groups that occur in sentence final position (//), and marked breath-groups that occur in the middle of sentences (/). They note that the juncture // corresponds phonetically to a rise in pitch whereas the juncture / corresponds phonetically to a sustentation of pitch. This phonetic distinction may simply be a coarticulation effect. When a speaker uses a marked breath-group in the middle of a sentence, he may not complete the tensioning of his laryngeal muscles at the end of the marked breath-group before he begins to relax these muscles for the breath-group that follows. Similar phenomena occur for the segmental features (cf. Lindblom, 1963, for a careful study of coarticulation effects in vowels).

These two utterances are phonetically identical except for the different intonation contours. Since the notion of an underlying phrase marker is not present in taxonomic "antimentalistic" grammars, the "meaning" of the utterance must be conveyed by the morphemes that are present in the superficial structure. Utterances (C) and (C′) form a "minimal pair" with respect to intonation, and they have different meanings; hence the pitch contours are morphemes. Moreover, since the "morphemes" were composed of individual pitches, the latter were said to be "phonemes."

Unfortunately, the same pitch contours often have rather different meanings when they occur in different sentences. Stockwell (1960*a*), for example, makes this comment:

> There is a good deal of evidence . . . that intonation patterns are the absolutely minimal differentiators of numerous utterance tokens though such evidence is always disconcerting in the difficulty it offers anyone who tries to assign semantic values to such differences in a way that will yield consistent results in a variety of contexts.

The way out taken by Trager and Smith was to state that the meaning of the intonation contour was the speaker's attitude toward the words of the sentence, which is sufficiently vague to fit any example. Much of the preoccupation of later taxonomic studies with intonation perhaps stems from the desire to find some phonetic cues that would explain how sentences are semantically interpreted. Intonation seemed to provide a new set of "phonemes" that could permute with all the segmental phonemes to provide a greatly expanded set of semantic interpretations.

The main function of intonation in the Trager-Smith *Outline of English Structure* is, as they noted, to provide an "objective" basis for immediate constituent analysis. Trager and Smith observed that the intonation pattern could sometimes segment the speech signal into "phonemic phrases" [9] that reflected the constituent structure when utterances like (C) and (C′) were produced. They erred, however, in assuming that the intonation reflected the constituent structure within all sentences. Normally, a speaker will produce an entire sentence on a single unmarked breath-group (pitch "morpheme" 231# in Trager-Smith notation). It is only when the speaker is trying to disambiguate the sentence that he will consistently segment smaller constituents by means of intonation. For nonambiguous sentences virtually any part of the constituent structure of the derived

[9] We shall use the term "phonemic phrase" in place of the Trager-Smith term "phonemic clause."

phrase marker can potentially be delimited by means of breath-group division. When a speaker pauses to breathe, he obviously can stop talking at any word, though he usually stops at some "major" break, that is, a node nearer to the "top" of the tree diagram. People know how to recognize immediate constituent structure simply because they know the syntactic rules of the langauge that govern constituent structure, as well as the lexicon of the language. They can recognize a phrase simply because it is a well-formed phrase.

If it were necessary to have acoustic signals that provided specific cues for immediate constituent analysis, it would obviously be impossible to understand written texts. It is only when ambiguity arises that intonation becomes important.[10] A speaker will normally not bother to divide a sentence into breath-groups because it is usually not necessary. However, Trager and Smith wanted to have "objective" cues for immediate constituent analysis, and so many utterances were transcribed as though they always were produced with complex intonation patterns. These "objective" phonemic transcriptions have, however, been accepted with reservations by other linguists who, in theory, agreed with Trager and Smith on the utility of "objective" cues. Sledd (1955*a*), in his review of the *Outline of English Structure,* comments that

> Anyone who has attempted to analyze or teach the English patterns of pitch and stress knows that competent observers may vigorously disagree and that a single observer may disagree with himself so often as to make secure confidence in his own judgments painfully difficult. . . .

The results of a controlled psychoacoustic experiment (Lieberman, (1965) demonstrate that competent linguists do not consider simply the physically present acoustic signal when they transcribe the pitch and stress "phonemes" of an utterance according to the Trager-Smith system. In this experiment two linguists who were quite familiar with this system transcribed the utterances of two speakers who each read the words *they have bought a new car* as though they were a statement, a question, a message expressing fear, a message expressing happiness, etc. The fundamental frequency and amplitude contours of the utterances were then measured. The utterances were also electronically processed to yield a set of stimuli in which a fixed vowel /a/ had a fundamental frequency and envelope amplitude contour

[10] An obvious parallel can be made with orthographic punctuation. Commas are essential only when a sentence might be ambiguous if the derived constituent structure was not indicated. Commas are otherwise not necessary for the understanding of the sentence. Trager and Smith, in effect, put all the commas into their transcriptions.

that varied in the same manner as the original speech signal. The following observations followed from the data of this experiment:

1. When two competent linguists independently transcribe a set of sentences that include "emotional" as well as "normal" utterances, 60 percent of the pitch levels and junctures of the two Trager-Smith transcriptions vary.

2. The Trager-Smith pitch levels do not correspond to discrete relative ranges of fundamental frequency. These comments apply even when the data were limited to the transcriptions made by a single linguist who carefully transcribed the tape-recorded sentences of a single talker.

3. The pitch levels of the Trager-Smith system do not even reflect the relative pitch levels of a single utterance of a single talker when it is transcribed by a single linguist. The fundamental frequency that corresponds to pitch level 1, for example, may be identical to or greater than the fundamental frequency that corresponds to pitch level 2. The pitch levels reflect the relative fundamental frequency only during segments of speech in which there is continuous voicing.

4. A subclass of utterances was transcribed more consistently and accurately than the rest of the stimulus ensemble. These utterances were produced on either a single unmarked breath-group or a single marked breath-group. These contours were always transcribed by the linguists in terms of the "suprasegmental morphemes" 231#, 232/, or 232//. When the single contour extended over an entire unemotional utterance, the pitch levels bore a reasonable relationship to the actual fundamental frequency contour of the utterance. However, in other instances, contours having the same "shape" but different fundamental frequency ranges were transcribed with exactly the same pitch levels and junctures. The linguists apparently responded to the suprasegmental breath-groups rather than to any pitch levels. For example, in Figure 5.1, the fundamental frequency contours of two of the utterances are plotted. Fundamental frequency is plotted with respect to the ordinate and time with respect to the abscissa. Note that the final portion of fundamental frequency contour *B* (from approximately 0.6 seconds to the end of stimulus) bears the same Trager-Smith transcription as the entire contour *A* in Figure 5.1, though the fundamental frequencies of the two contours are markedly different.

This example, which is typical of other instances in the data sample of this experiment, indicates that certain contours are perceived as complete entities. The linguist apparently "hears" contour *A* in Figure 5.1 and the final portion of the stimulus in contour *B* in the same way. He therefore assigns the same Trager-Smith transcription to both stimuli, though they involve rather different fundamental frequencies. The linguist's perception seems to be organized in terms of suprasegmental breath-groups rather than segmental "phonemic" pitch levels, though he uses the pitch levels to transcribe the breath-groups.

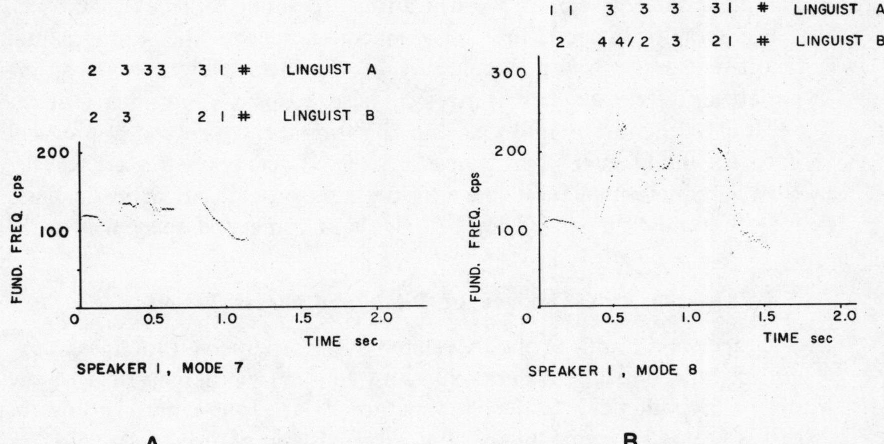

Figure 5.1 Two fundamental frequency contours demonstrating that the "pitch levels" of the Trager-Smith "phonemic" notation often have no direct acoustic basis.

The sentence *They have bought a new car* was spoken with the two fundamental frequency contours *A* and *B*. The segmental intonation transcriptions of two trained linguists are marked for both utterances. Note that the final portion of fundamental frequency contour *B* (from about 0.6 sec to the end of the stimulus) bears the same Trager-Smith transcription as the entire contour *A* though the fundamental frequencies of the two contours are markedly different. The linguists apparently responded to the suprasegmental breath-groups rather than to any pitch levels.

5. The linguists heard stimuli in which the fundamental frequency and amplitude contours of the complete sentences were accurately reproduced as modulations of a fixed vowel. When the linguists transcribed these contours, each linguist changed 50 percent of the pitch levels and junctures of his transcription vis-à-vis his transcription of the complete sentence where he, of course, heard the words of the message. The transcriptions of the fixed vowels were more accurate representations of the actual fundamental frequency contours than the transcriptions of the complete speech signal where the linguists heard the words of the message.

6. When the linguist heard the complete speech signal, he was

able to transcribe four degrees of stress. However, when the linguist heard the fixed vowels that were accurately modulated with the fundamental frequency and amplitude contours of the original speech signal, he was unable to transcribe accurately more than two degrees of stress, stressed or unstressed. Only 7 percent of the secondary stresses and none of the tertiary stresses that were transcribed for the complete speech signal were transcribed under these conditions. These results suggest that in connected speech the fundamental frequency and amplitude contours of the speech signal can differentiate only two degrees of stress. These acoustic quantities (fundamental frequency, amplitude, and duration) can provide a physical basis for the listener's perception of stressed versus unstressed vowels. Vowel reduction phenomena may perhaps provide an acoustic basis for differentiating a third level of stress in connected speech.

5.5 On the Independence of Pitch and Stress Levels

Trager and Smith explicitly relate stress to perceived loudness (*op. cit.*, p. 36), but they do not state how loudness is perceived. In view of the hypothetical "objective" nature of the phonemic entities in this system, it seems likely that stress is supposed to be directly related to some physical attribute of the acoustic signal. Although the highest pitch level of each "suprasegmental morpheme" almost invariably coincides with the primary stress, stress and pitch are supposed to be independent entitites.

Trager and Smith are, in a sense, correct when they state that pitch levels and stress levels relate to different structural levels. The Trager-Smith pitch levels are often used, in effect, to transcribe the marked and unmarked breath-group. The Trager-Smith levels, insofar as they relate to the actual prominence of vowels in the speech signal, are transcriptions of the segmental feature [+ P_s], which under certain conditions plays a part in acoustically manifesting linguistic stress.[11]

Since the suprasegmental breath-group is a more basic feature in the hierarchy of the grammar than the segmental feature [P_s], the two features clearly have a different status. However, at the acoustic and articulatory level the segmental feature [+ P_s] interacts with the suprasegmental breath-group. The "phonemic pitch" and "phonemic stress" levels of the Trager-Smith analysis are thus related, since they were directed at providing an accurate "objective" transcription of the acoustic signal.

[11] We shall discuss this topic in Chapter 7.

6 The Marked Breath-Group and Questions

In this chapter we shall discuss some of the syntactic rules that relate marked breath-groups to questions. Sentences that end with a rising intonation have traditionally been associated with questions in English and other languages. Hadding-Koch (1961, p. 9), for example, cites a medieval rule for liturgical recitation from Munster which states that a fall in pitch corresponds to periods, a small rise to commas, and a large rise to interrogatives.[1] Jones (1932) and Armstrong and Ward (1926) give many examples of questions that are produced with Tune II. However, not all questions in English end with a rising intonation; Trager and Smith (1951) and Pike (1945), indeed, claim that intonation is not related to the grammar. It supposedly conveys only the attitude of the speaker.[2] The notation of deep structure is not present in the grammars envisioned by Pike or Trager and Smith. If one considers the deep underlying structure as well as the superficial structure, certain regularities are apparent in the relationship between questions and intonation.

[1] The rule was written as shown here:

Sic can-ta com-ma, sic du-o punc-ta: sic ve-ro punc-tum. Sic sig-num in-ter-ro-ga-ti-o-nis?

[2] We have already discussed one of the linguistically motivated functions of the breath-group in Chapter 5, where we also briefly reviewed some of the known effects of emotion on intonation. Intonation clearly does convey the emotion or attitude of the talker. Indeed, the entire speech signal probably does. However, the marked breath-group is clearly related to the deep phrase markers of questions through syntactic rules.

6.1 The Formation of Questions in a Number of Languages

Let us first consider the formation of questions in a number of languages besides English. The same general results will hold for English, which we shall treat in more detail. In Japanese a question that takes the answer yes or no can be formed in two different ways. Abe (1955) notes that a statement like the expression *Darekakita* (Somebody came) can be turned into a question by the addition of the interrogatory particle *ka.* The sentence becomes *Darekakitaka?* It usually retains the falling statement intonation. In Japanese, as in most languages, "neutral" statements usually conclude with falling pitch. However, *Darekakita* can be also turned into a question by concluding the sentence with a rising intonation. The question can also be formed by using the interrogatory particle and rising intonation. The utterance still remains a normal question. (He also states that Ida C. Ward noted a similar phenomenon in the Yoruba language.)

Peškovskij (1930) observes that in Russian a question can be formed by using an interrogatory particle *li,* in which case the pitch may fall at the end of the utterance as it does for Russian statements, or else by the use of rising intonation without the particle, for example, *vy student?*

A similar effect also seems to take place in Chinese.[3] Chang (1958), in his study of the Chengtu dialect, noted that a particle with a rising intonation at the end of the sentence indicates that it is a question. The particle has a falling intonation when the sentence is a statement. The phonemic tone of the last syllable of the sentence and the sentence intonation interact.[4] A high-falling phonemic tone may become a level tone when it occurs at the end of a question that has a rising intonation. In contrast, questions may be signaled by syntactic forms in other Chinese dialects.[5] The yes-no question *Did Joe eat his soup?* in Mandarin Chinese may take the form *Joe ate or did not eat his soup.* The sentence ends with a falling intonation.

Danes (1960) notes that in Czech a special interrogatory contour is used ". . . only in yes or no questions which would not otherwise

[3] I am indebted to Mr. T. R. Hofmann, who pointed out the phonetic information for Chinese.

[4] In tone languages the sentence intonation is apparently superimposed on the individual tones (cf. Chapter 4).

[5] F. Lee, personal communication.

differ sufficiently, either lexically or grammatically, from statements." He also observes that German uses a special interrogative contour with yes-no questions: "In Russian, on the contrary, with yes or no questions containing the interrogative particle *-li* this special question contour is not used."

Hadding-Koch (1961, p. 17) states that in Finnish the interrogative is marked by an interrogatory particle and that the sentence intonation for the question is like that of the statement. In Spanish, she observes, the only thing that distinguishes an interrogative question of the form *Is my father coming?* from the statement *My father is coming* is the intonation. Both the statement and the question can have the same word order. They differ only in that the question concludes with rising pitch while the statement concludes with a falling pitch. In Swedish, interrogatory sentences usually involve both obligatory word order inversion and rising pitch at the end of the sentence.[6]

Daniel Jones's *Intonation Curves* (1909) reveals that in French the interrogatives formed by means of word order inversion, such as *Entends-tu?* conclude with a rise in pitch. Interrogatives can also be formed by simply concluding the sentence with a rise in pitch. Questions that use *wh*-words, like *who* or *what,* end with falling pitch in French. French yes-or-no interrogatives can also be formed using the particle *est-ce que*; the intonation then falls at the end of the sentence. Jones's curves show that English yes-or-no interrogatives have a rising intonation when they are formed by inverting the order of the subject and auxiliary verb. Yes-no questions in English like *John came home?* have only a rise in intonation at the end of the sentence. However, there are some marginal English interrogatives that contain special interrogatory phrases like *I suppose* or *I wonder* and end with a falling pitch. English questions with words like *why* or *what* also end with falling pitch.

De Bray (1961) notes that in Serbo-Croatian there are two main sentence intonations: "(1) a falling type, used in statements, commands, wishes, questions with an interrogative word initially, or questions with the enclitic 'li' as second word"; and (2) a rising intonation used in questions without an interrogative word. Lehiste (1961), in her acoustic study of the accents of Serbo-Croatian, finds that the sentence intonation interacts with the word accents on the final syllable of a sentence. This finding is, of course, consistent with the data

[6] Swedish and German interrogative questions apparently can also have as a phonetic output a generally high pitch that is sustained throughout the entire sentence (cf. Chapter 4).

of Chapter 4, which indicated that the terminal falling subglottal air pressure of the unmarked breath-group and the increase in laryngeal tension of the marked breath-group occurred during the last 150–200 msec of phonation.

Abramson (1962) notes that Thai, another tone language, can also form questions by adding a rising intonation to a word or phrase that is unmodified in all other respects.

In Table 6.1 we have grouped sixteen languages according to some of the ways in which questions are formed. The rows of the table indicate whether the language can form a question: (1*A*) by insert-

TABLE 6.1 Languages Grouped According to the Ways in Which Questions Can Be Formed

		I. Pitch falls at end of sentence.	II. Pitch rises, usually at end of sentence.
(1)	*A*. Special particle or phrase or word	Mandarin Chinese Finnish Russian French Japanese English Serbo-Croatian	
(2)	*A*. Word order inversion		Swedish French English German
	B. No changes in word order		Thai Czech Spanish Japanese English French Russian Yoruba Serbo-Croatian Chengtu dialect (Chinese)

The languages in the upper row have question forms in which special particles, words, or phrases occur. The languages in the lower row have question forms that do not have special "question" words or particles. The columns of the table indicate whether the language has a phonetic form in which a rising intonation contour can differentiate the question from statements. Note the "trading" relationship between intonation and special segmental phonetic elements.

ing a special interrogatory particle or phrase, such as *li* in Russian or *I suppose* in English (or by the use of *wh*-words like *who* or *what*); (2*A*) by a process or word order inversion (which may involve the use of auxiliary verbs in some cases); or (2*B*) without any change in word order. The columns of the table indicate whether the language has a phonetic form in which a rising intonation contour can differentiate the question from statements. Neutral statements conclude with a falling pitch in all of these languages.

In all of these languages the underlying phrase markers of the questions must have morphemes that indicate that the sentence is a question. The underlying phrase markers undoubtedly all contain the morpheme *Q* and a *wh*-morpheme attached to some noun phrase or the sentence adverbial (cf. Katz and Postal, 1964; Chomsky, 1965). Table 6.1 seems to show that the recoverability of the deep phrase marker is ensured after the syntactic and phonologic components of the grammar act on the deep phrase marker. The phonetic outputs either have special *wh*-words, or they are uttered on breath-groups that end with a rising intonation. The listener is able to deduce that a question has been asked, because he either hears a special word or hears a sentence final marked breath-group. In a loose sense a question can be signaled either by means of intonation or through a special word or words. A more precise characterization of this substantive linguistic universal would seem to be that under certain conditions the constituent *Q* and the *wh*-morpheme may be deleted by certain transformations. These transformations mark the sentence final breath-group. We shall consider English questions in detail in the following section, which should explicate this notion.

6.2 English Question Formation: Diachronic and Synchronic Aspects

We shall follow, in broad outline, the syntactic analysis of questions that is presented in Katz and Postal (1964, pp. 79ff.). We shall show that the generation of the sentence final marked breath-group follows from the general principle of the recoverability of the underlying phrase marker. As Katz and Postal point out,

> This principle requires that the distortions produced by the transformational removal of elements from a P-marker be unique. That is, a transformation T which operates by deleting elements or substituting for elements can apply to a P-marker only if the output of T on the P-marker permits unique recovery of that P-marker, given a description of T. The motivation for this principle . . . . which receives its formulation

in the general theory of linguistic descriptions, is both syntactic and semantic.

The syntactic evidence for this principle consists of evidence about particular natural languages which shows that the simplest transformational grammar involves this constraint. The semantic motivation for this principle is that the deep phrase marker is the input for the semantic component of the grammar (cf. Fodor and Katz, 1963). When a listener hears the phonetic output of the derived phrase marker, or reads the orthographic transcription, he must be able to reconstruct the deep phrase marker in order to arrive at a semantic interpretation of the utterance.

In Figure 6.1 a simplified version of the underlying deep phrase

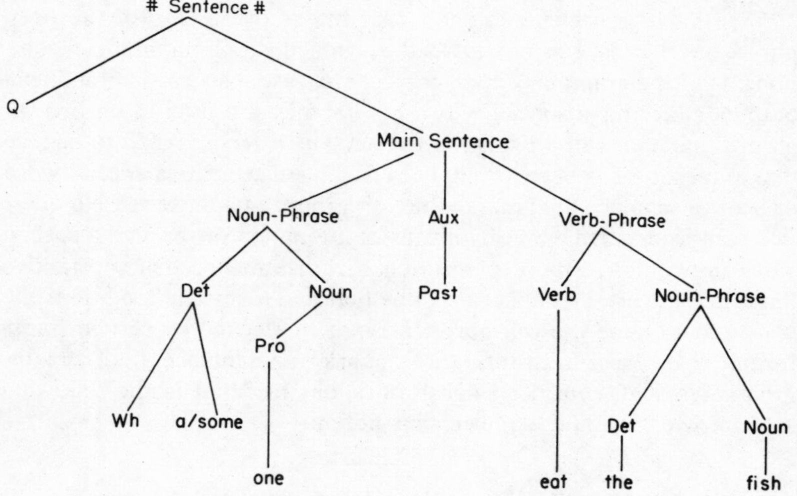

Figure 6.1

marker[7] of the sentence *Who ate the fish?* is presented, as a "tree" diagram. Note the presence of the morphemes *Q* and *wh-* in the underlying phrase marker. As Katz and Postal (*op. cit.*, p. 89) state,

> The *Q* morpheme indicates semantically only that the sentence is a question, i.e., a paraphrase of an appropriate sentence of the form *I request that you answer.* . . . The function of *wh* is, however, to specify the element or elements of the sentence that are 'questioned'.

[7] This simplified phrase marker is by no means complete (cf. Chomsky, 1965), but it is adequate for the purposes of our exposition.

In Figure 6.2 the underlying phrase marker of the sentence *What did the boy eat?* is presented. The following ordered transformational rules are required for these underlying structures:

(T1) $\underset{1}{\# + Q}, \underset{2}{X}, \underset{3}{\text{Noun Phrase}}, \underset{4}{Y} \Rightarrow 1324$
where 3 dominates *wh*

(T2) $\underset{1}{\# + Q}, \underset{2}{X}, \underset{3}{\text{Noun Phrase}}, \underset{4}{\text{Tense} + Y}, \underset{5}{Z} \Rightarrow 12435$
where 2 dominates *wh* and *Y* is the part of the Aux adjacent to the tense marker.

The string {*Q* + *wh* + some + one} in the derived phrase marker has the phonetic shape *who,* while the string {*Q* + *wh* + some +

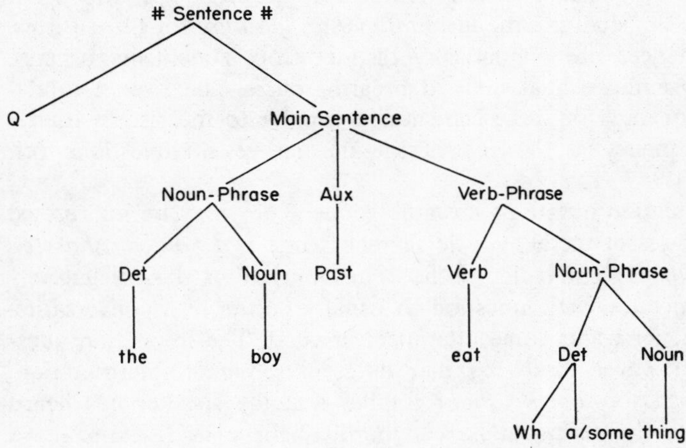

What did the boy eat ?

Figure 6.2

thing} has the phonetic shape *what.* The basic breath-group assignment rule spans each sentence with an unmarked breath-group. The sentences thus both end with a falling intonation contour.

The yes-no questions can be handled in a number of ways. Katz and Postal, for example, shift *Q* to the end of the sentence (*op. cit.,* p. 104). A morphophonemic rule then directly maps *Q* into a rising intonation. Schubiger, in a traditional grammatical analysis (1935), simply stated that yes-no interrogatives end with a rising intonation.

These discussions, however, do not furnish any insight into the possible function of intonation in these sentences. They do not, for example, formally explicate the reasons that might underlie the fact that for so many different languages the phonetic output of a question involves either special words or a rising intonation. Why do the yes-no questions of some languages, like English, always have a rising sentence final intonation? Why does English have sentences like *Joe ate the soup?* as well as *Did Joe eat the soup?* Why does *Joe ate the soup?* seem to have a different meaning from *Did Joe eat the soup?*

At least three types of "simple" yes-no questions occur in English. There is the "normal" yes-no question like *Did Joe eat the soup?* The question is neutral in the sense that it does not indicate whether the speaker believes that Joe ate the soup or that Joe did not eat the soup. The speaker wants to know what happened. In contrast to the normal yes-no question, sentences like *Joe ate the soup?* also occur in English. We shall use the term *intonation question* for these forms. These sentences are phonetically distinct from statements because they have sentence final marked breath-groups. The rise in fundamental frequency for these sentences is similar to the rise in fundamental frequency at the end of the normal yes-no questions (cf. Chapter 4).

The intonation questions are ambiguous. They may be interpreted as paraphrases of metalinguistic sentences like *Did you say that Joe ate the soup?* The so-called "echo" question is thus the deleted version of a metalinguistic question. It usually occurs in a conversation when a listener wants some utterance repeated. The intonation question can, however, have a rather different semantic interpretation. The sentence *Joe ate the soup?* implies that the speaker has heard that Joe ate the soup but he can hardly believe it. It expresses a measure of doubt that is not conveyed by the normal question *Did Joe eat his soup?* The intonation question *Joe ate the soup?* is not neutral. It is a somewhat rhetorical question. The speaker has already formed an opinion, and he does not really need any confirmation. The reply to the question *Are you going to drive down that rutted road?* is either yes or no. The reply to the question *You're going to drive down that rutted road?* is either a confirmatory silence or an explanation to the effect that the road is not really rutted, or that your car has a good suspension, or that it is the only way you can reach your destination, etc. The speaker already knows that you are going to drive down the road. The underlying phrase markers of the intonation questions must reflect these differences. We shall

TABLE 6.2 Representative Quotations from the *Oxford English Dictionary* for Direct Questions Involving *Whether*

Category 1

ca. 1000 *The Holy Gospels in Anglo-Saxon, Northumbrian and Old Mercian Versions etc.*, W. W. Skeat ed., 1871–1887, John IV. 33,

Hwæðer ænizȝ man him mete brohte?

ca. 1300 *Havelok the Dane, The Lay of ca. 1300,* Early Eng. Text Soc. 1868, 292,

Godrich . . . seyde, "Hweþer she sholde be Quen and leuedi ouer me?"

ca. 1300 *Cursor Mundi (The Cursur of the World) A Northumbrian Poem of the 14th Century in Four Versions,* Early Eng. Text Soc. 1874–1892, 5178,

Louerd! quer i sal him euer se?

1588 King, A., translation of *Canesius' Catechisme or Schort Instruction of Christian Religion,* Scottish Text Soc. 1901, 67,

Quhat is Battisme? and quhidder it be necessare to all mankynd?

Category 2

ca. 1000 *The Holy Gospels in Anglo-Saxon. . . .* , Matt. XXI. 25,

Hwæðer wæs iohannes fulluht, þe of heofonum, þe of mannum?

ca. 1400 Caxton *The Pylgremage of the Soule; from the French of G. de Guilleville ca. 1400* (Caxton 1859), I, XXX. 34,

Whether shal the lord refuse this seruaunt either els he shal receyue hym?

1450–1530 *The Myroure of Oure Ladye, Containing a Devotional Treatise on Devine Service etc.*, Early Eng. Text Soc. 1873, I, XVIII. 48,

Whither comst thow to chyrche to slepe or to wake?

1595 Shakespeare, *King John,* I, i, 134,

Whether hadst thou rather be a Faulconbridge, . . .
Or the reputed sonne of Cordelion?

1599 Shakespeare and others, *The Passionate Pilgrime,* vii. 17,

Was this a lover, or a Letcher whether?

1713 Berkeley, G. W. *Three Dialogues Between Hylas and Philonous,*

Whether does doubting consist in embracing the Affirmative or Negative side of a Question?

1822 Shelley, P. B. *Prose Works,* 1888, II. 115,

Whether do you demonstrate these things better in Homer or Hesiod?

Category 3

1549 Latimer, H. *The Fyrste(-Seuenth) Sermon Preached Before the Kynges Maiestye* (Arber 1869), 38,

Whither wyl he alowe a subiect to much?
Whether haue any man here in England to much?

develop an analysis for the yes-no questions that explicates these semantic differences and is consistent with the treatment of the general *wh* questions.

In Table 6.2 we have cited several representative quotations from the *Oxford English Dictionary* for direct questions involving *whether*. The sentences cover the period from about 1000 to that of contemporary English. Throughout this period yes-no questions could also have a phonetic form that is equivalent to the contemporary "normal" English yes-no questions. In earlier periods the verb adjacent to the tense marker was preposed, as in *Went John home?* These interrogative sentences conclude with a rising intonation.

The following analysis seems relevant for the period that starts at about the year 1000 and ends at the beginning of the seventeenth century.

1. English had a subjunctive mood. The base component of the grammar could generate phrase markers having the form shown in Figure 6.3.

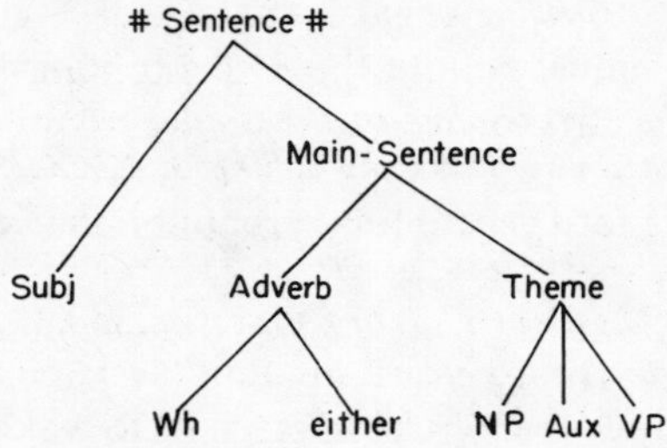

Figure 6.3

2. The base component also generated phrase markers that had the form shown in Figure 6.4.

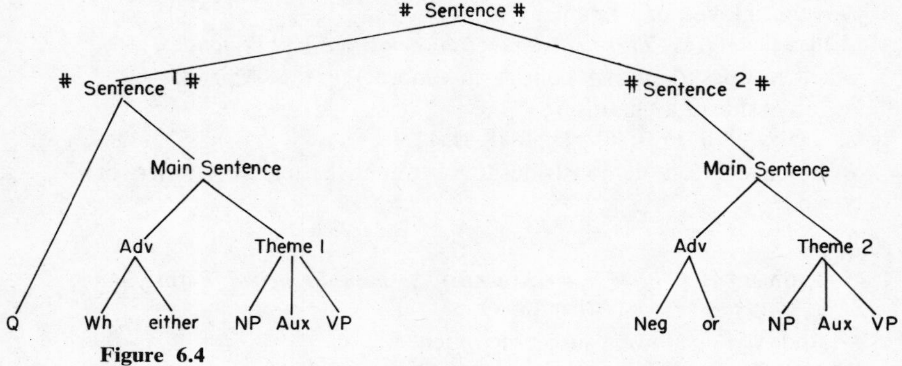

Figure 6.4

The phrase structure rules of the base component of the grammar contained these rules:

Sentence → Sentence—Sentence
Sentence → $\begin{Bmatrix} Q \\ \text{Subj} \end{Bmatrix}$—Main Sentence
Main Sentence → (Adv)—Theme
Adv → (*wh*)—(Neg)—Adv
Theme → Noun Phrase—Aux—Verb Phrase
Noun Phrase → Det—Noun
etc.

Type 1 and type 2 deep phrase markers underlie the data listed in categories 1 and 2 in Table 6.2. Rule (T2), or rather a modified version of it, (T2′), which transposes the entire verb, operates on these phrase markers. Rule T2′ would have the following form:

(T2′) # + Q, X, Noun Phrase, Tense + W, $Z \Rightarrow$ 12435
1 2 3 4 5
where 2 dominates *wh* and W is the verb adjacent to the tense marker.

Rule (T2′) was probably replaced with rule (T2) in the fifteenth century. An optional transformation (T3) deleted theme 2 when themes 1 and 2 were identical.[8]

(T3) # [Q, Adv, [NP-Aux-VP]], ## [Adv, [NP-Aux-VP] ,] #
1 2 3 Th-1 S1 4 5 Th-2 S2 6
⇒ 1,2,3,4,6
where 2 dominates *wh*,
4 dominates Neg,
3 = 5.

The operation of rule (T3) in contemporary English relates sentences like *Did he hit you or not?* to sentences like *Did he hit you or didn't he hit you?* Rule (T4), a second optional transformation, resulted in a sentence in which *or not* was deleted.

(T4) # Q, Adv, NP-Aux-VP #,# Adv # ⇒ 123
1 2 3 4
where 2 dominates *wh* and 4 dominates Neg.

The grammar could thus operate to form sentences like those in category 3 in Table 6.2, like *Whither wyl he alowe a subiect to much?* Throughout this period the string $\left\{\begin{Bmatrix} Q \\ \text{Subj} \end{Bmatrix} + wh + \text{Adv}\right\}$ in the de-

[8] NP = Noun Phrase, VP = Verb Phrase, N = Noun, etc.

rived phrase marker had the phonetic shape *whether*. Rule (T5) is an optional transformation that could operate throughout this period to produce sentences in which *whether* was deleted.

$$\text{(T5)}\quad \begin{bmatrix} \xleftarrow{\hspace{6em}} [-BG] \xrightarrow{\hspace{6em}} \\ \#, \begin{Bmatrix} Q \\ \text{Subj} \end{Bmatrix} - wh - \text{Adv, Theme 1}\ \#,\ X,\ Y\# \\ 1 \quad 2 \qquad\qquad\qquad 3 \qquad 4 \quad 5 \end{bmatrix} \Rightarrow \begin{bmatrix} \leftarrow [+BG] \rightarrow \\ 1, 3, 4, 5, \# \\ \end{bmatrix}$$

where X = Adv and Adv dominates Neg and Y = Theme 2 = Theme 1 or $X = Y$ = Null,

where the breath-group spans the entire sentence. Rule (T5) formally characterizes the "trading" relationship between the marked breath-group and the string $\{Q + wh + \text{Adv}\}$. The presence of one or the other of these entities in the derived phrase marker aids the recoverability of the underlying phrase marker. Rule (T5) was optional until the beginning of the seventeenth century.

Note that rules (T2) or (T2′), the auxiliary inversion rule, cannot apply to the type 1 deep phrase markers because of the presence of the subjunctive mood morpheme *Subj*. The sentences in category 1 in Table 6.2 all have the nominal preceding the auxiliary and main verbs. Dahlstedt (1901) and the editors of the *Oxford English Dictionary* regard sentences like those in category 1 in Table 6.2 to be examples of the subjunctive mood. The earlier Old English examples were inflected in the subjunctive mood since the presence of the morpheme *Subj* also made obligatory subjunctive marking transformations applicable. These transformations later became inoperative, and the superficial manifestations of the subjunctive for the most part disappeared except for the absence of Aux inversion. The subjunctive sentences express uncertainty or speculative inquiry. The interlocutor does not really expect to get a yes-no reply. However, it is hard always to be really certain on semantic grounds about what constitutes a subjunctive and what constitutes a "neutral" question. Let us for the moment assume that the sentences listed under category 1 in Table 6.2 have type 1 deep phrase markers. We shall see that this leads to an insight into the grammar of contemporary English.

After the beginning of the seventeenth century *whether* disappeared in sentences like those listed in categories 1 and 3 in Table 6.2. Rule (T5) became obligatory. In *Hamlet,* Act III, Scene I, the following conversation occurs:

HAMLET: Ha, Ha! Are you honest?
OPHELIA: My Lord?
HAMLET: Are you fair?

Whether still occurs in sentences like those listed in category 2 in Table 6.2, since rule (T5) cannot operate because theme 2 is not identical to Theme 1. Hamlet thus says,

> Whether 'tis nobler in the mind to suffer
> The slings and arrows of outrageous fortune
> Or to take arms against a sea of troubles

Thus for contemporary English the two deep phrase markers that follow would result in the sentences (A) *John ate the fish?* and (B) *Did John eat the fish?, Did John eat the fish or didn't he eat the fish?,* and *Did John eat the fish or not?* Rules (T2) and (T5) operate[9] on phrase marker A to produce the sentence *John ate the fish?* Rules (T2) and (T5) operate on phrase marker B to produce the "tag" question *Did John eat the fish or didn't he eat the fish?* Rules (T2),

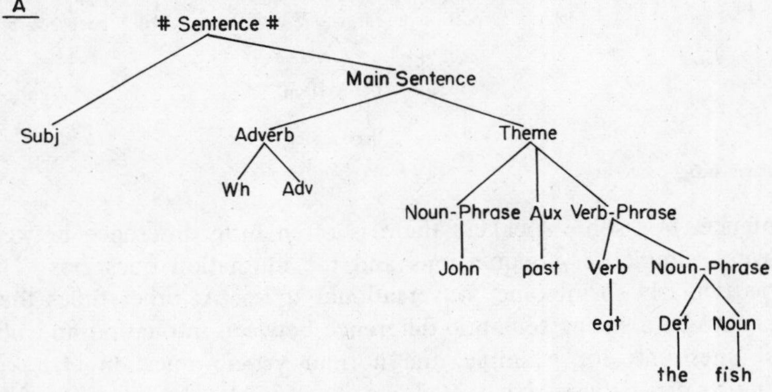

Figure 6.5

(T3), and (T5) operate on phrase marker B to produce the tag question *Did John eat the fish or not?* Rules (T2), (T3), (T4), and (T5) operate on phrase marker B to produce the "simple" question *Did John eat the fish?* The semantic interpretations of the two tag questions and the simple question that have underlying phrase marker B are identical, and our analysis mirrors this fact since the optional

[9] Obviously, many other rules figure in the shaping of the derived phrase maker and the phonetic output; cf. Chomsky (1957, 1965) and Chomsky and Halle (1966) for pertinent discussions of the syntactic and phonologic components of the grammar.

transformations neither add nor bring any new semantic information.

To many speakers of English, *John ate the fish?* denotes a certain air of rhetorical doubt relative to the other sentences. This slight semantic difference is explicated in this analysis through the presence of the subjunctive morpheme in the phrase marker that underlies this

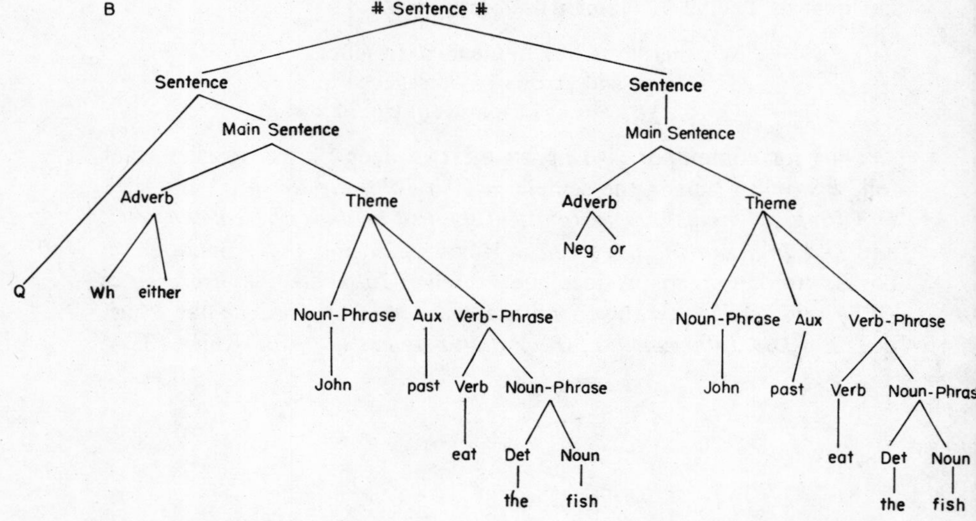

Figure 6.6

sentence. For some speakers there is often little difference between normal, simple yes-no questions and the intonation questions. This is particularly so in some conversational styles. At other times there seems to be a strong semantic difference between intonation and normal questions, for example, the normal yes-no question *Are you going to drive down that rutted road?* versus *You're going to drive down that rutted road?* The wide variation in the semantic distinctness of the normal and the intonation yes-no question is perhaps a function of the marginal status of the subjunctive mood in English. Perhaps the projection rules of the semantic component of the grammar assign a conditional status to the subjunctive, that is, the mood is subjunctive if the subjunctive constituent is present in the deep phrase marker and if other conditions are met.

This analysis of the intonation questions is consistent with the other syntactic manifestations of the subjunctive mood in English. We stated that the manifestations of the subjunctive are for the most part absent in contemporary English. This is not strictly so, and sentences like *If I were the Queen of . . .* and *If I were there . . .*, commonly occur. The verb is modified by the presence of the subjunctive constituent. In contrast to the subjunctive inflection in these examples, the verb in the subjunctive intonation question *I was there?* is not modified. This phenomenon is, however, quite consistent with the inflectional system of English. Chomsky (1965, p. 221) points out that case in English is determined by the position of the noun in the surface structure rather than in the deep structure. The pronoun in the sentences *He was struck by a bullet* and *He is easy to please* is in each case the direct object of the verb in the underlying deep structure. Nevertheless, the form is *he* rather than *him*. Rule (T5) deletes the subjunctive constituent; the verb in the derived phrase marker of the sentence *I was there?* is therefore not inflected.

7 Prominence, Stress, and Emphasis in American English

In this chapter we shall discuss some of the acoustic manifestations of linguistic stress in American English.[1] In particular, we shall consider the role of the segmental feature [+ P_s]. We shall present evidence to demonstrate that perceived linguistic stress is often a secondary manifestation of the derived constituent structure. The listener mentally "computes" the linguistic stress by means of the derived constituent structure of the utterance. He determines the derived constituent structure by means of the words of the sentence, by the breath-group division that we covered in Chapter 6, or through "disjuncture." Finally, we shall discuss the acoustic properties of disjuncture in detail.

7.1 Definitions of Prominence, Stress, and Emphasis

There is a great deal of uncertainty in linguistic and phonetic literature with respect to the terms "prominence," "stress," and "emphasis." We shall try to preserve the following distinctions.

7.1.1 Prominence. We shall use the term "prominence" for the occurrences of the distinctive feature [+ P_s]. Perceptually, prominence is therefore the perceived "loudness" of a vowel relative to its environment. The acoustic correlates of prominence are duration, fundamental frequency, and sound pressure level (or amplitude).

[1] We shall also briefly consider some similar effects in German.

Prominence thus will refer to the occurrence of the segmental feature $[+ P_s]$.

7.1.2 Stress. We shall reserve the term "stress" for the abstract entities that are generated by the phonologic rules of the "stress cycle." Most studies of English agree that the vowels of words, short phrases, and sentences are differentiated by relative degrees of stress or "loudness." [2] Sweet (1892) differentiated ". . . three degrees of stress or loudness . . . strong, half strong, and weak. . . ." Jesperson (1907) used four levels of stress; Bloch and Trager (1942) and Trager and Smith (1951) also used four levels of "phonemic stress" for English. On the other hand, Pike (1945) believes that ". . . only one phonemic innate stress contrast can be demonstrated to exist in English. . . ." Jones (1932) is vague about the number of levels of stress that can be perceived when single words or short phrases are uttered. However, he notes that in connected speech only two degrees of stress need be transcribed.

Stress in these studies is a phonetic element that has definite acoustic correlates in the speech signal that are independent of the acoustic correlates of the segmental phonemes.[3] Chomsky, Halle, and Lukoff (1956) and Chomsky and Halle (1966) have shown that cyclical phonologic rules will assign a set of stress "levels" to the vowels of a word or phrase. These stress levels that are assigned to a word are a function of the phonemic structure of the word, its syntactic function (e.g., whether it is a noun or a verb in the derived phrase marker), and the constituent structure of the derived phrase marker.

Chomsky and Halle (1966) have suggested that stress gradations can readily be explained if it is assumed that, as a universal principle, rules assigning primary stress (indicated by 1) require stress lowering in all previously stressed syllables. Therefore, in order to account by general rules for the location of prominence in English sentences, it will be necessary to assign secondary, tertiary, etc., stress to some

[2] Stress level 1 is the "strongest" stress, level 2 is "weaker" than 1, level 3 is weaker than 2, etc.

[3] Except for Jones, who notes that stress may be perceived by virtue of the listener's knowledge of the structure of the language rather than by means of any special acoustic cues (1932, p. 227):

> When a strong stress is given to a syllable incapable of receiving any noticeable increase of loudness, a person unfamiliar with the language would be unable to tell that a stress was present. . . . A person familiar with the language would not perceive the stress objectively from the sound . . . but he perceives in a subjective way; the sounds he hears call up to his mind (through the context) the manner of making them, and by means of immediate "inner speech" he knows where the stress is.

syllables. For example, the words *easy* and *chair* both have a primary stress when they are produced as isolated words:

1
[easy]
1
[chair]

When they are produced in the phrase *easy chair* the stress rules assign primary stress to *easy*. The stress on *chair* is therefore lowered:

1 2
[easy chair]

This principle is consistent with the data that follow in this chapter, since it implies that the listener can calculate the secondary and tertiary stresses once he knows where the primary stress is. The phonologic rules shift only the primary stress, but each time they assign primary stress to some vowel they lower the stress levels on all other vowels. If the listener thus perceives where the prominence is, he can calculate the stress levels of the other vowels by using his knowledge of the phonologic rules that assign primary stress. The listener also has to know the constituent structure of the derived phrase marker because the phonologic stress rules operate in terms of the derived constituent structure and the segmental feature bundles (the phonemes).

In most cases the listener deduces the constituent structure of the language through the words of the utterance. He simply knows what may constitute a well-formed phrase or sentence. In certain cases, the constituent structure of a phrase may be ambiguous. We shall show that in these cases the acoustic feature of "disjuncture" may be used to disambiguate the constituent structure of the derived phrase marker in a manner analogous to the disambiguation of sentences by breath-group division.

7.1.3 Emphasis. We shall use the term "emphasis" to identify instances where the distinctive feature $[+P_s]$ produces extra prominence on the vowel or vowels of a word (and its consonants), apart from the stress that the vowels of the word would have received from the phonologic stress rules. In other words, emphasis is prominence that is not predicted by the stress cycle. It may result from the presence of an emphatic morpheme in the underlying deep phrase marker. The syntactic component of the grammar results in a derived phrase marker where the segmental feature $[+P_s]$ can follow from the presence of emphatic elements in the deep phrase marker.[4] In Chapter 4, for example, we presented a group of sentences where either the word *soup* or the word *Joe* was emphasized in the sentences *Joe ate his soup* and *Did Joe eat his soup?* The vowels of the emphasized monosyllabic words were marked with the feature [+ P_s]. The term "contrastive stress" could have been used for emphasis, but it might cause some confusion. We want to preserve the distinction between the distinctive feature [+ P_s] and its underlying source. The phonologic feature [+ P_s] in the phonetic output can be the manifestation of either emphasis in the underlying phrase marker or, in certain circumstances, the "stronger" stresses generated by the phonologic stress cycle. In itself it has no more "meaning" than the phonologic feature [+ voicing].

7.2 Some Phonetic Manifestations of Stress

Let us start by considering the simplest case, the manifestations of stress when two-syllable words are carefully spoken in isolation. In parts *A* and *B* of Figure 7.1, quantized sound spectrograms and plots of the fundamental frequency and subglottal air pressure with respect to time have been presented for speaker 1 reading the words *rebél* and *rébel* in isolation (cf. Chapter 4). Each word was produced on a separate unmarked breath-group.

The segmental feature [+ P_s] occurred on the stressed vowel in each case. Compare the plots of subglottal pressure with those in Figures 4.10 and 4.11. In Figure 4.10 [+P_s] was not placed on any vowel. In Figure 4.11 [+ P_s] was placed on the vowel of the word *Joe*. Speaker 1 consistently used the archetypal articulatory correlate of [+ P_s] to produce prominence; that is, he used a momentary increase in the subglottal air pressure of approximately[5] 4 to 6 cm H_2O. In parts *A* and *B* of Figure 7.1 each isolated word has been produced on a short breath-group, and the peak subglottal pressure occurs on the vowel marked with primary stress. In the data presented in Chapter 4, it often was not evident whether the peak subglottal air pressure occurred on a single vowel or whether it was deliberately placed on an entire syllable. These utterances, which were produced at a slower, more deliberate rate, show that the scope of [+ P_s] is a single vowel.

[4] See Klima (1964) for a discussion of emphasis and some of its other phonetic manifestations.

[5] These values must be regarded as only an approximation since the relationship of true subglottal pressure to the measured balloon pressure has been quantitatively determined only for steady-state or quasi-steady-state conditions; cf. Chapter 4.

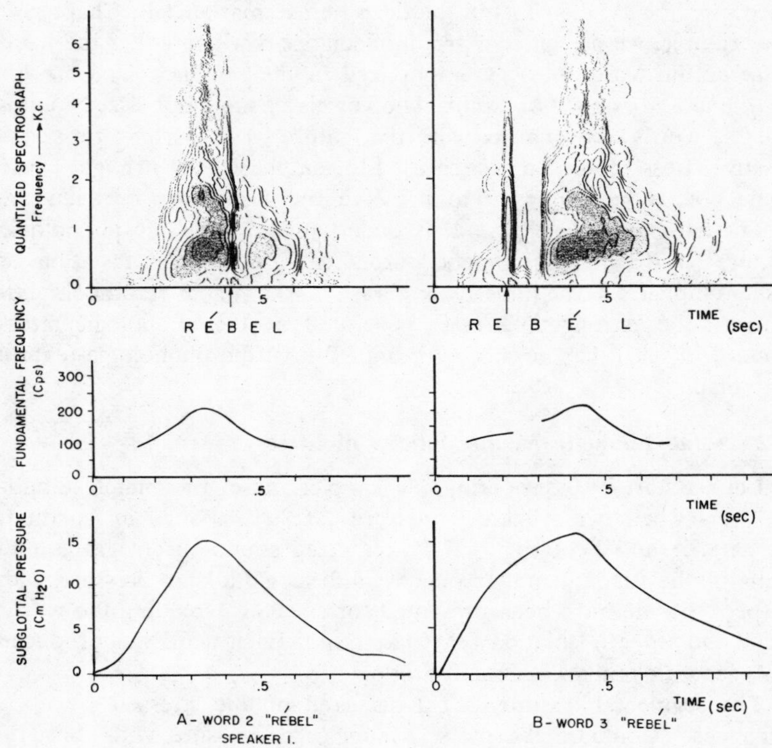

Figure 7.1 Acoustic and physiologic data for speaker 1 reading the two isolated words *rébel* and *rebél*.
Fundamental frequency and subglottal air pressure are plotted as functions of time. Quantized wide-band (300-cps analyzing filter bandwidth) spectrograms are also presented. Each contour line of the spectrogram represents a 6-db increment in amplitude. Synchronizing pulses that are marked by means of vertical arrows (after 0.4 sec and 0.2 sec) are also indicated on the spectrograms.

The prominent vowels have the peak fundamental frequencies, amplitudes, and durations. The unstressed vowels have been reduced. The acoustic correlates of primary linguistic stress in this two-syllable word pair are thus in agreement with acoustic studies by Lieberman (1960), Hadding-Koch (1961), and Ladefoged and McKinney (1963), as well as psychoacoustic studies by Fry (1955, 1958). The distinction that occurs in all of these studies is, however, binary. The stressed vowel of the bisyllabic word is prominent, whereas the other vowel is not prominent. Can "degrees" of prominence differentiate intermediate levels of stress? Can a listener compute some sort of "prominence" function from the fundamental frequency, amplitude,

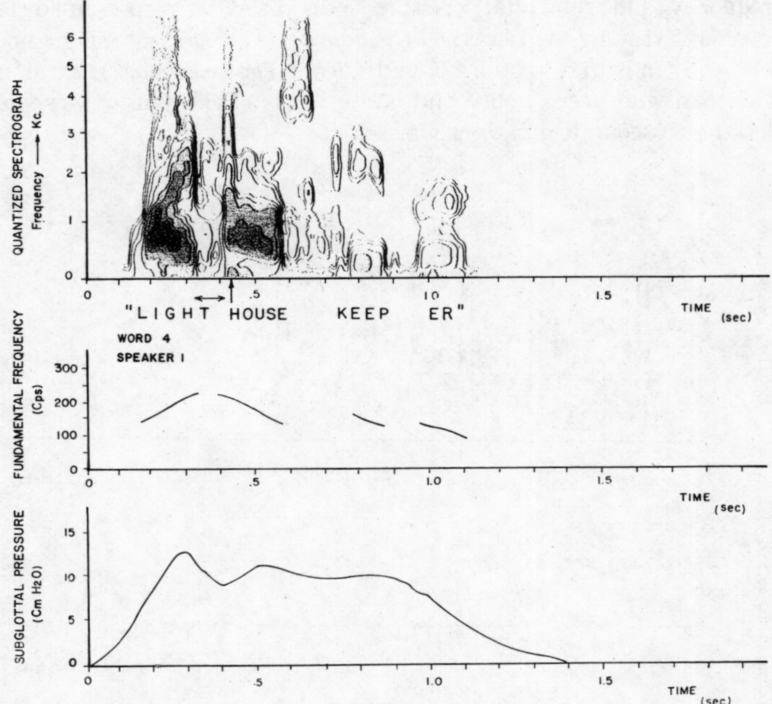

Figure 7.2 Acoustic and physiologic data for speaker 1 reading the isolated phrase (*light house*) (*keeper*), meaning someone who tends to a lighthouse. The "disjuncture" or interval between vowels of *light* and *house* is marked by a horizontal arrow below the spectrogram.

and duration of each vowel, and differentiate stress level 1 from stress level 2 and further differentiate stress level 2 from stress level 3? The results of a number of independent psychoacoustic experiments suggest that listeners can make only binary categorical distinctions along the dimension of prominence when they listen to connected discourse.[6] However, what categorical distinctions can be made when a word or phrase is spoken in isolation?

In Figures 7.2 and 7.3, quantized spectrograms and fundamental

[6] The experiment discussed in Chapter 5 (Lieberman, 1965) demonstrated that amplitude, f_0, and duration (the acoustic correlates of $[+P_s]$ in connected speech) can differentiate only two degrees of stress, level 1 versus everything else. Hadding-Koch (1961) found that the stress levels assigned by listeners, other than level 1, were randomly distributed. Armstrong and Ward (1926) and Jones (1932, 1962) transcribe only two degrees of stress for connected speech, as does Pike (1945). Lisker, in a personnal communication, notes that students of the Trager-Smith notation consistently produce random results with respect to differentiating the intermediate stress levels.

frequency and subglottal pressure plots have been presented for speaker 1 reading the phrase (*light house*) (*keeper*), meaning someone who tends to a lighthouse, and (*light*) (*house keeper*), meaning a woman who keeps house and is not heavy. Each phrase was produced on a separate breath-group.

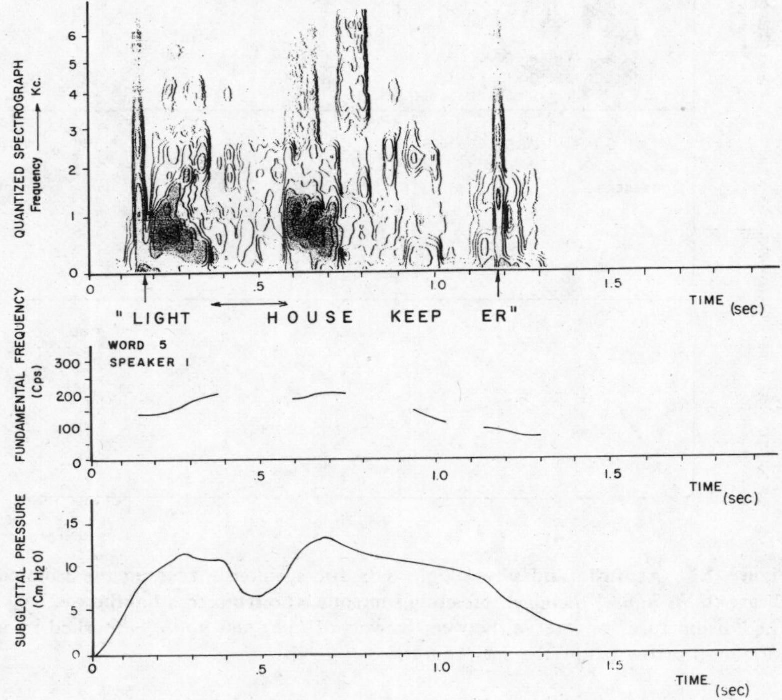

Figure 7.3 Acoustic and physiologic data for speaker 1 reading the isolated phrase (*light*) (*house keeper*), meaning a woman who is not heavy.
The disjuncture or interval between the vowels of *light* and *house* is marked by a horizontal arrow below the spectrogram. Note that this disjuncture is longer than the disjuncture marked in Figure 7.2.

The linguistic stress predicted by the stress rules for the utterance
1 3 2 4
plotted in Figure 7.2 is *light house keeper*. Note that the fundamental frequency, amplitude, and duration of the vowel of *house,* which is assigned stress level 3, are greater than those of the vowel /i/ in *keeper,* which is assigned stress level 2. The fundamental frequencies of the vowels in *light* and *house* are about the same, though *light* bears stress level 1 while *house* bears stress level 3. The peak ampli-

tude of the first formant of *light* is, however, 6 db greater than that of *house*. Note the duration of the interval between the vowels of *light* and *house,* which is marked with an arrow on Figure 7.2. This duration was accurately measured from a conventional wide-band (300-cps analyzing filter bandwidth) spectrogram on which the beginning and end of phonation were clearly visible. It is presented in Table 7.1,

TABLE 7.1 Measurements of Duration, Average Fundamental Frequency, Peak Fundamental Frequency, Minimum Fundamental Frequency, and Peak Amplitude Derived from Figures 7.2 and 7.3

Figure 7.2							
Stress Pattern	1		3		2		4
	light	———	house	———	keep	———	er
Duration segment (msec)	180	40	170	190	90	100	120
Average fundamental frequency (cps)	190		180		140		110
Peak fundamental frequency	225		220		160		130
Minimum fundamental frequency	130		130		125		90
Peak amplitude (db)	48		42		30		24

Figure 7.3							
Stress Pattern	2		1		3		4
	light	———	house	———	keep	———	er
Duration segment	240	220	160	180	90	110	110
Average fundamental frequency	165		200		130		90
Peak fundamental frequency	210		210		150		100
Minimum fundamental frequency	140		190		110		70
Peak amplitude (db)	48		48		30		30

where the duration, average fundamental frequency, maximum and minimum fundamental frequency, and relative amplitude (to the nearest 6-db step above the noise level of the spectrogram) of each vowel of the utterances plotted in Figures 7.2 and 7.3 are presented.

In Figure 7.3 the same data are presented for (*light*) (*house keeper*) which should have the stress pattern *light house keeper*. The average fundamental frequency of the vowel of *house* is higher than
(stress numbers printed under *light house keeper*: 2 1 3 4)

that of *light,* though both vowels have the same peak fundamental frequency. Both vowels have the same relative peak amplitude. The vowel /i/ in *keeper* has almost the same amplitude, duration, and fundamental frequency in Figure 7.2 and Figure 7.3. Note that the duration of the interval (marked by means of an arrow) between the vowels of *light* and *house* is 220 msec in Figure 7.3, whereas it is only 40 msec in Figure 7.2. The duration of the interval between /ay/ of *light* and /i/ in *keeper* is, however, quite similar in both utterances.

Now, what acoustic cue differentiates these two utterances? The answer to this question is that the disjunctures, which we shall define

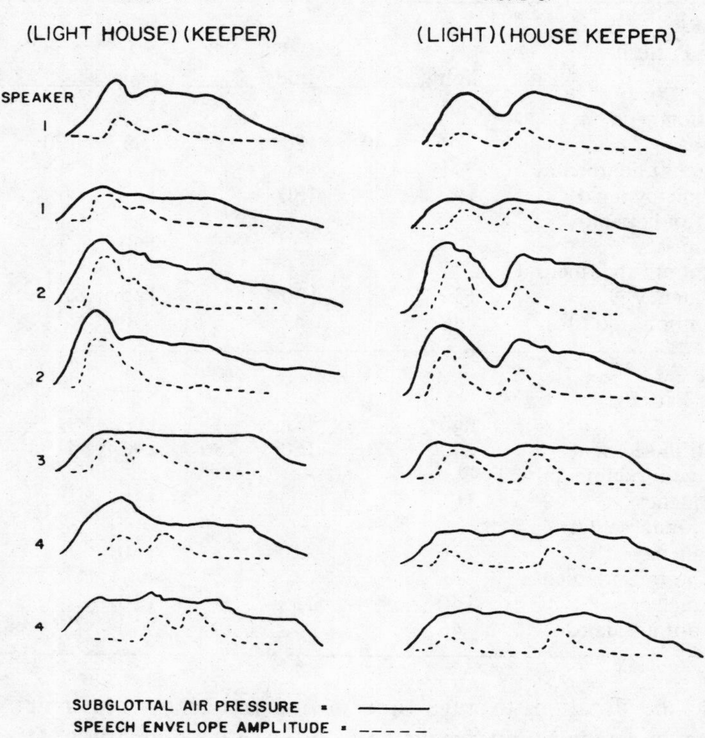

Figure 7.4 Subglottal air pressure and speech envelope amplitude plotted for speakers 1, 2, 3, and 4 reading the isolated phrases (*light house*) (*keeper*) and (*light*) (*house keeper*).

The subglottal air pressure is marked by means of a solid line, while the envelope amplitude is marked by means of a broken line. Note that the duration of the interval between the peaks of the speech envelope amplitude function always correlates with the derived constituent structure.

as the intervals between the vowels, are the relevant acoustic cues. Bolinger and Gerstman (1957) first observed this effect in an experiment in which they used tape-splicing techniques to change the utterance (*light house*) (*keeper*) into (*light*) (*house keeper*) and vice versa by simply changing the interval between *light* and *house*. We replicated their results using a digital computer to "splice" intervals of speech, without any noticeable experimental artifacts.[7]

In Figure 7.4 subglottal air pressure functions and envelope amplitude functions of (*light house*) (*keeper*) and (*light*) (*house keeper*) are plotted for the four talkers who were recorded in the physiological experiment that we discussed in Chapter 4. Note that the peak subglottal air pressure cannot be correlated with stress level 1. The duration of the interval between the two air pressure peaks always correlates with the constituent structure of the utterances. The disjuncture rather than the magnitude of the air pressure peak differentiates the utterances.

Similar effects also seem to occur in German. In Figure 7.5 spec-
2 4
trograms are presented of the two German phrases *eine Handvoll*
1 2 3 1
Kirschen and *eine Hand voll Kirschen* as they were spoken by a native speaker of German. In Table 7.2 the durations and average fundamental frequencies of the vowels and the durations of the disjunctures are tabulated for the utterances in Figure 7.5. Note that the acoustic correlates of prominence do not divide into any ordered classes that would support a series of stress levels. The disjunctures marked on Figure 7.5 again seem to indicate the differing constituent structures of these utterances. The disjuncture may be filled as it is in this case with the fricative. It does not have to be a silent pause.

It is conceivable that the disjunctures are themselves acoustic correlates of stress levels. We might think of a system in which vowels were either prominent or not prominent and where the length of the disjuncture between two prominent vowels was inversely proportional to the difference between the two stress levels. The data, however, do not support this hypothesis. In Figure 7.5, for example, the disjunc-

[7] The speech signal is sampled 10,000 times per second and quantized along a linear scale with 7 bits using an analog-to-digital converter and a PDP-1 computer. The digit sequence is recorded on magnetic tape. A computer program is used to display the waveform on a scope and simultaneously play the signal. The operator can mark any part of the waveform to the nearest 0.0001 sec and remove any interval to a storage tape. Up to 30 sec of speech can be stored, divided, and recombined. If "cuts" are made at zero crossings in the vicinity of intervals of comparative silence, or the beginning or end of voicing, objectional transients can be minimized.

ture between *voll* and *Kirschen* is identical for *A* and *B*. The same situation occurs in Figures 7.2 and 7.3. The duration of the disjuncture between *house* and /i/ of *keeper* is similar, though the stress levels of the vowels are dissimilar. What seems to be happening is that the increased duration of the disjuncture in Figure 7.3 and Figure

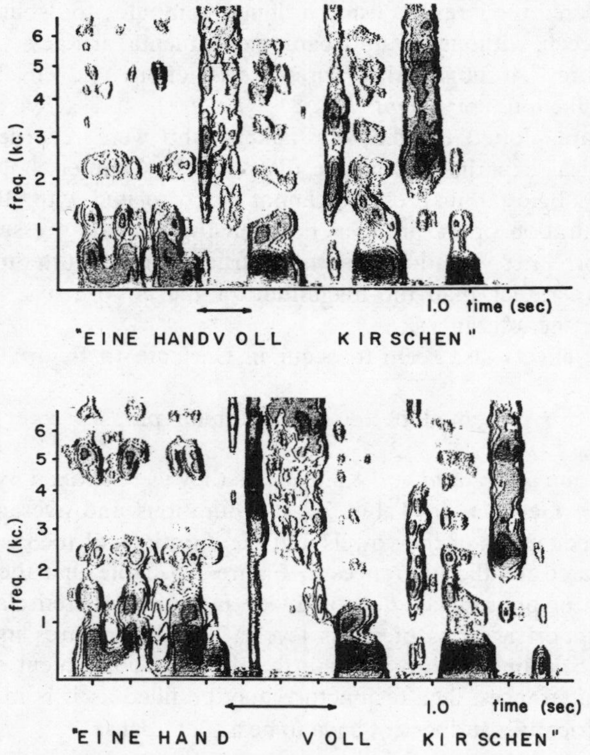

Figure 7.5 Quantized spectrograms for a native speaker of German reading the isolated phrases *eine Handvoll Kirschen* and *eine Hand voll Kirschen*. The disjunctures between the vowels of *Hand* and *voll* are marked by means of horizontal arrows. Note that the duration of the disjuncture correlates with the derived constituent structure.

7.5*B* indicates the constituent structure of the utterance. As we shall see in the examples that follow, the disjunctures manifest those aspects of the constituent structure that may not be evident from the rest of the stimulus ensemble.

In connected speech, disjuncture may still be used to mark constituent structure. In Figure 7.6 spectrograms of the phrase *light house keeper* are presented for the instances when it was spoken by speaker

TABLE 7.2 Measurements of Duration, Average Fundamental Frequency, and Amplitude Derived from Figure 7.5

	2		4		1	
	(Hand	______	voll)	______	(Kirschen)	eine Handvoll Kirschen
Duration segment (msec)	350	140	150	50	470	
Average fundamental frequency (cps)	90		90		90	
Peak amplitude (db)	30		30		30	
	2		3		1	
	(Hand)	______	(voll	______	Kirschen)	eine Hand voll Kirschen
Duration segment (msec)	440	260	130	60	360	
Average fundamental frequency (cps)	80		70		70	
Peak amplitude (db)	36		36		36	

1 in complete sentences. The context furnished by sentence 1,[8] *The life of a light house keeper formerly was very lonely,* indicates the appropriate constituent structure, as does sentence 4, *Our maid weighed 180 pounds, but the Joneses had a light house keeper for more than twenty years.* The disjunctures still mark the constituent structure, probably because the speaker was aware of the contrast when he carefully read each sentence.

The context of the entire sentence actually overrides the effect of the disjunctures. It is possible to use a digital computer to "excise," or cut out, the *light house keeper* phrases from each sentence and switch them without causing any objectional artifacts.[9] It is then impossible to hear any difference between the stress patterns of the altered sentences and the original sentences. In sentence 1, one hears the phrase as (*light house*) (*keeper*) whether or not the original sentence or the sentence with the phrase excised from sentence 4 is heard. The context of the entire sentence indicates the appropriate constituent structure, and the listener "hears" the correct stress pattern.

It is difficult to assess the extent to which disjuncture reflects constituent structure in normal speech. In Figure 7.7, spectrograms are presented for a male native speaker of American English who read

[8] In the list in Table 4.1.

[9] Using the same technique that we discussed on page 153.

these phrases: A—(*light house*) (*keeper*), B—(*light*) (*house keeper*), and C—(*light*) (*heavy weight*). Each phrase was read in isolation in sequence. The disjuncture between the first two words is marked. Note that phrases A and B are differentiated by disjuncture, whereas C is not. The constituent structure of phrase C is relatively unambiguous

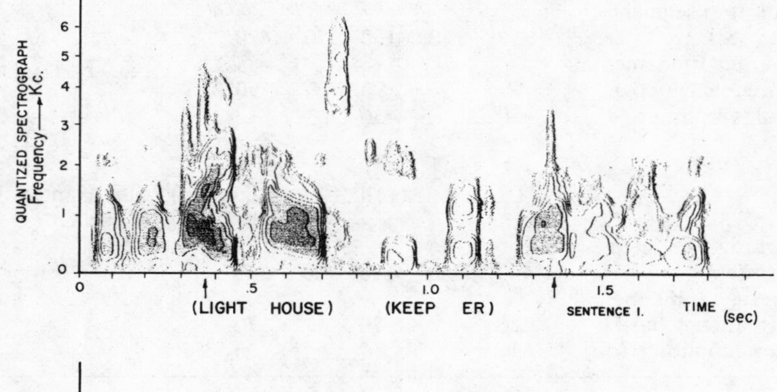

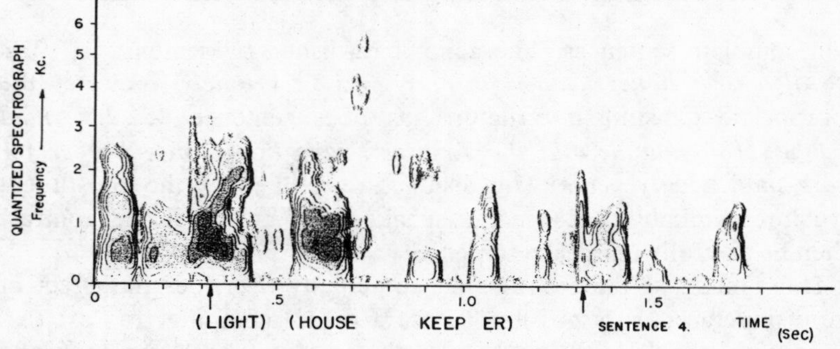

Figure 7.6 Quantized spectrograms of the words *light house keeper* read in the context of the sentence *The life of a light house keeper formerly was very lonely* (sentence 1) and the sentence *Our maid weighed 180 pounds, but the Joneses had a light house keeper for more than twenty years* (sentence 4). Note that the disjuncture between the vowels of *light* and *house* is greater in sentence 4.

if only the string of segmental phonetic elements is considered. The speaker apparently does not bother to increase the disjuncture between the vowels of *light* and *heavy*. Instead, he utters the phrase at an even rate. The junctural contrast is wiped out. The speaker apparently uses only the minimum effort that is sufficient to ensure that the utterance will be understood. In Figure 7.8 the spectrograms of the same three utterances are presented for a second male native speaker of American English. Note that the duration of the disjunc-

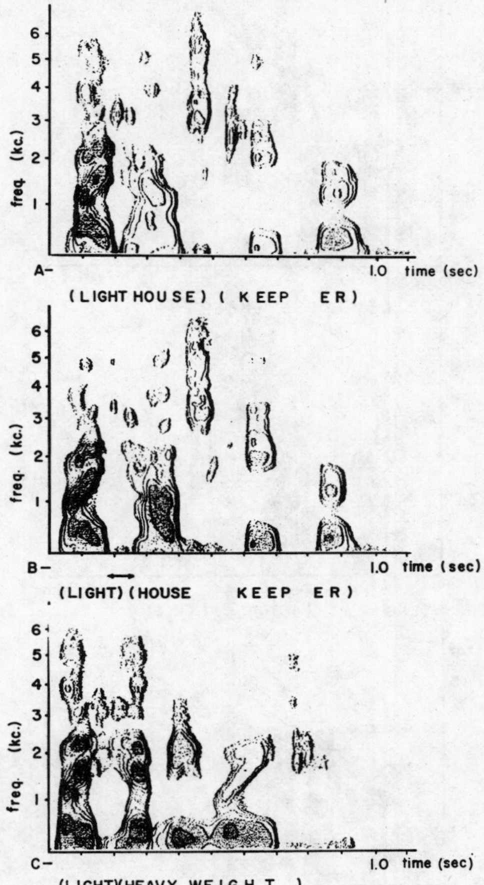

Figure 7.7 Quantized spectrograms of a male speaker reading these isolated phrases: A — (*light house*) (*keeper*), B — (*light*) (*house keeper*), and C — (*light*) (*heavy weight*).

The disjuncture between *light* and *house* is marked for utterance *B*. Note the absence of a similar disjuncture between *light* and *heavy weight* in utterance *C*. The derived constituent structure of utterance *C* is relatively unambiguous if only the string of words is considered.

ture between the word *light* and the rest of the utterance reflects the constituent structure of each phrase. In this instance the disjuncture is especially short for A, quite long for B, and of an intermediate duration for C. The relative ambiguity of the constituent structure of each phrase as derived from its words affects the degree to which the disjunctures reflect the constituent structure. Words that are more

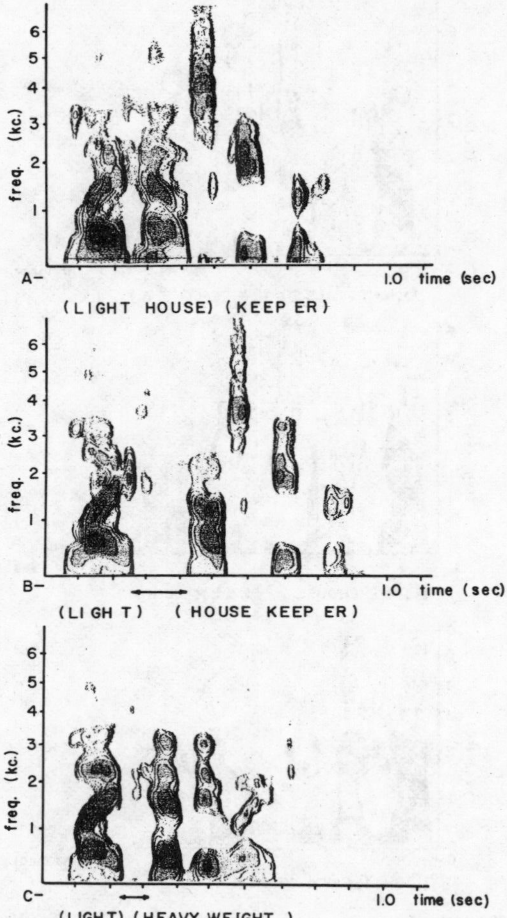

Figure 7.8 Quantized spectrograms of a different male speaker reading these isolated phrases: *A* — (*light house*) (*keeper*), *B* — (*light*) (*house keeper*), and *C* — (*light*) (*heavy weight*).
The disjunctures after *light* are marked for utterances *B* and *C*. Note that the disjuncture is shorter in utterance *C*.

closely related tend to be separated by shorter disjunctures when the constituent structure may be in doubt. Note that in all these examples the disjunctures between *house* and *keeper* never change appreciably. There is no need to modify these disjunctures though the constituent structure is different, because the modification of the disjuncture between *light* and *house* provides enough information for the listener to interpret the utterance correctly.

In summation, we might conceive of a process whereby the phonetic outputs of linguistic stress were formed in the following manner:

1. Let X be the "stress level" of each vowel which is assigned by the phonologic rules.
2. All vowels where $X \leq X_i$ are marked $[+ P_s]$.
3. All vowels where $X > X_i$ are $[- P_s]$.
4. All vowels where $X \geq X_j$ are reduced.

The magnitudes of X_i and X_j are functions of the rate at which the speaker is talking, the context, etc. In rapid discourse, X_i might equal 0, and no vowels would be marked $[+ P_s]$ as the result of linguistic stress. In careful speech, X_i probably equals 1.

Disjunctures would manifest the constituent structure where it would otherwise not be clear from the total context of the message. The perception of the "weaker" degrees of stress always follows from the listener's application of the rules of the grammar on the derived phrase marker. However, the derived phrase marker is manifested by different phonetic signals in different situations. The "weaker" stress levels thus are, in effect, computational "indices" that are functions of the derived constituent structure and the stress assignment rules of the language. A listener perceives these stress levels by means of a process of internal computation. Some of the stress levels can be mapped out in terms of various acoustic phenomena under certain conditions,[10] but only a finite number of weaker stress levels can in any eventuality be directly mapped out acoustically.

7.3 Categorization versus Discrimination

We have stated that prominence exercises only a binary function with regard to the perception of linguistic stress. Many of the objections to this view may stem from a basic confusion between categorical and comparative decisions. For example, under optimal conditions, the threshold for detecting a difference in frequency between two successively presented sinusoidal tones is of the order of 1 part in a 1000 (Rosenblith and Stevens, 1952; Harris and Stuntz, 1950). On the basis of comparative judgments of this type, it has been estimated that human listeners can distinguish about 350,000 different pure tones (Stevens and Davis, 1938). In contrast to this differential

[10] A trained speaker, for example, can modulate his voice for pedagogic purposes and produce a special prosodic signal. However, this is analogous to using a pencil to tap out the sequence of stress levels and is not typical of even carefully read normal speech.

sensitivity is the relative inability of a listener to identify and name (i.e., categorize) sounds presented, not for direct comparison, but for individual identification. Pollack (1952), for example, has shown[11] that listeners can consistently identify no more than four or five pure tones when each tone is individually presented for identification. The gross disparity between the estimate of human performance that is based on a projection of human discriminatory abilities and the actual categorical performance reflects the basic difference between categorical and comparative decisions.

It is, for example, possible to produce the sentence *Joe ate his soup* with virtually any degree of prominence on *Joe*. If two of these utterances are successively presented to a listener, he will be able to discriminate extremely small differences in prominence. If the listener were asked to state what each utterance "meant," he would undoubtedly associate many fine shades of "meaning" with each degree of prominence. The "shades of meaning" might reflect some of the emotional attributes of intonation, or they might refer to incidents in the listener's life history. Many of the "minimal intonation pairs" that are discussed in linguistic literature are comparative. They may have some relevance to the emotional aspects of intonation, but they are not directly relevant to the linguistic aspects of intonation. Linguistic decisions are categorical. Two male speakers may produce the vowel /a/ with formant frequencies $F_1 = 720$, $F_2 = 1080$, and $F_3 = 2600$ cps for one talker and $F_1 = 720$, $F_2 = 1110$, and $F_3 = 2700$ cps for the other talker. The two vowels will both be categorized as /a/ though listeners can easily discriminate between the two sounds (Stevens, 1952).

Geisler, Molnar, *et al.* (1958) performed an interesting experiment in which listeners were asked to categorize short "clicks" according to their loudness. Listeners were seated one at a time in an anechoic chamber and monaurally presented with 0.1 msec clicks through a PDR-10 headphone. The clicks were presented at 5-second intervals, and the amplitudes of the clicks were varied in either 5- or 10-db steps in three sessions over a range of intensity that went from 10 to 80 db or from 35 to 80 db over the mean threshold of the subjects taking part in the experiment. Twenty listeners heard these stimuli. The listeners were asked to place the stimuli in five categories. The performance of the subjects varied. Some subjects were unable to form five categories. One listener, for example, classified most of the stimuli that were less than 40 db in the "weakest" category and

[11] Pollack expressed his results in terms of information transmitted (cf. Shannon, 1948). The rate of information transferred was 2.0–2.3 bits.

placed the stimuli that were over 40 db into one of the other four categories without regard to their relative intensity. Essentially, he formed only two categories. Other listeners were able to form five categories. Each listener's performance was remarkably stable and remained unaffected by further training.[12] The listeners apparently had different categorization procedures. These results contrast with those reported by Pollack (1953), who investigated the categorization of pure tones according to amplitude. He found that listeners could consistently form the equivalent of three to four categories. The differences in the performance of the listeners when they listened to clicks rather than to sustained pure tones may reflect the use of linguistic criteria by some listeners and nonlinguistic criteria by others, just as the performance of the listeners in the Hadding-Koch and Studdert-Kennedy (1964) experiment (cf. Chapter 4) reflected the use of linguistic rather than "pure" psychoacoustic criteria.

One additional comment can be made regarding the possible import of psychoacoustic experiments that deal with "elementary" auditory cues like pure tones. Pollack (1952), as we noted, found that listeners could form the equivalent of four out of five categories with respect to frequency. If language made optimum use of the potential to form these psychoacoustic categories, we might expect to find some language where four or five "pitch levels" had a phonemic status. However, it is impossible to find any examples where four or five static pitch levels each have a phonemic status. Languages like Chinese, which have phonemic pitch contours, instead build up the pitch phonemes out of the binary distinctive features high pitch, low pitch, rising and falling (Chang, 1958). Linguistic "codes" apparently avoid making extreme demands on the human auditory system. They operate with a "margin for error." Since loudness can be categorized, under optimum conditions, to only three or four levels, it is not surprising to find that only two degrees of prominence function as linguistic cues in connected speech.

[12] Personnal communication from C. E. Molnar.

8 On the Perception and the Production of Speech

In the previous chapters we have discussed some of the acoustic and articulatory correlates of the breath-group and [P_s]. We noted that listeners often seem to perceive intonation and stress by means of a process of "analysis by synthesis" in which they make use of their knowledge of the articulatory gestures that are involved in the production of speech. The listeners "decode" the input speech signal by using their knowledge of the constraints that are imposed by the human articulatory "output" apparatus. In a sense we have proposed a "motor" theory of speech perception since we have suggested that there is a close relationship between the inherent properties of the speech output mechanism and the perceptual recognition routine.

In recent years Liberman and his colleagues at Haskins Laboratories have suggested that ". . . a reference to articulation helps the listener to decode the acoustic signal . . ." in the perception of the segmental phonemes (Liberman, Cooper, Harris, and MacNeilage, 1963; Liberman *et al.,* 1966). In support of this theory they have presented experimental evidence indicating that the distinctness of phonetic categories is often paralleled by differences in articulation that are more distinct and invariant than the differences in the acoustic signal. The relation between phoneme and articulation is often more nearly one-to-one than is the relation between phoneme and acoustic signal.

The perception of intonation and stress is apparently similar to the perception of the segmental phonemes. The listener must perform a certain amount of direct acoustic "preprocessing," which obviously must precede any "analysis by synthesis." Fundamental frequency, for example, must be perceived. The listener may then make use of his knowledge of the articulatory constraints and employ "analysis by synthesis." He may indeed partially ignore the acoustic signal and "fill in" phonetic features, using his knowledge of the syntactic and semantic constraints of the language and the total social context of the message.

There is a great deal of experimental evidence to support the view that speech is often both produced and perceived by this process. The listener apparently comprehends the message by a process of "hypothesis formation" that involves analysis-by-synthesis where the context guides the recognition routine. The listener may consider a comparatively large "chunk" of speech, and he is often able to "guess" what the speech signal should be from the context that is furnished by the "chunk." The speaker, in turn, simplifies his articulatory control problem, knowing when the listener probably will be able to guess what the message should have been. The speaker may neglect to manipulate his articulatory apparatus precisely when he believes that the listener will be able to guess what he should have said from the context of the message.

Miller and Isard (1963), for example, have shown that the grammatical structure and "meaningfulness" of a sentence affect the perception of individual words in the message. Listeners were asked to "shadow"—to repeat aloud afterwards—exactly what the speaker said for a set of 50 grammatical sentences, 50 anomalous sentences, and 50 ungrammatical strings of words that were all formed from the same words. For example, the following are grammatical sentences:

Accidents kill motorists on the highways.
Trains carry passengers across the country.
Bears steal honey from the hive.

The following are anomalous sentences that had similar grammatical structures but lacked "sense":

Trains steal elephants around the highways.
Accidents carry honey between the house.
Bears shoot work on the country.

Typical ungrammatical strings are:

Around accidents country honey the shoot.
On trains hive elephants the simple.

Eighty-nine percent of the grammatical sentences, 80 percent of the anomalous sentences, and 56 percent of the ungrammatical strings were shadowed correctly.

Lieberman (1963*c*) showed that in fluent speech a speaker may neglect to articulate a word carefully when he knows that it can be inferred from the context in which it occurs. In this experiment the word *nine* in the sentence *A stitch in time saves nine* was recognized 50 percent of the time when it was isolated from its context. The word *nine* was also spoken in the sentence *The number that you will hear is nine.* It was identified 90 percent of the time when it was isolated from this context. The presence of the word *nine,* of course, was almost redundant in the first sentence, and the speaker therefore neglected to articulate it carefully. Similar effects took place for other words that were spoken in the middle of other sentences. The words *borrower* and *lender* were both poorly articulated when they occurred in the sentence *Neither a borrower nor a lender be.* Listeners could identify *borrower* only 45 percent of the time and *lender* 10 percent of the time when each was isolated from the sentence. The same words were identified 80 and 40 percent of the time, respectively, when they were isolated from the sentence *The* ——— *were all imprisoned.* The entire context of these sentences therefore plays a part in determining how essential any particular word is. The listener probably performs a preliminary acoustic analysis of the speech signal and identifies whatever phonetic features he can from the acoustic signal. He then forms a hypothesis regarding the phonetic character of the segments that he cannot identify from the acoustic signal, and he applies the rules of the phonologic and syntactic components of the grammar to obtain a hypothetical underlying phrase marker. If the semantic interpretation of the hypothetical underlying phrase marker is reasonable and is consistent with the conversation, the social context, etc., then the listener accepts the hypothesis regarding the acoustically indistinct parts of the utterance and "hears" them distinctly. If the hypothetical underlying phrase marker is not satisfactory, then the listener may try another phonetic hypothesis, or he may simply not understand what has been said.

These effects are quite pronounced in conversational speech. Pollack and Pickett (1964) in an experiment excised words and groups of words from normal conversational speech. Conversational speech was individually recorded from four female college students. The speakers were participating in a psychoacoustic experiment and were waiting in an anechoic chamber for the test to proceed. The experimenter engaged each speaker in a conversation that was recorded with a condenser microphone on a high-quality magnetic tape recording. The talkers were informed the following week that they had been recorded, and they reported that they had been completely unaware of this. The acoustic signal was thus recorded under virtually optimum conditions. Short segments of speech were electronically "excised" from the tape recordings. An electronic gate was first adjusted at a word so the sounds of the preceding and the following words were inaudible. The end of the gate was then adjusted so that the following word was also audible, and the procedure of widening the gate to include more and more words was repeated until the width of the gate reached 2000 msec. Listeners were then asked to identify the words of the excised segments. The listeners first heard the segment that contained a single word. They then heard the sample that contained two words. The procedure was repeated until the listeners heard the 2000-msec gate. It was found that, on the average, the listeners were not able to identify 80 percent of the words until the gate width was at least 1000 msec.

It is quite interesting to listen to these excised segments. The words do not gradually become more intelligible as the gate width increases. As the gate width gradually increases, the speech signal remains unintelligible until a critical gate width is reached, and the signal suddenly seems perfectly clear. The listener gradually receives more and more acoustic information as the gate's width increases. However, the acoustic signal in itself is insufficient to identify the phonetic content of the message uniquely. Some of the distinctive features that specify each phonetic segment probably can be determined from the available acoustic signal. Other distinctive features cannot be uniquely identified. The listener therefore forms a hypothesis concerning the probable phonetic content of the message that is consistent with the known features. However, he cannot test this hypothesis for its syntactic and semantic consistency until he gets a fairly long segment of speech into his temporary processing space. The speech signal therefore remains unintelligible until the listener can successfully test a hypothesis. When a hypothesis is confirmed, the signal abruptly becomes intelligible. The acoustic signal is, of course, necessary to provide even a partial specification of the phonetic signal. However, these experiments indicate that in many instances the phonetic signal that the listener "hears" is internally computed.

The listener mentally constructs a phonetic signal that incorporates both the distinctive features that are uniquely characterized by the acoustic signal and those that he hypothesizes in order to arrive at a reasonable syntactic and semantic interpretation of the message. In some instances the acoustic signal may be both necessary and sufficient to specify uniquely the phonetic elements of the message. This usually occurs when a talker is asked to read aloud nonsense syllables or isolated words. The talker, of course, "knows" that the message will not allow the listener to test any reasonably complex phonetic hypotheses. The speaker therefore carefully articulates the message.

The speaker's decisions on the relative precision with which he must specify the phonetic elements of the message in the acoustic signal must be made in some interpretive component of the grammar. The speaker must weigh the anticipated linguistic competence of the hearer as well as the linguistic context furnished by the entire sentence, the semantic context of the conversation, and the total context of the social situation. A speaker may, for example, talk more distinctly to a foreign student when he believes that the listener is unfamiliar with the grammar of the language. A husband may talk less distinctly to his wife when he knows that she is familiar with his particular dialect. The listener's process of phonetic hypothesis formation also takes place in this interpretive component. To the extent that aspects of the total linguistic competence of the talker or the listener are involved, this interpretive component is part of the grammar. Obviously, the effects of inebriation or of marbles in the mouth on the production or perception of speech are linguistically unpredictable. The linguistically predictable aspects of the interpretive component, which we shall term the "production" component, should be considered as part of the grammar since they are part of the human linguistic competence.

In Figure 8.1 we have sketched a block diagram of the grammar. The output of the phonologic component feeds into a block that we have labeled the "production" component. The production component mediates between the phonetic representation and the speech production and auditory apparatus of the human which, in turn, relate the abstract linguistic structure to the acoustic speech signal. The production component schematically represents the ability of a person to bring his total knowledge of the grammar, the social context, the message set, etc., to bear on either simplifying the articulatory control problem or interpreting the auditory signal. In some ways the speech signal that ultimately results can be viewed as an approach to an optimal code. The speaker tends to include no more information in the speech signal than is necessary to convey his message in a given situation. The listener in a given situation brings all the information that he has available to bear on the problem of "decoding" the acoustic signal. The production component is part of this block diagram since it is a buffer between the phonetic output and the acoustic signal. The pathways into the production component on Figure 8.1 have the status of all connections on block diagrams. They do not indicate how the pathway is actually effected. They do indicate that

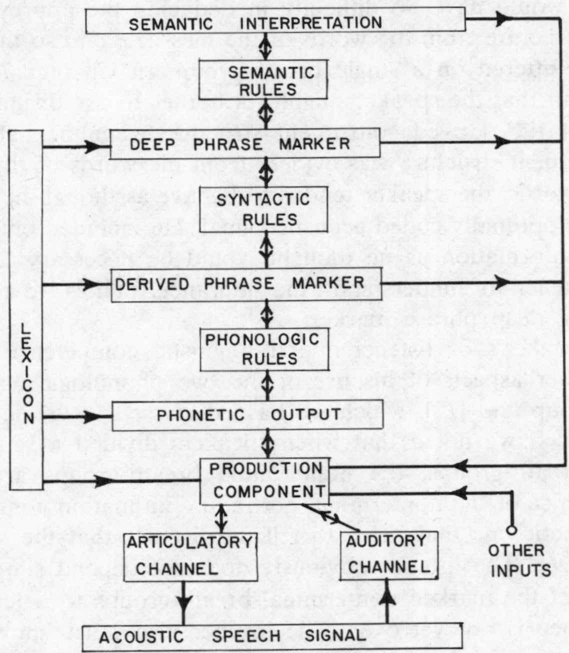

Figure 8.1 Block diagram of the grammar.
The output of the phonologic component feeds into the production component. The production component represents the ability of a person to bring his total knowledge of the grammar, the social context, the message set, etc., to bear either on simplifying the articulatory control problem in the production of speech or on "decoding" the acoustic signal. The listener's perceptual recognition routine may involve a process of hypothesis formation in which semantic factors, the derived constituent structure, and a knowledge of the articulatory constraints of speech production are all considered.

there *is* a pathway. The "motor theory of perception" in this model simply describes one aspect of the listener's total linguistic competence that may be invoked in the perceptual recognition routine.

We briefly mentioned some "production" effects that involved intonation in Chapters 5 and 7. In Chapter 5 we noted that the division of a sentence into breath-groups might be viewed as a production effect that is directed at making the recovery of the deep phrase marker possible. We stressed the fact that the division of a sentence into breath-groups that manifested the constituent structure of the derived phrase marker usually did not occur when the constituent structure was evident from the words of the utterance, or from the total context of the utterance. The speaker knew that the listener probably would have no difficulty in deducing the appropriate constituent structure from the words of the message, and so the sentence would be uttered on a single breath-group. In Chapter 7 we again pointed out that the speaker might not bother to use disjuncture as a marker of the derived constituent structure when he believed that the constituent structure was evident from the words of the message. In other words, the speaker tended to behave as though he were producing an optimally coded acoustic signal. He included only as much acoustic information as he thought would be necessary for the potential listener to "understand" the utterance, that is, to recover the underlying deep phrase marker.

The speaker's or listener's total linguistic competence obviously affects other aspects of his use of the two phonologic features, the breath-group and $[P_s]$, which we have discussed in detail. In Chapters 4 and 5 we noted that when speakers divided a sentence into several breath-groups, the nonterminal breath-groups are marked. The presence of the nonterminal not-falling intonation contour serves as a phonetic cue that helps to tell the listener that the sentence is not yet over. The listener obviously does not depend simply on the presence of the marked nonterminal breath-groups to determine that the sentence is not yet over. The listener also must know the syntactic structure of English. He must know what strings of words can form a phrase or a sentence. The presence of $[+ BG]$ is simply an additional phonetic cue that helps the listener reach a decision as to whether he has heard the complete sentence or part of the sentence. He still has to know, for example, the rules that govern the admissible forms of yes-no questions since the marked breath-groups may have been generated by the *wh*-deletion rule (cf. Chapter 6) rather than the breath-group division rule.

When a speaker breaks a sentence up into several breath-groups, the presence of the nonterminal marked breath-groups may sometimes be quite important for indicating that the sentence is not over. Consider the string of words *I saw the boy who fell down the stairs.* If these words were uttered on one normal breath-group, the listener would hear the sentence *I saw the boy who fell down the stairs.* The underlying phrase marker of this sentence, which contains a relative clause, is similar to the underlying phrase markers of the two simpler sentences *I saw the boy* and *The boy fell down the stairs*. The intonation indicates that the string of words *I saw the boy who fell down the stairs* constitutes a complete sentence. If the same string of words is uttered on two normal breath-groups

[I saw the boy] [who fell down the stairs]

the listener will treat the speech signal as though two sentences were uttered, the simple declarative sentence *I saw the boy* and the interrogative sentence *Who fell down the stairs?* The underlying phrase marker of each sentence will be derived independently. The underlying phrase marker and semantic interpretation of the interrogative sentence *Who fell down the stairs?* will, of course, be quite different from the underlying phrase marker and semantic interpretation of the relative clause in the sentence *I saw the boy who fell down the stairs*. The presence of the first marked breath-group is thus very important if the speaker wants to break up the sentence *I saw the boy who fell down the stairs* into two breath-groups, since the listener has no other way of telling[1] that the two strings of words [*I saw the boy*] and [*who fell down the stairs*] are not independent sentences. However, there are many instances where a sentence may be divided into two breath-groups and where it is not particularly essential to mark the first breath-group because the listener can tell from the words of the utterance that the sentence is not yet over. If the breath-groups segment the utterance at a word that is an impossible end or beginning point for a sentence, then the speaker may not bother to mark the nonterminal breath-group. There is no need to use any special phonetic cue to indicate that the sentence has not yet ended, because the words of the two breath-groups themselves indicate that they belong to the same sentence. The listener knows what constitutes a well-formed sentence.

Armstrong and Ward (1926) in their study of English intonation commented that ". . . there are so many cases in connected speech where we have to rise [in pitch] at the end of the first intonation group that it is a relief to fall when the choice is at all possible." They give the following examples of sentences in which the first breath-groups are not marked by a rising or steady pitch at its end:

He strolled aimlessly about the road kicking stones out of his path.
She shook hands and said she was glad he had come.
I shall tell him about it when I come home Saturday.
I go home at six generally.
Well he didn't come as a matter of fact.

[1] In the absence of other context, such as previous parts of the conversation.

Cowan (1936) in his instrumental study has literally hundreds of similar examples.[2] He collected a large number of plots of fundamental frequency and acoustic amplitude as functions of time for a group of actors reading dramatic passages. Some of his speakers always end nonterminal breath-groups with a rising pitch, while some of his speakers omit this gesture when the words of the sentence indicate that the sentence cannot end (or start) at the pause.

In short, the use of nonterminal marked breath-groups to indicate that a sentence has not yet ended bears the same relation to the total ensemble of acoustic cues as do other articulatory gestures. It may be omitted by some speakers where its presence can be easily inferred from the total stimulus ensemble. The linguistic aspects of intonation that we have discussed, like other phonologic aspects of the language, may be modified by production effects. In connected fluent speech where production effects are usually apparent, these features may be omitted or grossly distorted.

[2] It is interesting to note that Cowan's instrumental study shows far more cases of nonterminal normal breath-groups than does the Armstrong-Ward perceptual analysis. Instruments cannot infer the presence of a cue from the structure of the language. Linguists, however, may "hear" acoustic signals where none exist.

9 A Survey of Some Recent Linguistic Studies of Intonation

In this chapter we shall discuss, for the most part, analyses of British and American English that were published in the twentieth century. Instrumental studies based on measurements of the acoustic signal have been feasible only during the past thirty years, and they are still quite difficult to perform; therefore most of these analyses are based upon observations by phoneticians and linguists. We shall not attempt to discuss every recent linguistic analysis of English intonation, but we shall try to discuss some of the studies that have most influenced current trends.

The goal of most of these studies has been the development of a notation for the objective representation of intonational phenomena. Some of the studies have attempted to relate certain aspects of intonation to linguistic structure in a systematic way. However, these attempts have for the most part been unsuccessful.

Three fundamentally different approaches have evolved since 1900. One approach, typified by the British school that has become identified with Daniel Jones, has made use of suprasegmental "tunes" that, on the acoustic level, are quite similar to the breath-group. The second approach, which also has been largely identified with British phoneticians, has described pitch contours by means of "tones" that occur on specific vowels. The sequence of tones that may rise and fall determines the intonation pattern of the utterance. Some of the linguists who employ these tones group the tones into suprasegmental "tone-patterns." While the "tunes," or "tone-patterns," are often related to certain sentence types, most of these studies do not attempt systematically to relate intonation to a formal grammar.

The third approach has been developed principally by American linguists who tried to apply the segmental techniques of taxonomic phonemics to intonation. In these studies intonation has been analyzed in terms of segmental pitch levels, stress levels, and junctures. The segmental elements, however, have been grouped into suprasegmental "phonemic phrases," "phonemic clauses," and "suprasegmental morphemes." An attempt has been made to relate these suprasegmental elements to the constituent structure of the sentence. However, these studies have been preoccupied, in general, with the problem of furnishing "objective" cues for immediate constituent analysis and with providing "morphemes" that will yield a semantic interpretation of a sentence directly from the superficial phrase marker.

We shall first discuss the British "tone" and "tune" analyses before we go on to the American "phonemic" descriptions and other analyses that do not quite fit into any of these categories.

9.1 Henry Sweet (1892), *New English Grammar*

Although Sweet's *New English Grammar* was published in 1892, the phonetic elements[1] that Sweet briefly outlined in it in two pages (pp. 228–229) are the basis of all of the "tone" analyses that have since been published. Sweet set up "three degrees of stress or loudness . . . strong, half strong, and weak. . . . Sounds which can occur only in unstressed syllables are called weak. . . . Intonation is either level, rising or falling. . . . The level tone may be either high or low and the other tones may begin in a high or low pitch." Sweet also stated that "When excited we speak in a high pitch or key, when depressed in a low key. The non-level tones can pass through different intervals, the greater the interval, the more emphatic the tone becomes."

Sweet had two other "compound" intonation symbols: ∨, which meant a falling intonation followed by a rising intonation, and ∧, which meant a rising followed by a falling intonation. Both of these compound tones could start at either a high or a low pitch. Sweet seemed to equate intonation with the pitch or fundamental frequency of the voice and stress with loudness. It seems quite clear that by loudness he meant the perceptual impression of loudness and not any acoustic measurement of the speech waveform. Sweet appears to

[1] These phonetic elements have a long history and were probably first used by Walker (1787).

have used this notation simply to transcribe intonation. He was using the tones as phonetic symbols in a manner analogous to the segmental IPA notation for vowels, consonants, etc.

Recent research (Lieberman, 1965) shows that Sweet's intonation notation can be used to transcribe the intonation patterns of English utterances quite accurately. A trained linguist can accurately transcribe the change in fundamental frequency of a segment of speech relative to its immediate surroundings by using this notation.

9.2 Daniel Jones (1909), *Intonation Curves*

Although Jones was quite familiar with Sweet's notational system, he performed a quasi-instrumental study of intonation. He obtained a set of recordings of English and French conversations and dramatic readings. He listened to those records and lifted the "needle off the gramophone" at regular intervals and noted the pitch that he last heard on a musical scale. When he was in doubt, he repeated the passage. He then placed a phonetic transcription of the recordings under the pitch notations. These transcriptions are probably quite accurate, since the ear can resolve variations smaller than 1 cps in

9. An English postmaster, then, is also a banker?

10. He is to a certain extent.

11. But any important business, I suppose, devolves on the head offices?

12. Just so. The nearest of these is the head district office at Charing Cross.

13. Oh, that is where I have had my poste-restante letters addressed to. I will go there.

14. I imagine even the grocers, or any other branch office would keep letters for you, if marked: "To be left till called for."

Figure 9.1 Pitch transcriptions reproduced from Daniel Jones (1909), *Intonation Curves*.
Jones transcribed pitch on a musical scale by lifting the needle off a phonograph record at regular intervals and noting the pitch. A phonetic transcription is placed under each pitch transcription.

the fundamental frequency of vowel-like sounds (Flanagan and Saslow, 1958).

In Figure 9.1 some of these curves are reproduced for English conversations. Jones published these recordings without any general comments except for noting that perhaps there were more breaks and inflections in the contours of each sentence because the subjects spoke quite carefully for the recordings. Jones does not attempt to discuss the "meaning" of the contours. He simply states that the contours are useful pedagogic aids. However, Jones's ready acceptance of the "two tune" theory of Armstrong and Ward (1926) was probably due, in part, to the fact that their theory fits the data in *Intonation Curves.*

9.3 H. E. Palmer and W. G. Blandford (1924), *A Grammar of Spoken English on a Strictly Phonetic Basis*

Palmer and Blandford in this study employ Sweet's tones, but they group them into suprasegmental "tone-patterns." They attempt to relate the use of these tone-patterns to various types of sentences, but they fail to differentiate the emotional aspects of intonation from the linguistic aspects.

They use high or low falling tones, which they mark as ↘ or ↘, high or low rising tones, marked by ↗ or ↗, and one "rise-fall-rise" tone, which they mark ∼↗. Each nucleus tone is preceded by a "head" and followed by a "tail." The heads and tails essentially connect the nucleus tones in connected speech. Six "tone-patterns," each consisting of a head and a nucleus, are described. They "may be designated by the following symbols and numbers":[2]

1 ⌐↘ 2 ∫↗ 3 ∧↘ 4 ⌐↗ 5 ⌐∼↗ 6 ∧↗ (p. 16)

(Tone-pattern 4 has two alternate forms.) The "tails" that go with these tone-patterns continue in the direction established by the nucleus tone when a sentence is spoken on only one tone-pattern. When several tone-patterns occur in one sentence, the "tail" of one tone-pattern must join the "head" of the next tone-pattern. The tone-patterns are supposed to have definite "functions and meanings," which are set forth on pages 18–24 of the study by Palmer and Blandford.

Tone-pattern 1 is used "In statements having the nature of 'declarations' or 'assertions' . . . commands . . . questions beginning with an interrogative word . . . and 'rhetorical' questions. It is the

[2] Palmer, in a slightly earlier work (1922), used the same system of tones but did not try to group them into tone-patterns.

pattern that occurs with by far the greatest frequency." Tone-pattern 2 is used in "assertions" and "special questions with a one word prominence," such as "Where?" Its use "implies 'then in that case,' 'that being so.' " Tone-pattern 5 "expresses a certain kind of contrast, the semantic nature of which is most difficult to define or even describe. It implies concession. . . ." Tone-pattern 6 also has "semantic and stylistic functions . . . [that] are difficult to describe." Tone-pattern 4 is used for yes-no interrogatives and "echo" questions, and tone-pattern 3 is used in "statements . . . having the nature of comments." The rest of the book's treatment of intonation is concerned with the special "meanings" that occur in sentences having several tone-patterns.

Palmer and Blandford note that stress and pitch are interrelated, and they define stress in terms of "force of utterance" (p. 5). They state that the linguistic stress indicates "which syllable of a word is eligible for becoming the nucleus of a tone group . . ." (p. 6).

The division of the intonation pattern into a head, nucleus, and tail seems to be rather arbitrary, as are many of the "meanings" set forth in this book. One soon gets the impression that every possible intonation pattern has its own subtle, arbitrary meaning.

The studies of Schubiger (1935), Kingdon (1939), and Jassem (1952) all follow essentially the pattern of this study. A reasonably accurate phonetic transcription of a large corpus of utterances is associated with a vast catalog of "meanings," and the linguistic aspects of intonation are never clearly differentiated from the emotional aspects.

9.4 L. E. Armstrong and I. C. Ward (1926), *Handbook of English Intonation*

This work attempts to differentiate the emotional aspects of intonation from its linguistic function. The authors state that

> The aims of this work are primarily pedagogic; attention is given to the simplest forms of intonation used in conversation. . . . The writers are aware that there are other varieties and deeper subtleties of intonation than are here recorded. Such variations, however, are not essential for correct and good English, and their absence would not be missed by anyone who had not made a special study of intonation [p. 1].

Armstrong and Ward define "stress" in terms of breath force. They state that a speaker stresses the important words in a sentence: "If he feels one idea to be important he stresses the words embodying that idea, if many ideas, he stresses many words." They define "intonation" in terms of perceived pitch. The authors note that

> These two elements, stress and intonation, are very closely connected. So close is the connection, indeed, that it is often difficult to decide whether stress or intonation or a combination of the two is responsible for certain effects [p. 3].

A word spoken in isolation may have a certain stress pattern. However, "in connected speech this word stress is often dropped [p. 3]." When sentences are spoken slowly, ". . . slight variations in intonation and stress are to be observed which would not occur in quick speech. Some of the syllables which would normally be unstressed . . . have some stress. . . . These variations are not essential. . . ."

Armstrong and Ward transcribe the over-all sentence intonation by a series of dots and dashes. Each dot marks the relative pitch of an unstressed syllable, and each dash marks the relative pitch of the stressed syllable. The vertical position of the dot or dash reflects the relative pitch of each syllable.

The most important aspect of this system is that two "tunes" are defined. Tune I essentially starts on a medium pitch and continues on this pitch with some upward variations on stressed syllables until the end of the sentence, when the pitch falls rapidly. Tune II starts at either a high or a middle pitch and gradually falls, but it ends with rising or level pitch. Sentences are divided into "sense-groups," and each "sense-group" is an intonation group that *may* have the contour of Tune I or II.[3] In short sentences that have only one "sense-group" Tune I is used for statements and imperatives. Tune II is used for some interrogative yes-no questions and for sentences in which the speaker wishes to imply some uncertainty.

Longer sentences may consist of many sense-groups. They note that

> I. Different people divide their speech into different sense-groups, and there is a corresponding difference in their intonation groups.
>
> II. A speaker varies his sense-groups and consequently the rhythm and intonation of the passage he is reading or speaking, according to the style of his subject matter and the speed or deliberation with which he speaks.
>
> III. In conversational style the sense-groups are longer than in description or narration. The more deliberate the speech the more groups are made. . . .

[3] Armstrong and Ward really use the terms "sense-group" and "intonation group" rather interchangeably. They never attempt a definition of "sense-group."

Tune II is usually used in longer sentences for sense-groups that do not terminate the sentence. Tune I occasionally can be used for nonterminal sense-groups in long sentences under certain conditions.

Sentences of this type are, for the most part, co-ordinate sentences or phrases with a logical, though not necessarily a grammatical, dependence on each other. If in the speaker's mind the logical connection is very close, the first intonation group may be said with the second tune. But there are so many cases in connected speech where we have to rise at the end of the first group that it is a relief to fall when a choice is at all possible [p. 26].

In Figure 9.2 some transcriptions from this study are reproduced.

Armstrong and Ward, in effect, isolated the acoustic and perceptual manifestations of the breath-group. The two tunes are both

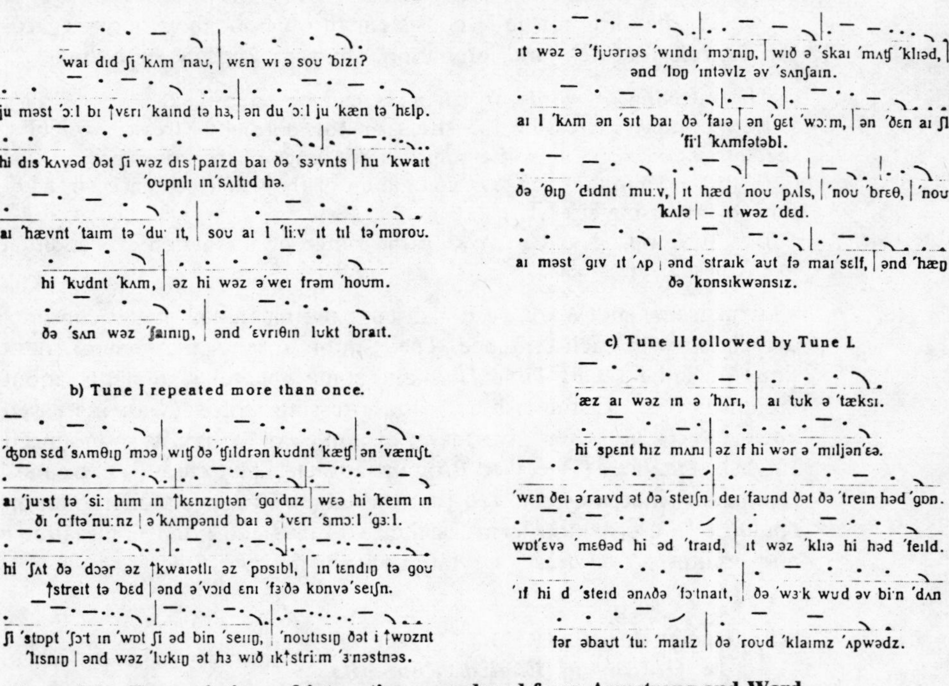

Figure 9.2 Transcriptions of intonation reproduced from Armstrong and Ward (1926), *Handbook of English Intonation.*

Each dot marks the relative pitch of an unstressed syllable, and each dash marks the relative pitch of a stressed syllable. The vertical position of the dot or dash reflects the relative pitch of each syllable. Two "tunes" are defined. Tune I starts on a medium pitch and continues with upward variations on stressed syllables until the end of the sentence, where the pitch then falls rapidly. Tune II, in contrast, ends with a level or rising pitch.

suprasegmental. Tune I is equivalent to the unmarked breath-group, while Tune II is equivalent to the marked breath-group. The height of the syllables in their transcription is a phonetic transcription of the fundamental frequency variations that are superimposed on the breath-group.

Armstrong and Ward also noted that stress, which is equivalent to the "force of utterance" $[+P_s]$, may interact with the tunes. They differentiate perceived prominence from stress and intonation. They note, for example, that

> When the speaker wants to pick out a certain word (or words) and distinguish it from others in the sentence by making it specially prominent, he does so chiefly by a change in intonation. Increase of stress often accompanies this change, but it does not ever appear to be essential [p. 48].

However, they are not quite consistent throughout their book regarding the roles of stress and intonation. On page 26 they state that

> The meaning of words or sentences can be intensified.
>
> I. By simply increasing the stress on the normally stressed syllables, the intonation remaining the same as for unemphatic utterance.
>
> II. By widening the range of intonation of the whole sentence (in addition to increasing stress).
>
> III. By lowering and narrowing the range of intonation (in addition to increasing the stress).

Armstrong and Ward do not discuss the meanings of the contours associated with each sentence. They simply discuss the general functions of Tune I and Tune II, make some general statements about "intensifying," "distinguishing," and stressing words (with increased vocal effort) and then give many examples of correctly pronounced English sentences (Received Pronunciation). Their study is extremely significant since they realized that the linguistic aspects of intonation could be transcribed in terms of the two tunes and pitch (intonation) and breath-force (stress) deviations from the two tunes.

9.5 Daniel Jones (1932), *An Outline of English Phonetics*

In this work Jones adopted the Tune I–Tune II Armstrong-Ward analysis, and he expands on it. He states that intonation can be used to "make the meaning" of an utterance clearer, and he gives an "operational definition" of the relationship between intonation and "sense-groups":

Pauses are continually being made in speaking. They are made (1) for the purpose of taking breath, (2) for the purpose of making the meaning of the words clearer.

It is usual to employ the term breath-group to denote a complete sentence that can conveniently be said with a single breath, or, in the case of very long sentences, the longest portions that can conveniently be said with single breaths.

Pauses for breath are normally made at points where pauses are necessary or allowable from the point of view of meaning.

Sentences are usually divisible into smaller groups between which pauses may be made, though they are not essential. The shortest possible of such groups (i.e., groups which are not capable of being further subdivided by pauses) are called sense-groups. Each sense-group consists of a few words in close grammatical connection, such as would be said together in giving a slow dictation exercise [p. 254].

Jones notes that "Intonation is a . . . different thing from stress." Intonation is essentially defined as perceived pitch. He relates prominence, stress, and intonation as follows:

In every spoken word or phrase there is at least one sound which is heard to stand out more prominently than sounds next to it [p. 55].

The prominence of a given sound may be increased or diminished by means of any one of the three sound attributes, length, stress, or intonation, or by combinations of these. A common and effective means . . . is to increase the stress. In English increase of stress is generally accompanied by a modification of intonation and sometimes by an increase of length [p. 228].

It is important not to confuse stress and prominence. The prominence of a syllable is its general degree of distinctness, this being the combined effect of the timbre, length, stress and intonation of the syllabic sound. The term "stress" refers only to the degree of force of utterance, it is independent of length and intonation, though it may be combined with these [p. 228].

Jones says essentially that stress and intonation are independent at the articulatory level. Prominence is a perceptual quantity that may be effected by either stress or intonation. To Jones, stress seems to be an articulatory gesture, and he explicitly states that its perception involves a knowledge of the structure of the language and "analysis-by-synthesis":

When a strong stress is given to a syllable incapable of receiving any noticeable increase of loudness, a person unfamiliar with the language would be unable to tell that a stress was present. . . . A person familiar with the language would not perceive the sound objectively from the sound . . . but he perceives it in a subjective way; the sounds he hears call up to his mind (through the context) the manner of making them, and by means of immediate "inner speech" he knows where the stress is [p. 227].

It is not entirely clear whether he thinks that all "prominent" sounds may be also perceived from the listener's linguistic analysis of the context or whether he thinks that only stress can be perceived in this way. He may believe that only stress can be perceived in this way, since his reasoning seems to follow from the articulatory facts peculiar to stress, that is, that increased force of utterance or breath may occur on a sound having low inherent sonority (such as a nasal).

Jones's definitions of stress, intonation, and prominence are quite clear, and his subjective evaluations of their acoustic correlates have, for the most part, been substantiated by psychoacoustic and acoustic experiments (cf. Chapter 2). He also clearly expresses the notion that intonation can potentially be used to clarify the meaning of a sentence though, of course, he does not state how a sentence is understood.

Although Jones rather carefully defines stress [+ P_s], he does not note that inherently it is a different type of entity from the suprasegmental tunes. Jones's insights into the perception of stress are, nevertheless, interesting.

9.6 L. Bloomfield (1933), *Language*

Bloomfield's treatment of intonation and stress is not so important for its detail as for the direction in which it channeled later American "phonemic" analyses. Much of the subsequent American work is an expansion and codification of Bloomfield's basic premises and assumptions. In contrast to Jones, who differentiated perceived prominence from stress (force of utterance) and the acoustic correlates of stress, Bloomfield implies that perceived loudness is equal to stress. The perceived loudness is equated to the intensity of the acoustic signal: "Stress—that is, intensity or loudness—consists in greater amplitude of the sound waves . . . [p. 110]."

Bloomfield's definition of stress seems to reflect his preoccupation with "objective" measurements. Bloomfield's followers treat stress and pitch as independent phenomena, which they are if stress is simply supposed to be the amplitude of the acoustic signal and pitch the fundamental frequency. However, stress is also supposed to be equivalent to perceived loudness, and it is clear that the perception of the loudness of a short segment of speech involves its amplitude, duration, and fundamental frequency (cf. Chapters 2, 4, and 7).

Bloomfield asserts that pitch phonemes constitute separate morphemes and carry their own meanings independent of the words of a sentence:

> Differences in pitch . . . are used in English, and perhaps in most languages as secondary phonemes . . . pitch is the acoustic feature where gesture-like variations, non-distinctive but socially effective, border most closely on genuine linguistic distinctions [p. 114].
>
> . . . The pitch phonemes in English are not in principle attached to any particular words or phrases, but vary, with differences in meaning, in otherwise identical forms [p. 116].

The pitch phonemes, however, have other functions in speech. Intonation is supposed to play a part in expressing "the actor-action construction" in "the favorite" English sentence forms (p. 172). Bloomfield points out (pp. 170–171) that

> In English and many other languages, sentences are marked off by modulation, the use of secondary phonemes. In English, secondary phonemes of pitch mark the end of sentences, and distinguish three main sentence-types: John ran away [.] John ran away [?] Who ran away [¿].
>
> This use of secondary phonemes to mark the ends of sentences makes possible a construction known as *parataxis,* in which two forms united by no other construction are united by the use of only one sentence-pitch. Thus if we say *It's ten o'clock* [.] *I have to go home* [.] with the final falling pitch of a statement on *o'clock,* we have spoken two sentences, but if we omit this final pitch (substituting for it a pause pitch), the two forms are united . . . into a single sentence. . . .

This function, of course, sounds rather like a vague version of the functions of Tune I and Tune II in connected speech.

Bloomfield, in effect, argues that intonation contours must be morphemes because intonation carries meaning. Since the intonation contours are determined by various pitches, these pitches must be phonemes. He also notes that these pitch "phonemes" play a role in forming syntactic "constructions." The principal effects of Bloomfield's work were to channel subsequent studies toward the isolation of these "pitch phonemes" and the explicit characterization of their role in defining syntactic "constructions."

9.7 B. Bloch and G. L. Trager (1942), *Outline of Linguistic Analysis*

Bloch and Trager in their section on phonetic analysis briefly discuss the ". . . PROSODIC FEATURES of QUANTITY (length), STRESS (loudness), and TONE (pitch); the last two are grouped together as features of accent [p. 34]." They do not discuss either quantity or tone in detail. "Tone levels (higher and lower) and tone contours (rising, level, falling, etc.) may be indicated by accent marks over the letters, by superior numerals with assigned values, or by other devices [p. 35]."

Though they initially define stress in terms of loudness they also note the classical articulatory definition in terms of force of utterance. They observe that stress may depend "also in part on the pitch of the voice. Different grades ('loud,' 'half-loud,' 'strong,' 'weak,' etc.) are commonly indicated . . . [p. 35]." Several degrees of stress are necessary to distinguish English words. About the only departure from Jones's treatment of stress is that Bloch and Trager imply that several degrees of stress must always be indicated in order to distinguish English words, whereas Jones feels that though several degrees of stress may be perceived when a word is spoken in isolation, only two degrees of stress, stressed versus unstressed, must be discerned when words are spoken in fluent speech.

Juncture is also briefly mentioned. They note on page 35 that "The three words *nitrate, night-rate,* and *dye-trade* illustrate three ways of joining sounds in the sequence -[ajt]-." They add that the aim of a phonetic transcription is "to record as accurately as possible all features of an utterance or a set of utterances which the writer can hear. . . ."

9.8 R. S. Wells (1945), "The Pitch Phonemes of English"

Wells professes (p. 28) to have applied "to pitches . . . all the principles and methods of segmental phonemics." (Segmentation, biuniqueness, and no overlap are all supposed to apply to this analysis.) He specifies (p. 30) that "There are four pitch phonemes, designated by Arabic numerals from 1 (lowest) to 4 (highest)." Although he proposes to use the technique of complementary distribution, he is not bothered by the following fact:

In proving the existence and distinctness of the four pitch phonemes by minimal contrast, we ought to consider the same string of segmental phonemes with minimally contrasting pitch contours imposed on it; but it is difficult to find one such string equally well adapted to two minimally contrasting contours [p. 32].

Wells asserts that the pitch phonemes "are organized into meaningful sequences called pitch morphemes, which are the strict analogues of segmental morphemes composed of segmental phonemes" (p. 34). However, he does not state what these morphemes are or what meanings they may possibly carry or, for that matter, how they can be reasonably compared to the segmental morphemes in view of the passage quoted from page 32.

Wells follows Bloomfield's lead. He takes a group of 19 sentences (pp. 31–32) which presumably have meaning differences that are the result of different intonation morphemes. He transcribes these pitch "morphemes" by means of four numbered pitch levels,[4] and he notes that these strings of numbers contrast. He says that he has therefore demonstrated a set of phonemic contrasts. However, the differences in meaning that Wells notes follow either from the deep structure of the sentences or the emotional aspects of intonation. The phonetic reality of these number sequences is, moreover, rather dubious (cf. Chapter 5).

Wells's study also contains some additional phonetic deficiencies. He notes that contour 231 is the most usual contour in American English (the unmarked breath-group) and that pitch phoneme 3 always occurs on the main stress. Nevertheless, he criticizes Palmer for relating pitch and stress. In addition, Wells has no way of indicating rapid glides in pitch. This defect was corrected by the Pike and Trager-Smith "phonemic" analyses, which, nevertheless, retained the four phonemic pitches that Wells uses in this paper.

9.9 K. L. Pike (1945), *The Intonation of American English*

The phonemic aspects of Pike's analysis are based on the premise that pitch contours are independent morphemes.

English words have basic, intrinsic meanings . . . that are indicated only by the requisite consonants, vowels, and stress, and a context where such a meaning is possible; in that sense that lexical meaning is intrinsically a part of the word itself and not dependent on extraneous phenomena such as pitch produced by emotion.

The intonation meaning is quite the opposite. . . . Rather than con-

[4] Ripman in 1922 used from three to five numbers to represent the pitch levels of syllables in a connected text. Ripman, however, did not make any claims about the phonemic nature of these pitch levels.

tributing to the intrinsic meaning of the word, it is merely a shade of meaning added to or superimposed upon that intrinsic lexical meaning, according to the attitude of the speaker. . . . In English, then, an INTONATION MEANING modifies the lexical meaning of a sentence by adding to it the SPEAKER'S ATTITUDE toward the content of the sentence (or an indication of the attitude with which the speaker expects the hearer to react) [p. 21].

. . . all speakers of the language use basic pitch sequences in similar ways under similar circumstances.

In English, many intonation contours are explicit in meaning. Whenever a certain sequence of relative pitches is heard, one concludes that the speaker means certain things over and above the specific meanings of the words themselves [p. 20].

Pike wishes to "follow Bloomfield's attempt at a phonemic analysis of intonation," and he has devised the "mechanical details of a technique for discovering the contrastive levels of pitch of a system such as English contains" (p. 11).

Before we get involved with the significant details of Pike's analysis, it would be well to point out that Pike does not find *any* contours that are "explicit in meaning." He usually does not even try to give the meanings of the contours that he describes in this book. When he does, it is apparent that a particular contour never has a specific meaning. On page 51, for example, he gives four different sentences that illustrate the function and the meaning of one contour (contour 03-2). The contour has four different meanings in the four sentences. The only element common to the four different meanings is that they involve "supplementation" of some type. However, on page 53 the same contour implies a question.[5] Pike notes that "meanings were very difficult to define—and are still subject to revision" (p. 2).

9.9.1 Pitch Levels. Pike describes intonation contours in terms of four pitch levels and two "pauses." The four pitch levels are relative levels and may vary from one person to the next; they may even vary in the speech of the same person from time to time. The pitch levels are numbered from 1 to 4; level 1 corresponds to the highest and level 4 to the lowest relative pitch. Pike notes that "this number is not an arbitrary one. . . . The four levels are enough to provide for the writing and distinguishing of all of the contours that have differences of meaning so far discovered. . . . A description in terms of five or six levels would leave many theoretically possible combinations of pitches unused" (p. 26).

9.9.2 Pauses. There are two "pauses" in this analysis. The "ten-

[5] The contour is a marked breath-group.

tative" pause, denoted by [/], "tends to sustain the height of the final pitch of the [preceding] contour" though there may be "occasional slight drift upward." The final pause, [//], "modifies the preceding contour (or contours) by lowering in some sense the normal height of the contour" (p. 31). Furthermore,

> Of the two pauses, the tentative one tends to occur at all places where the attitude of the speaker includes uncertainty, or nonfinality [p. 32].
>
> The final pause occurs where the speaker's attitude, at the time of pause, is one of finality, and for this reason occurs most often at the end of statements.
>
> Frequently, pauses in the middle of sentences separate large grammatical units such as clauses, or separate smaller units in such a way as to contribute to their internal unity. In the next illustration a routine pause separates clauses; in the second illustration the pauses . . . set off the units *three plus two:*
>
> | If | ′Tom goes, | ′I | will | ′too |
> |---|---|---|---|---|
> | 3– | °2–4–3/ | 2–4– | –4–3 | °2–4// |
>
> | ′Two, | times | ′three | ′plus | two, | is | ′ten |
> |---|---|---|---|---|---|---|
> | °2–4–3/ | 4– | °2 | °1– | –4–3/ | 3– | °2–4// |
>
> [p. 33].

Pike is thus somewhat more explicit than Jones with regard to using pauses to clarify the "meaning" of a sentence.

9.9.3 Stress. Pike notes that

> . . . one—and only one—phonemic innate stress contrast can be readily demonstrated to exist in English, utilizing words which differ by stress, but have the same vowel and consonant phonemes . . . (i.e., word pairs minimally different by stress).
>
> . . . no analysis of stress can be valid if it fails to account for its relation to intonation . . . [p. 82].

Pike explicitly relates stress to intensity on page 83.

9.9.4 Primary and Precontours.[6] The intonation contour of a sentence can be divided into "primary" and "precontours." Pike also observes that

[6] Pike's treatment of precontours is rather like the treatment of the unstressed syllables at the start of Tune I or Tune II by Jones and Armstrong and Ward. The pitch of these syllables follows the pitch of the start of the tune that follows. Palmer and Kingdon adopt the same treatment for their "heads" and "tails," which occur on unstressed syllables.

A stressed syllable constitutes the BEGINNING POINT for every primary contour; there is no primary contour without a stressed syllable, and every heavily stressed syllable begins a new contour . . . the beginning of the primary contour will be shown by the degree sign [°] placed before the number of the pitch level [p. 27].

Immediately preceding the stressed syllable of a primary contour there will oftentimes be one or more syllables which . . . are unstressed. These syllables may be called PRECONTOURS, and depend for their pronunciation on the syllables which follow them [p. 29].

9.9.5 The Subdivision of Sentence Contours

A single contour is not necessarily exactly as long as a sentence. One sentence may have several contours . . . [p. 20].

When a phrase becomes quite long, the contour may be subdivided, since a long contour is somewhat awkward to pronounce; sometimes contours may be spread out over long sequences of syllables without being subdivided; at other times the stresses and arrangement of words cause even a five syllable phrase to be divided [p. 24].

In the first part of his book, Pike apparently uses the term "contour" to mean the actual acoustic pitch contours that occur when a speaker utters a sentence. On page 34, however, Pike suddenly redefines "contour" to mean a potential pitch contour that *could* occur if a speaker produced a primary contour on each stressed syllable. Pike then uses the term "rhythm unit" to mean what "contour" used to mean before page 34, that is, the pitch contours that the speaker actually produces. The presentation is rather confusing since Pike does not indicate that he has redefined "contour" to mean a potential rather than an actual pitch contour.

English sentences are spoken with recurrent bursts of speed, with long or short pauses or with intonation breaks between. A sentence or part of a sentence spoken with a single rush of syllables uninterrupted by a pause is a RHYTHM UNIT [p. 34].

Potentially a rhythm break may occur after the end of any word at all, but the potential after a primary contour is much stronger than elsewhere. A slightly slower rate of utterance will often break a complex rhythm unit into two simple units, even without a marked change of the speaker's attitude or attention, simply by introducing a pause after the first primary contour. In general, pauses can be introduced elsewhere in the sentence only when the speaker changes his attitude, or speed, or emphasis quite sharply [p. 37].

The only significant difference between Pike's discussion of "rhythm units" and "primary contours" and Jones's treatment of "breath-groups" and "sense-groups" (aside from the fact that Jones is much clearer and does not pretend to be giving a "phonemic" solution) is that Pike stresses the point that there are preferred ways of dividing a sentence into breath-groups.

9.9.6 Vocal Quality. Pike also discusses "other intonation characteristics that may be affected or caused by the individual's physiological state—anger, happiness, excitement, age, sex and so on" (p. 20). He states that

> Excited speech tends to use WIDE INTERVALS between the pitch levels of the intonation contours. Monotonous, weary, or professional style tends to utilize NARROW INTERVALS. Excited speech tends to be relatively FAST, whereas deliberate, or whining, or grief-filled speech tends to be relatively SLOW. Excited speech, further, tends to be HIGH in general pitch or KEY, whereas grief or scorn tends to be LOW [p. 100].
>
> In general, a qualitative characteristic is applicable to an entire utterance, or series of utterances, or even to one's entire speaking time. This is quite different from an intonation contour which is usually limited to a short phrase [p. 100].

The two most significant aspects of Pike's analysis are his isolation of the "pauses" that occur at the end of "rhythm units" and his observation that the acoustic modifications that reflect emotion affect the entire utterance rather than part of it. It is rather surprising that Pike did not notice the similarities between his analysis and the Tunes I and II of the Armstrong-Ward analysis.

9.10 R. S. Wells (1947), "Immediate Constituents"

In this paper, Wells makes the point that the "pitch morphemes" also have the function of indicating the immediate constituent structure of the utterance. He notes that

> One can be sure that any segmental morpheme which ends the scope of a pitch morpheme also ends a constituent (or else the whole utterance); but it is not always true that the beginning of the scope of a pitch-morpheme similarly coincides with the beginning of a constituent (or of the utterance). If, in our orthography, we marked a parenthetical expression by placing a closing parenthesis) at the end but no corresponding opening parenthesis (at the beginning, we should have a parallel to the manner in which the beginning and end of the scope of a pitch-morpheme may be said to mark the limits of a constituent.

The "scope" of a pitch morpheme is the sequence of segmental morphemes that it is supposed to modify. The purport of this paper is that the pitch contours and pauses have the express purpose of dividing a sentence into phrases and furthermore of indicating the relationship between these phrases. This, of course, implies that the pitch contours of each sentence are determined by the sentence's immediate constituent structure.

9.11 G. L. Trager and H. L. Smith (1951), *Outline of English Structure*

Superficially, the Trager-Smith analysis of the prosodic features resembles Pike's. Trager and Smith use four phonemic pitch levels. Number 1 corresponds to the speaker's lowest relative pitch and number 4 to his highest relative pitch level. There are three terminal junctures that correspond to Pike's two "pauses." The terminal juncture [#] phonetically means a fall in pitch. It corresponds to Pike's "final pause." The terminal symbols [//] and [/], respectively, correspond to a rise in pitch and a sustention of pitch. They correspond to Pike's "tentative pause," which either sustained the height of the pitch level that preceded it or involved a "slight drift upwards." One additional juncture, which is transcribed as /+/, is used in this analysis. The principal function of this "internal juncture" is to indicate phonetic cues that separate words or parts of certain compound words during fluent speech. Four "phonemic" stress levels also are used. The levels are marked with the following symbols: /′ ˆ ˋ ˘/. Primary stress, designated by /′/, is the loudest stress. (Stress is defined psychoacoustically in terms of loudness.) The secondary stress, /ˆ/, occurs only in compound words or phrases in which the "internal juncture," /+/, occurs. Secondary stress is thus one of the phonetic cues of the "internal juncture" phoneme. (Smith and Trager, of course, regard all these elements as phonemic.)

One function of this complex notation, which can be regarded as an elaboration of Pike's notation joined to the Bloch-Trager stress and juncture notation, is to differentiate prosodic contours that have different meanings (using the term "prosodic contour" to mean a complex of stress, pitch, and junctural phenomena that occur in an utterance transcribed with this system). The sentence

2 3 1 1
Hôw + do + thèy + stúdy / nôw + wè've + gôt + thèir + bóoks #?

which we have copied using standard orthography and the Smith-Trager prosodic transcription (from p. 44) is supposed to represent the way this sentence is spoken: "If attention is to be centered on the problem they have in studying. . . ." If the question is asked with polite interest rather than insistence, it is supposed (p. 44) to be spoken thus:

3 1 1
Hów + do + thèy + stûdy / nôw + wè've + gôt + thèir + bóoks//?

One of the fundamental differences between Pike and Trager-Smith is that where Pike differentiated between the "pitch contours" that could potentially occur in a sentence and the "rhythm units" that were the pitch patterns that actually occurred, Trager and Smith discuss only those prosodic patterns that actually occur. Trager and Smith say essentially that the primary function of the prosodic features is to divide the sentence into linguistic units[7] and that each linguistic unit *always* is represented by a prosodic pattern (or class of prosodic patterns) that is actually present in the acoustic speech signal. They note that

> The contribution of the phonological analysis of stress, juncture, and intonation patterns . . . is . . . that it makes these techniques [the recognition of immediate constituents and part of speech syntax] into solidly established objective procedures, removing once and for all the necessity of defending one's subjective judgments as to what goes with what [p. 77].

They take the position that the phrase *at the little market near the corner* (p. 51) is always divided into two smaller phrases, *at the little market* and *near the corner,* by the presence of special intonation patterns that "always contain at least one pitch phoneme, and end in one of the terminal junctures. . . ." In other words, we do not group these words because we know the grammar of English and therefore know how phrases are formed. We group them because special acoustic signals are always present.

We can see a steady progression from Pike to Wells to Trager-Smith. Pike notes that there are potential pitch contours that may be realized by a speaker to make the meaning of a sentence clearer. Wells points out that these potential pitch contours are tied to the

[7] Trager and Smith note that within each phrase the words are delimited by the stresses and the internal juncture which also reflect the morphological structure of the words of the phrase. They state that "Suprasegmental morphemes consisting of patterns of stress, with the possibility of including plus junctures, are called SUPERFIXES" (p. 56).

A "morphemic word" is defined as an actual word plus its superfix. A "morphemic phrase" is defined as several words plus an over-all phrase superfix. They add that "the phrase superfix is found to be statable always in terms of the morphological nature of the included words and as an element superseding their superfixes in accordance with regular correlations" (p. 57).

structures, that is, the immediate constituent analysis of the superficial phrase marker. However, he still allows for some variation and uncertainty in the way that the pitch contours signal the immediate constituent structure to the listener. Smith and Trager, however, tie the pitch contours directly to the immediate constituent structure. They imply that these pitch contours are always physically realized. The suprasegmentals always provide "acoustic" cues that tell the listener how to divide the sentence for syntactic analysis. The Trager-Smith analysis of intonation is thus the logical extension of Bloomfield's hunt for "objective" facts. The "objective" facts have been related here to the level of immediate constituents.

In Chapter 6 we briefly reviewed the results of an experiment (Lieberman, 1965) demonstrating that the pitch levels and stresses of the Trager-Smith system often have no physical basis. The linguist acquainted with the system may fill in the pitch and stress notation that is appropriate for the immediate constituent analysis of the utterance he hears. He determines the phrase structure of the utterance through the words of the message rather than through any special phonetic cues.

The great value of the Trager-Smith analysis is that it correctly noticed that the intonation of an utterance could reflect its immediate constituent structure. Wells had recognized this, and Trager and Smith refined the segmental analysis of intonation, but they went too far. The "phonemic clause" was defined in terms of the segmental pitch phonemes that were used to transcribe an utterance. As we noted in Chapter 5, breath-groups can delimit the constituent structure of a derived phrase marker. Under the conditions that we discussed in Section 5.1.2 the division of a sentence into breath-groups can aid in the recovery of the deep phrase marker when the sentence would be ambiguous if the derived constituent structure were not manifested. The situation is quite parallel to the use of commas in the orthography.

Trager and Smith saw that the intonation patterns of certain utterances could change their "meanings." However, since the notion of an underlying phrase marker does not occur in their grammar, they assumed that the difference in meaning somehow was part of the intonation itself. Since intonation contours can have many different meanings, it must be possible to form many different intonation "morphemes." It obviously would be absurd to say that Tune II has, for example, 50 different "meanings." Hence, there must be many pitch "phonemes" that can be concatenated into many pitch "morphemes." Unfortunately, the only elements of the Trager-Smith system that do seem to have a reasonably consistent physical basis are the "morphemes" 231# and 232// (or 232/), which are equivalent notations for the unmarked breath-group and the marked breath-group.

The distinction that Trager and Smith draw between pitch levels and stress levels is in a sense justified since the segmental pitch "phonemes" serve as a notation for the suprasegmental "phonemic clauses." The phonemic clauses really reflect the potential division of the utterance into breath-groups, whereas the stress levels reflect prominence $(+ P_s)$ and the subordination principle (cf. Chapter 7). Thus insofar as the stress and pitch levels reflect the segmental feature $[P_s]$ and the suprasegmental breath-group, they relate to features that are far apart in the hierarchy of phonologic features.

9.12 Z. Harris (1944), "Simultaneous Components in Phonology"

In this study, Harris attempted to analyze intonation in terms of suprasegmental morphemes at a time when many other linguists were attempting segmental analyses. Harris, like Bloomfield, states that intonation contours are morphemes,

> . . . pitch and stress have been found to constitute the elements of special morphemes . . . they constitute morphemes by themselves independent of the rest of the speech with which they are simultaneous [p. 182].

However, in contrast to the theories of Pike, Wells, Trager and Smith, these morphemes are clearly suprasegmental:

> . . . the pitch sequence is a single component whose length is that of a whole utterance or phrase [p. 190].

Harris offers no procedures whereby these "special morphemes" may be identified. He notes that

> . . . the components described in this paper are not complete physical events; therefore they cannot actually be substituted for each other to see if any two of them are free variants or repetitions of each other [p. 201].

The intonation morphemes, in other words, cannot be separated from the lexical contexts with which they are supposed to be simultaneous.

9.13 R. H. Stetson (1951), *Motor Phonetics: A Study of Speech Movements in Action*

In this work Stetson claims that he can study "the movements of speech" without regard to their linguistic function. Stetson makes this comment:

Motor phonetics is the study of the skilled movements involved in the process of handling articulatory signals. Motor phonetics deals with the organized series of actual syllables or nonsense syllables shaped by the language mechanism. "Phonetic" refers to such physiological processes in the study of the signals of a language independent of the meaning of the signals [p. 6].

However, one could reasonably argue that Stetson was studying the phonologic component of French and English, since he did confine his study to the words, phrases, and admissible "nonsense syllables" of these languages. The principal difficulty with this interpretation is that Stetson pursued his investigation without regard to any linguistic frame of reference, and so it is sometimes difficult to see whether he is discussing a significant aspect of the language or some idiosyncrasy of the particular speaker.

Stetson attempts to develop a consistent physiological model for the production of the suprasegmental aspects of speech. The basis of this physiological model is Stetson's view of the physiology of the lungs. He apparently believed that the chest was similar to a hand bellows. He believed that when the chest was inflated, the air in the lungs was *not* under pressure in the absence of the activity of the muscles between the ribs (the intercostal muscles). He says that

When the chest is slightly inflated for speaking, the air is not under pressure; like a hand bellows for blowing a fire, the volume is increased, but the nozzle is open and there is no flow of air. . . .

If one makes quick strokes of the hands while holding the inflated air bellows, the nozzle emits little pulses of air; as the quick strokes are repeated the air pulses reduce the volume of the air, and the arm muscles must bring the boards of the bellows closer and closer to accommodate for the loss of air.

In much the same way the vocal apparatus makes a series of vowel syllables, "Oh, Oh, Oh. . . ." The chest is inflated by the larger muscles, the quick strokes for each air pulse are made by the short muscles between the ribs, and as the chest volume gets less and less, the larger outside muscles and the abdominal muscles accommodate the walls and floor of the chest to the changing volume.

The muscles between the ribs [intercostals] produce the syllables "Oh, Oh, Oh . . ." as units included in the slower movement of the breath-group which is made by the larger muscles of the chest and abdomen. The rapid muscle contractions [of the intercostals] are like ripples of the wave of the expiratory movement of the breath-group [pp. 1–2].

Stetson's physiologic model is unfortunately erroneous. The air in the inflated lungs *is* under pressure. The elastic recoil force that is generated by the distended walls of the chest is the primary motive force for expiration (cf. Chapters 2 and 4). Indeed, the loss of elasticity by the walls of the chest is one of the pathologic conditions that characterizes pulmonary emphysema, where the patient has difficulty in expiration.[8] The function of the intercostal muscles is, moreover, in doubt. It is not even clear whether they are expiratory muscles (Agostoni, 1964). Even if they were expiratory muscles, and even if a peak subglottal air pressure occurred on each syllable when it was produced as part of a string of stressed syllables, it would be difficult to ascertain which muscles contracted to produce the peak pressure without extensive data on the entire respiratory muscle complex and the alveolar air pressure and lung volume. Stetson's measurements of gastric pressure cannot be accurate measures of the pressure of the air in the lungs as he claims. He does not compensate for the effects of the elastic recoil force on the pleural pressure since he apparently did not know how the respiratory system normally functions. The only aspect of Stetson's theory that seems to have a firm basis is the subglottal air pressure function that is associated with the breath-group, that is, a positive air pressure function normally associated with an expiration bounded by inspirations. Stetson's physiological definition of the breath-group reads as follows:

> The breath-group is an abdominal movement; the driving rectus and parietal muscles of the abdomen reciprocate with the diaphragm and the thoracic muscles. This movement groups the syllable pulses and adjusts the chest-abdomen to the slight reduction in volume due to the outgo of the chest pulses [p. 32].

This is wrong since the elastic recoil force of the lungs actively reduces the volume of the lungs during expiration.

Stetson's study is, in short, misleading in its conception of the articulatory maneuvers involved in inspiration and the production of speech. Its data also are often erroneous. The principal value of this study is that it focused some attention on the linguistic role[9] of subglottal articulatory maneuvers.

[8] Dr. Jere Mead, Harvard School of Public Health.

[9] Twaddell (1953), in an interesting paper, attempts to define the Trager-Smith junctures and other transitions in terms of Stetson's model. He states, for example, that "The first step is to define pause with utmost rigor as an inspiration" (p. 438). He assumes that "The preinspiration transitions /#, // / are produced by characteristic actions of the abdomen-diaphragm musculature. . . ." He also notes that "With /+/ the controlling mechanism is the intercostal musculature." Twaddell defines other transitions in terms of the "internal intercostal action" and the "external intercostal action," etc. (p. 441). Twaddell essentially uses a binary notation for these definitions, which are based on Stetson's incorrect model.

9.14 M. Bierwisch (1965), "Regeln für die Intonation deutscher Sätze"

Bierwisch, in a recent study of German sentence intonation, which to some degree complements our study, demonstrates that it is possible to generate an intonation contour for a German sentence if only the superficial syntactic structure, primary accents, and "syntactic intonation markers" (SIM) are considered. Bierwisch defines "intonation" in terms of the perceived pitch contour of the utterance. He notes that the fundamental frequency of the utterance is the primary acoustic correlate of intonation. Bierwisch's study is similar to our analysis, and he believes that accent, or stress, is an abstract characteristic of the sentence that is determined by its derived phrase marker.

The syntactic intonation markers include Question and Emphasis morphemes. Boundary symbols are introduced that always mark the end of sentences and that can mark the ends of clauses within the sentence. The potential points at which boundary symbols can be located are determined through algorithms that take account of the derived constituent structure and the distribution of accented vowels. These algorithms place some necessary restrictions on the division of a sentence into breath-groups.

Bierwisch uses the boundary symbols, the primary accents, and the SIM to generate a linguistically determined intonation contour, which he carefully differentiates from the possible emotional aspects of intonation in marked contrast to the Trager-Smith and Pike analyses. By means of a complex set of segmental rules Bierwisch, in essence, generates a breath-group between each set of boundary symbols. The breath-group extends over the entire sentence if no boundary symbols occur within the sentence. If the sentence has several boundary symbols, then it is divided into several breath-groups. The presence of the question SIM essentially marks the breath-group. Bierwisch points out that it results in a pitch rise at the end of the sentence.

Bierwisch transcribes his breath-groups by means of a pitch contour that ascends and descends in a number of steps. Each step occurs on an accented syllable. In effect, Bierwisch is using a phonetic transcription that is not unlike Jones's (1932). He connects the stressed syllables by means of horizontal and vertical lines.[10] However, he does

[10] This phonetic transcription was motivated by a psychoacoustic study by Isačenko and Schädlich (1963), who synthesized intonation contours in terms of small frequency steps with a Vocoder. The experimental procedures of this study make it difficult to evaluate its results. It is not quite clear whether

not claim that the fundamental frequency of the speech signal is a series of discrete steps. He notes that the phonetic transcription is not equivalent to the output of the articulatory apparatus. Instead, he regards it as an input to a universal articulatory theory that also accepts the emotional state of the speaker as an input. Bierwisch thus does not actually generate the acoustic output signal, though his phonetic output is transcribed as a pitch contour. Since Bierwisch notes that the fundamental frequency is the primary acoustic correlate of perceived pitch, it would be less confusing if he used some measure other than pitch for the transcription of his phonetic output.

Bierwisch considers the effects of emotion on intonation, and he considers the possibility of generating special intonation morphemes in the base component of the grammar. He correctly concludes that this course is inadvisable. Emotion affects all aspects of speech production. If we include rules for emotion in the deep structure, we should also have to include an entire repertoire of "emotional phonologic features" as well as optional emotional syntactic rules to account for the deletions and insertions that are characteristic of certain emotional styles. Instead, Bierwisch correctly proposes that the effects of emotion be superimposed on the phonetic output of the grammar.

Bierwisch maintains that the scope of the breath-group is suprasegmental since the boundary symbols delimit the constituent structure of the derived phrase marker. However, he does not explicitly use the breath-group as a phonologic feature. The position of each "pitch step" in the contours that Bierwisch generates by means of his segmental rules may or may not be syntactically determined. The data that we presented in Chapter 4 and the data in the studies of Cowan (1936), Denes (1959), Uldall (1960), and Hadding-Koch (1961) suggest that these small variations often have no syntactic significance. In any event, these variations probably should be treated as departures from the breath-group. Bierwisch indeed discusses this possibility. The incorporation of the feature breath-group into his analysis would greatly simplify its phonologic rules.

---

the psychoacoustic data are statistically significant or whether the responses are meaningful, since the listeners were essentially asked to discriminate between sets of signals rather than to categorize them; cf. Chapter 7 for a discussion of categorization versus discrimination.

References

Abe, I. (1955), "Intonation patterns of English and Japanese," *Word, 11,* 386–398.

Abramson, A. S. (1962), *The Vowels and Tones of Standard Thai: Acoustical Measurements and Experiments,* Part III, *Intern. J. Am. Ling., 28.*

Agostoni, E. (1964), "Action of respiratory muscles," *Handbook of Physiology, Respiration, I,* W. O. Fenn and H. Rahn, eds., American Physiological Society, Washington, D.C.

Agostoni, E., and Mead, J. (1964), "Statics of the respiratory system," *Handbook of Physiology, Respiration, I,* W. O. Fenn and H. Rahn, eds., American Physiological Society, Washington, D.C.

Armstrong, L. E., and Ward, I. C. (1926), *Handbook of English Intonation,* B. G. Teubner, Leipzig and Berlin.

Bell, C. (1848), *The Anatomy and Philosophy of Expression as Connected with the Fine Arts,* 4th ed., J. Murray, London.

Berko, J. (1958), "The child's learning of English morphology," *Word, 14,* 150–177.

Berry, J. (1953), "Some statistical aspects of conversational speech," in *Communication Theory,* W. Jackson, ed., Academic Press, New York.

Bierwisch, M. (1965), "Regeln für die Intonation deutscher Sätze," mimeographed manuscript.

Bloch, B., and Trager, G. L. (1942), *Outline of Linguistic Analysis,* Linguistic Society of America, Baltimore, Md.

Bloomfield, L. (1933), *Language,* Holt, New York.

Bolinger, D. L. (1949), "Intonation and analysis," *Word, 5,* 248–254.

Bolinger, D. L. (1957), "Intonation and grammar," *Language Learning, 8,* Nos. 1 and 2.

Bolinger, D. L. (1958), "A theory of pitch accent in English," *Word, 14,* 109–149.

Bolinger, D. L. (1961*a*), "Contrastive accent and contrastive stress," *Language, 37,* 83–96.

Bolinger, D. L. (1961*b*), "Ambiguities in pitch accent," *Word, 17,* 309–317.

Bolinger, D. L. (1961*c*), *Generality, Gradience; and the All or Nones,* Mouton, The Hague.

Bolinger, D. L., and Gerstman, L. J. (1957), "Disjuncture as a cue to constructs," *J. Acoust. Soc. Am., 29,* 778.

Boomer, D. S., and Dittmann, A. T. (1962), "Hesitation pauses and juncture pauses in speech," *Language and Speech, 5,* 215–220.

Borst, J. M., and Cooper, F. S. (1957), "Speech research devices based on a channel Vocoder," *J. Acoust. Soc. Am., 29,* 777.

Bosma, J. F., Lind, J., and Truby, H. M. (1964), "Respiratory motion patterns of the newborn infant in cry," in *Physical Diagnosis of the Newly Born, Report of the Forty-Sixth Ross Conference on Pediatric Research,* J. L. Kay, ed., Ross Laboratories, Columbus, Ohio, 103–116.

Bouhuys, A., Proctor, D. F., and Mead, J. (1966), "Kinetic aspects of singing," scheduled for *J. Appl. Physiol.*

Bühler, C., and Hetzer, H. (1928), "Das erste Verständnis für Ausdruck im ersten Lebensjahr," *Z. Psych., 197,* cited in Lewis (1936).

Bullowa, M., Jones, L. G., and Duckert, A. R. (1964), "The acquisition of a word," *Language and Speech, 7,* 107–111.

Chang, N. T. (1958), "Tones and intonation in the Chengtu dialect (Szechuan, China)," *Phonetica, 2,* 59–85.

Chiba, T. (1935), *A Study of Accent, Research into Its Nature and Scope in the Light of Experimental Phonetics,* Phonetic Society of Japan, Tokyo.

Chomsky, N. (1957), *Syntactic Structures,* Mouton, The Hague.

Chomsky, N. (1965), *Aspects of the Theory of Syntax,* The M.I.T. Press, Cambridge, Mass.

Chomsky, N., and Halle, M. (1966), *The Sound Pattern of English,* forthcoming, Harper and Row, New York.

Chomsky, N., Halle, M., and Lukoff, F. (1956), "On accent and juncture in English," *For Roman Jakobson,* M. Halle, H. Lunt, and H. MacLean, eds., Mouton, The Hague.

Cohen, M. R., and Drabkin, I. E. (1958), *A Source Book in Greek Science,* Harvard University Press, Cambridge, Mass.

Cooper, F. S., Peterson, E., and Fahringer, G. S. (1957), "Some sources of characteristic Vocoder quality," *J. Acoust. Soc. Am., 29,* 183.

Cowan, M. (1936), "Pitch and intensity characteristics of stage speech," *Archives of Speech,* Supplement I, 1–92.

Creelman, C. D. (1963), "Detection, discrimination, and the loudness of short tones," *J. Acoust. Soc. Am., 35,* 1201–1205.

Dahlstedt, A. (1901), *Rhythm and Word Order in Anglo-Saxon and Semi-Saxon with Special Reference to Their Development in Modern English,* E. Malmstrom, Lund, Sweden.

Danes, F. (1960), "Sentence intonation from a functional point of view," *Word, 16,* 34–54.

Darwin, C. (1872), *The Expression of Emotion in Man and Animals,* J. Murray, London.

De Bray, R. G. A. (1961), "Some observations of the Serbo-Croatian musical accents in connected speech," in *Study of Sounds,* Phonetic Society of Japan, Tokyo.

Denes, P. (1959), "A preliminary investigation of certain aspects of intonation," *Language and Speech, 2,* 106–122.

Draper, M. H., Ladefoged, P., and Whitteridge, D. (1959), "Respiratory muscles in speech," *J. Speech and Hearing Res., 2,* 16–27.

Dudley, H. (1939), "Remaking speech," *J. Acoust. Soc. Am., 11,* 169–175.

Egerod, S. (1956), *The Lungtu Dialect: A Description and Historical Study of a South China Idiom,* Ejnar Munksgaard Ltd., Copenhagen.

Faaborg-Andersen, K. (1957), "Electromyographic investigation of intrinsic laryngeal muscles in humans," *Acta Physiol. Scand., 41,* Suppl. 140.

Fant, C. G. M. (1960), *Acoustic Theory of Speech Production,* Mouton, The Hague.

Fant, C. G. M. (1961), "A new anti-resonance circuit for inverse filtering," *Speech Trans. Lab. Quar. Prog. Rept. 4/61,* 1–6, Stockholm.

Farnsworth, D. W. (1940), "High speed motion pictures of the human vocal cords," *Bell Lab. Rec., 18,* 203–208.

Ferrein (1741), *Mém. Acad. Paris.,* 409–432 (November 15, 1741).

Fink, B. R. (1962), "Tensor mechanism of the vocal folds," *Ann. Otolaryngol., 17,* 591–601.

Flanagan, J. L. (1958), "Some properties of the glottal sound source," *J. Speech and Hearing Res., 1,* 99–116.

Flanagan, J. L., and Saslow, M. G. (1958), "Pitch discrimination for synthetic vowels," *J. Acoust. Soc. Am., 30,* 435.

Fodor, J. A., and Katz, J. J. (1963), "The structure of a semantic theory," *Language, 39,* 170–210.

Fonagy, I. (1958), "Elektrophysiologische Beiträge zur Akzentfrage," *Phonetica, 2,* 12–58.

Fry, D. B. (1955), "Duration and intensity as physical correlates of linguistic stress," *J. Acoust. Soc. Am., 35,* 765–769.

Fry, D. B. (1958), "Experiments in the perception of stress," *Language and Speech, 1,* 126–152.

Garcia, M. (1855), "Observations on the human voice," *Proc. Roy. Soc., London,* 399–410.

Geisler, C. D., Molnar, C. E., Peake, W. T., Steinberg, C. A., and Weiss, T. F. (1958), "Judgments of the loudness of clicks," *Quarterly Progress Report,* No. 50, Research Laboratory of Electronics, M.I.T., Cambridge, Mass.

Goldman-Eisler, F. (1958), "The predictability of words in context and the length of pauses in speech," *Language and Speech, 1,* 226–231.

Hadding-Koch, K. (1961), *Acoustico-Phonetic Studies in the Intonation of Southern Swedish,* C. W. K. Gleerup, Lund, Sweden.

Hadding-Koch, K., and Studdert-Kennedy, M. (1964), "An experimental study of some intonation contours," *Phonetica, 11,* 175–185.

Halle, M., and Stevens, K. N. (1959), "Analysis by synthesis," *Proceedings of Seminar on Speech Compression and Processing,* Air Force Cambridge Research Center, AFCRC-TR-59-198.

Harris, C. M., and Weiss, M. R. (1963), "Pitch and formant shifts accompanying changes in speech power level," *J. Acoust. Soc. Am., 35,* 1876.

Harris, J. B., and Stuntz, S. E. (1950), *Am. Psychologist, 5,* 269.

Harris, Z. (1944), "Simultaneous components in phonology," *Language, 20,* 181–205.

Helmholtz, H. L. (1863), *Die Tonempfindung,* Berlin.

Hering, E., and Breuer, J. (1868), "Die Selbststeuerung der Athmung durch den Nervus vagus," *Sitzber. Akad. Wiss. Wien., 57(II),* 672–677.

Hermann, E. (1942), "Probleme der Frage," *Nachr. Akad. Wiss. Goettingen, 3–4.*

Hockett, C. F. (1958), *A Course in Modern Linguistics,* Macmillan, New York.

Holmes, J. N. (1963), "An investigation of the volume velocity waveform at the larynx during speech by means of an inverse filter," *Proceedings of Speech Communication Seminar,* Aug. 29–Sept. 1, 1962, Royal Institute of Technology, Stockholm.

Hoshiko, M. S. (1957), *Electromyographic Study of Respiratory Muscles in Relation to Syllabification,* Ph.D. dissertation, Purdue University, Lafayette, Ind.

Husson, R. (1950), Thesis, Faculty of Science, Paris.

Husson, R. (1955), "Physiologie de la vibration des cordes vocales," *Compt. Rend. Acad. Sci., 241,* 242–244.

Husson, R. (1957), "La vibration des cordes vocales (de l'Homme) sans courant d'air et les rôles d'une pression sous-glottique éventuelle," *J. Physiol. (Paris), 49,* 217–220.

International Phonetic Association (1949), *The Principles of the International Phonetic Association,* London.

Irwin, O. C. (1947), "Infant speech: Consonant sounds according to manner of articulation," *J. Speech Disorders, 12,* 397–401.

Ĭsacenko, A. V., and Schädlich, H. J. (1963), "Erzeugung künstlicher deutscher Satzintonationen mit zwei kontrastierenden Tonstufen," *Monatsber. Deut. Akad. Wiss. Berlin, 6.*

Isshiki, N. (1964), "Regulatory mechanism of voice intensity variation," *J. Speech and Hearing Res., 7,* 17–29.

Jackson, H. (1915), "Aphasia," *Brain, 38.*

Jakobson, R. (1942), "Kindersprache, Aphasie und allgemeine Lautgesetze," *Uppsala Universitets Arsskrift.*

Jakobson, R., Fant, C. G. M., and Halle, M. (1952), *Preliminaries to Speech Analysis,* Technical Report No. 13, Acoustics Laboratory, M.I.T.; reprinted by the M.I.T. Press, Cambridge, Mass.

Jakobson, R., and Halle, M. (1956), *Fundamentals of Language,* Mouton, The Hague.

Jassem, W. (1952), *Intonation of Conversational English,* Traveaux de la société des sciences et des lettres de Wroclaw, Seria A, no. 45, Wroclaw.

Jesperson, O. (1907), *A Modern English Grammar I,* E. Munksgaard, Copenhagen, and G. Allen and Unwin, London.

Jones, D. (1909), *Intonation Curves,* B. G. Teubner, Leipzig and Berlin.

Jones, D. (1932), *An Outline of English Phonetics,* 3rd ed., Dutton, New York.

Jones, D. (1962), *An Outline of English Phonetics,* 9th ed., W. H. Heffer & Sons, Cambridge, England.

Joos, M. (1962), in *Proceedings of 2nd Texas Conference on Problems of Linguistic Analysis in English,* University of Texas, Austin, Tex.

Karelitz, S., *Infant Vocalizations,* phonograph record CL 2669A, Long Island Jewish Hospital, New York.

Katsuki, Y. (1950), "The function of the phonatory muscles," *Japan. J. Physiol., 1,* 29–36.

Katz, J. J., and Postal, P. M. (1964), *An Integrated Theory of Linguistic Descriptions,* The M.I.T. Press, Cambridge, Mass.

Kersta, L. G., Bricker, P. D., and David, E. E. (1960), "Human or machine?" *J. Acoust. Soc. Am., 32,* 1502.

Kingdon, R. (1939), "Tonetic stress markers for English," *Le Maître Phonétique, 3.54,* 60–64.

Kingdon, R. (1958), *The Groundwork of English Intonation,* Longmans, Green & Co., London, New York, and Toronto.

Klima, E. S. (1964), "Negation in English," in *The Structure of Language,* J. J. Fodor and J. A. Katz, eds., Prentice-Hall, Englewood Cliffs, N.J.

Kurtz, J. H., *The Sounds of a Day-Old Baby,* tape-recording available from the Langley Porter Neuropsychiatric Institute, San Francisco, Calif., summarized in Ostwald (1963).

Ladefoged, P. (1961), in *Quarterly Progress Report, Speech Transmission Laboratory,* Royal Institute of Technology, Stockholm (October).

Ladefoged, P., and McKinney, N. P. (1963), "Loudness, sound pressure, and subglottal pressure in speech," *J. Acoust. Soc. Am., 35,* 454.

Landois, L. (1923), *Lehrbuch der Physiologie das Menschen,* 18th ed., Urban & Schwarzenberg, Berlin and Vienna.

Lehiste, I. (1961), "Some acoustic correlates of accent in Serbo-Croatian," *Phonetica, 7,* 114–147.

Lenneberg, E. (1964), *The Biological Basis of Speech,* manuscript.

Leopold, W. F. (1953), "Patterning in children's language," *Language Learning, 5,* 1–14.

Lewis, M. (1936), *Infant Speech, A Study of the Beginnings of Language,* Harcourt Brace, New York.

Liberman, A. M., Cooper, F. S., Harris, K. S., and MacNeilage, P. F. (1963), "A motor theory of speech perception," *Proceedings of the Speech Communication Seminar,* Speech Transmission Laboratory, Royal Institute of Technology, Stockholm (August 1962).

Liberman, A. M., Cooper, F. S., Harris, K. S., MacNeilage, P. F., and Studdert-Kennedy, M. (1966), "Some observations on a model for speech perception," *Proceedings of the Symposium on Models for *the Perception of Speech and Visual Form,* Boston, Mass. (November 1964).

Lieberman, P. (1957), "On vowel intonation," *Quarterly Progress Report,* No. 3, Research Laboratory of Electronics, M.I.T., Cambridge, Mass.

Lieberman, P. (1960), "Some acoustic correlates of word stress in American-English," *J. Acoust. Soc. Am., 32,* 451–454.

Lieberman, P. (1961), "Perturbations in vocal pitch," *J. Acoust. Soc. Am., 33,* 597–603.

Lieberman, P. (1963*a*), "Some acoustic measures of the fundamental periodicity of normal and pathologic larynges," *J. Acoust. Soc. Am., 35,* 344–353.

Lieberman, P. (1963*b*), "Laryngeal activity and the analysis and synthesis of speech," *J. Acoust. Soc. Am., 35,* 778.

Lieberman, P. (1963*c*), "Some effects of semantic and grammatical context on the production and perception of speech," *Language and Speech, 6,* 172.

Lieberman, P. (1965), "On the acoustic basis of the perception of intonation by linguists," *Word, 21,* 40–54.

Lieberman, P., and Lees, R. B. (1958), "Some acoustic correlates of vowel intonation," *Quarterly Progress Report,* No. 2, Research Laboratory of Electronics, M.I.T., Cambridge, Mass.

Lieberman, P., and Michaels, S. B. (1962), "Some aspects of fundamental frequency, envelope amplitude and the emotional content of speech," *J. Acoust. Soc. Am., 34,* 922–927.

Lieberman, P., and Soron, H. I. (1962), "Time relationship between the glottal and sound pressure waveforms . . . ," *J. Acoust. Soc. Am., 34,* 1976.

Lifshitz, S. (1933), "Two integral laws of sound perception relating loudness and apparent duration of sound impulses," *J. Acoust. Soc. Am., 5,* 31–33.

Lifshitz, S. (1935), "Apparent duration of sound perception and musical optimum reverberation," *J. Acoust. Soc. Am., 7,* 213–219.

Lindblom, B. (1963), *On Vowel Reduction,* Report No. 29, Speech Transmission Laboratory, Royal Institute of Technology, Stockholm.

Löwenfeld, B. (1927), "Reaktionen der Säuglinge auf Klänge und Geräusche," *Z. Psych., 104,* in Lewis (1936), p. 43.

Martin, S. E. (1957), review of C. F. Hockett, *Manual of Phonology* in *Language, 32,* 675–705.

Mead, J., and Agostoni, E. (1964), "Dynamics of breathing," in *Handbook of Physiology, Respiration, I.* W. O. Fenn and H. Rahn, eds., American Physiological Society, Washington, D.C.

Mead, J., and Milic-Emili, J. (1964), "Theory and methodology in respiratory mechanics with glossary of symbols," in *Handbook of Physiology, Respiration, I,* W. O. Fenn and H. Rahn, eds., American Physiological Society, Washington, D.C.

Mead, J., Proctor, D. F., and Bouhuys, A. (1965), in preparation.

Meader, C. L., and Muyskens, J. H. (1962), *Handbook of Biolinguistics,* Herbert C. Weller, Toledo, Ohio.

Menyuk, P. (1965), "Cues used in speech perception and production by children," *Quarterly Progress Report,* No. 77, Research Laboratory of Electronics, M.I.T., Cambridge, Mass.

Miller, G. A., and Isard, S. (1963), "Some perceptual consequences of linguistic rules," *J. Verbal Learning and Verbal Behavior, 2,* 217–228.

Miller, R. L. (1956), "Nature of vocal cord wave," *J. Acoust. Soc. Am., 28,* 159.

Moore, P., and von Leden, H. (1958), "Dynamic variations of the vibratory pattern in the normal larynx," *Folia Phoniat., 10,* 205–238.

Müller, J. (1848), *The Physiology of the Senses, Voice and Muscular Motion with the Mental Faculties,* W. Baly, translator, Taylor, Walton and Maberly, London.

Negus, V. E. (1949), *The Comparative Anatomy and Physiology of the Larynx,* Hafner, London.

Öhman, S., and Lindqvist, J. (1966), "Analysis-by-synthesis of prosodic pitch contours," *Quarterly Progress and Status Report,* 4/1965, Speech Transmission Laboratory, Royal Institute of Technology, Stockholm.

Ostwald, P. F. (1963), *Soundmaking: The Acoustic Communication of Emotion,* Charles C Thomas, Springfield, Ill.

Palmer, H. E. (1922), *English Intonation,* W. Heffer & Sons, Cambridge, England.

Palmer, H. E., and Blandford, W. G. (1924), *A Grammar of Spoken English on a Strictly Phonetic Basis,* W. Heffer & Sons, Cambridge, England.

Palmer, H. E., and Blandford, W. G. (1939), *A Grammar of Spoken English,* revised ed., W. Heffer & Sons, Cambridge, England.

Perkell, J. A. (1965), "Studies of the dynamics of speech production," *Quarterly Progress Report,* No. 76, Research Laboratory of Electronics, M.I.T., Cambridge, Mass.

Peškovskij, A. M. (1930), "Intonacija i grammatika," *Voprosy Metodik Rodrogo Jazyka Linguistiki, i Stilistiki,* pp. 95–108, Moscow and Leningrad.

Piersol, G. A. (1906), *Human Anatomy,* Lippincott, Philadelphia and London.

Pike, K. L. (1945), *The Intonation of American English,* University of Michigan, Ann Arbor, Mich.

Pollack, I. (1952), "The information of elementary audio displays," *J. Acoust. Soc. Am., 24,* 745–749.

Pollack, I. (1953), "The information of elementary audio displays, II," *J. Acoust. Soc. Am., 25,* 765–769.

Pollack, I., and Pickett, J. M. (1964), "The intelligibility of excerpts from conversation," *Language and Speech, 6,* 165–171.

Postal, P. (1964), "Constituent Structure: A Study of Contemporary Models of Syntactic Description," *Intern. J. Am. Ling., 30,* No. 1, Part III.

Pressman, J. J., and Kelemen, G. (1955), "Physiology of the larynx," *Physiol. Rev., 35,* 506–554.

Proctor, D. F. (1964), "Physiology of the upper airway," in *Handbook of Physiology, Respiration, I,* W. O. Fenn and H. Rahn, eds., American Physiological Society, Washington, D.C.

Revtova, L. D. (1965), "The intonation of declarative sentences in current English and Russian," presented at the 5th International Congress of Phonetic Science, Munster, Germany, August 16–22, 1964, summary in *Phonetica, 12,* 192.

Ripman, W. (1922), *Good Speech: An Introduction to English Phonetics,* E. P. Dutton & Co., London and Toronto.

Risberg, A. (1961), "Statistical studies of fundamental frequency range and rate of change," *Quarterly Progress Report,* 4/61, pp. 7–8, Speech Transmission Laboratory, Royal Institute of Technology, Stockholm.

Rosenblith, W. A., and Stevens, K. N. (1952), "Pitch discrimination data from two psychophysical methods," *J. Acoust. Soc. Am., 23,* 449.

Rubin, H. J. (1960), "The neurochronaxic theory of voice production—a refutation," *A.M.A. Arch. Otolaryngol., 71,* 913–920.

Rubinstein, B. (1964), unpublished memo, Seizure Clinic, Coney Island Hospital, New York.

Schafer, P. (1922), "Beobachtungen und Versuche an einem Kinde," *Z. Päd. Psych.,* in Lewis (1936), pp. 111–116.

Schubiger, M. (1935), *The Role of Intonation in Spoken English,* W. Heffer & Sons, Cambridge, England.

Schubiger, M. (1958), *English Intonation, Its Form and Function,* Max Niemeyer, Tübingen.

Shannon, C. (1948), "A mathematical theory of communication," *Bell Syst. Tech. J., 27,* 379–423.

Slawson, A. W. (1965), *Vowel Quality and Musical Timbre: A Psychoacoustic Comparison,* Ph.D. Thesis, Harvard University.

Sledd, J. (1955*a*), review of G. L. Trager and H. L. Smith, *Outline of English Structure* in *Language, 31,* 312–335.

Sledd, J. (1955*b*), review of C. C. Fries, *Structure of English* in *Language, 31,* 312–335.

Sonninen, A. (1956), "The role of the external laryngeal muscles in length-adjustment of the vocal cords in singing," *Acta Otolaryngol.,* Suppl. 130.

Soron, H. I., and Lieberman, P. (1963), "Some measurements of the glottal area waveform," *J. Acoust. Soc. Am., 35,* 1876.

Stetson, R. H. (1951), *Motor Phonetics,* North-Holland, Amsterdam.

Stevens, K. N. (1952), "The perception of vowel formants," *J. Acoust. Soc. Am., 24,* 450.

Stevens, K. N. (1960), "Towards a model for speech recognition," *J. Acoust. Soc. Am., 32,* 47–55.

Stevens, K. N. (1964), "Acoustical aspects of speech production," *Handbook of Physiology, Respiration, I,* W. O. Fenn and H. Rahn, eds., American Physiological Society, Washington, D.C.

Stevens, K. N., and Halle, M. (1964), "Remarks on analysis-by-synthesis and distinctive features," *Proceedings of Symposium on Models for the Perception of Speech and Visual Form,* Boston, Mass. (November 1964).

Stevens, K. N., Sandel, T. T., and House, A. S. (1962), "Perception of two-component noise bursts," *J. Acoust. Soc. Am., 34,* 1876–1878.

Stevens, S. S., and Davis, H. (1938), *Hearing: Its Psychology and Physiology,* Wiley, New York.

Stockwell, R. P. (1960*a*), review of Schubiger (1958), in *Language, 36,* 544.

Stockwell, R. P. (1960*b*), "The place of intonation in a generative grammar of English," *Language, 36,* 360.

Stockwell, R. P. (1961*a*), review of Kingdon (1958), in *Internat. J. Am. Ling., 27,* 278.

Stockwell, R. P. (1961*b*), in *Proceedings of 1st Texas Conference on Problems of Linguistic Analysis in English,* Austin, Texas.

Stockwell, R. P. (1962), in *Proceedings of 2nd Texas Conference on Problems of Linguistic Analysis in English,* Austin, Texas.

Stockwell, R. P. (1963), review of Bolinger (1961*c*) in *Language, 39,* 87.

Strenger, F. (1958), "Methods for direct and indirect measurement of the sub-glottic air-pressure," *Studia Linguistica, 12,* 98–112.

Sweet, H. (1892), *New English Grammar,* Part I, Clarendon Press, Oxford.

Timcke, R., von Leden, H., and Moore, P. (1958), "Laryngeal vibrations, measurements of the glottic wave," *A.M.A. Arch. Otolaryngol., 68,* 1–19.

Trager, G. L., and Smith, H. L. (1951), *Outline of English Structure, Studies in Linguistics,* No. 3, Battenburg, Norman, Okla.

Trendelenburg, W. (1942), *Arch. Sprach- u. Stimmheilk., 6,* 49, in Arnold (1957), "Morphology and physiology of the speech organs," *Manual of Phonetics,* L. Kaiser, ed., North-Holland, Amsterdam.

Trubetzkoy, N. S. (1939), *Grundzüge der Phonologie,* Traveaux du Cercle Linguistique de Prague 7, Göttingen; or the French translation by J. Cantineau, *Principes de phonologie,* Paris, 1949.

Twaddell, W. F. (1953), "Stetson's model and the supra-segmental phonemes," *Language, 29,* 415–453.

Uldall, E. (1960), "Attitudinal meanings conveyed by intonation contours," *Language and Speech, 3,* 223–234.

Van den Berg, Jw. (1954), "Sur les théories myo-elastique et neurochronoxique de la phonation," *Revue de Laryngol. de Bordeaux, 74,* 495–512.

Van den Berg, Jw. (1956), "Direct and indirect determination of the mean subglottic pressure," *Folia Phoniat., 8,* 1–24.

Van den Berg, Jw. (1957), "Subglottic pressure and vibrations of the vocal folds," *Folia Phoniat., 2,* 65–71.

Van den Berg, Jw. (1958), "Myoelastic-aerodynamic theory of voice production," *J. Speech and Hearing Res., 1,* 227–244.

Van den Berg, Jw. (1960*a*), "Vocal ligaments versus registers," *Current Prob. Phoniat. Logoped., 1,* 19–34.

Van den Berg, Jw. (1960*b*), "An electrical analogue of the trachea, lungs and tissues," *Acta Physiol. Pharmacol. Neerl. 9,* 361–385.

Van den Berg, Jw., Zantema, J. T., and Doornenbal, P. (1957), "On the air resistance and the Bernoulli effect of the human larynx," *J. Acoust. Soc. Am., 29,* 626–631.

Von Leden, H., and Moore, P. (1960), "Vibratory pattern of the vocal cords in unilateral laryngeal paralysis," *Acta Oto-Laryngol., 53,* 493–506.

Von Leden, H., Moore, P., and Timcke, R. (1960), "Laryngeal vibrations, measurements of the glottic wave, Part III, The pathologic larynx," *A.M.A. Arch. Otolaryngol., 71,* 16–35.

Vygotsky, L. S. (1962), *Thought and Language,* The M.I.T. Press, Cambridge, Mass.; Wiley, New York.

Walker, J. (1787), *The Melody of Speaking, Delineated or Elocution Taught Like Music,* published for the author, London.

Wells, R. S. (1945), "The pitch phonemes of English," *Language, 21,* 27–40.

Wells, R. S. (1947), "Immediate constituents," *Language, 23,* 81–117.

Widdicombe, J. G. (1964), "Respiratory reflexes," in *Handbook of Physiology, Respiration, I,* W. O. Fenn and H. Rahn, eds., American Physiological Society, Washington, D.C.

Wolff, P. H. (1966) "The natural history of crying and other vocalizations in early infancy," in *Determinants of Infant Behavior, IV,* B. Foss, ed., Methuen, London, scheduled for publication.

Index

Abramson, A. S., 39, 102, 132
Acoustic output of larynx, 7, 13, 20, 21
Acoustic theory of speech production, 5–8
Acquisition of language, 39
Air pressure perturbation effect, 54, 71, 98, 99
Analysis by synthesis, 31, 32, 48, 60, 61, 104–107, 163–168, 179
Archetypal articulatory gestures, 9, 27, 87, 88, 104–107, 147, 148
Archetypal breath-group, 26, 27, 53, 65–67, 87, 88, 96, 104–107
Archytas of Tarentum, 13
Armstrong, L. W., 28, 129, 169, 175–177
Audition, integrating effects in, 30

Bernoulli force, 15, 17, 18, 36
Bierwisch, M., 114, 194, 195
Bloch, B., 182
Bloomfield, L., 180, 181, 183, 190
Body pleythysmograph, 61
Bolinger, D. L., 152, 153
Bosma, J. F., 43
Bouhuys, A., 21, 61, 62
Breath-group
  acoustic and physiologic correlates of, 26, 27, 53, 65–100, 104–107
  archetypal, 26, 27, 53, 65–67, 87, 88, 96, 104–107
  of different languages, 27–29, 46, 105, 106
  division of sentences, 65, 108, 109–121
  examples of interactions with prominence, 69–72, 74, 76, 80, 81, 85–88, 93
  hypothetical interactions with prominence, 56
  idiosyncratic aspects of, 80, 81, 85, 86, 106, 107
  innate nature of, 2, 42–43
  innate referential, 42–44, 100
  interactions with tone features, 2, 101, 102, 107, 130–132
  span of, 2, 47, 65, 66, 104–121

Categorization versus discrimination, 159–160
Chang, N. T., 101, 130, 161
Chest register, 18–20
Children
  acquisition of language by, 39
  use of intonation by, 45–47
Chinese pitch phonemes, 101, 102, 130
Chomsky, N., 110, 120, 141, 143, 145
Coarticulation effects, 123
Constituent structure, 3, 108–120, 145, 146, 155–159
Context effects in perception, 3, 163
Cowan, M., 170

Darwin, C., 42, 43
Denes, P., 13, 122
Derived phrase marker, 111
  simplification of, 120, 121
Disambiguation by breath-group division, 108–120
Disjuncture, 152, 154–159, 185
Duration of expiration, 23–25, 65

Egerod, S., 102
Elastic recoil of lungs, 23–26, 54, 62, 93, 100, 192–193
Emotion, 42, 43, 121–122, 183, 184, 187, 195
Emphasis, 71, 72, 75, 141, 146, 147, 194
Esophageal air pressure
  measurement of, 43, 44, 62
  relation to subglottal air pressure, 62
Expiratory-inspiratory cycle, 23–26, 65, 100

Falsetto register, 12, 20–22
Fant, C. G. M., 8, 13, 29, 31
Farnsworth, D. W., 13, 22
Feedback control of phonation, 97
Flanagan, J. L., 13, 18, 29
Fonagy, I., 39
Formant frequencies, 7, 160
Functional load, 103
Fundamental frequency measurement, 68
Fundamental frequency versus subglottal air pressure, 77, 78, 82, 89, 95–98

German stress, 153, 194
Goldman-Eisler, F., 122

Hadding-Koch, K., 30, 35, 39, 48–61, 122, 131, 148, 149
Halle, M., 29, 31, 32, 40, 41, 141, 145
Harris, C. M., 13
Harris, Z., 191
Husson, R., 23
Hypothesis formation, 164–167

Idiosyncratic aspects of breath-group, 80, 81, 85, 86, 106, 107
Infant
  cries of, 41–44, 104
  use of intonation by, 42–45
Innate nature of breath-group, 2, 42–43, 104, 105
Innate referential breath-group, 53

Integrating effects in audition, 30
Intensity modulation, 21–23
Interaction
  of prominence and breath-group, 56, 69–76
  of segmental pitch phonemes with breath-group, 101, 102, 130–132
Intonation questions
  acoustic and physiologic correlates, 84, 91
  syntactic and semantic aspects, 136, 138, 141, 142
Isshiki, N., 20, 21, 98

Jakobson, R., 29–31, 39–41
Jones, Daniel, 28, 39, 109, 129, 131, 145, 149, 173, 174, 178–180
Joos, M., 28

Katz, J. J., 132, 133, 135

Ladefoged, P., 13, 97, 148
Larynx
  acoustic output, 7, 13, 20, 21
  activity of, 14–18, 22, 27
  anatomy of, 8–12
  photographs of, 11
Lenneberg, E., 24, 29
Leopold, W. F., 41, 45–47
Lewis, M., 44, 45, 47
Liberman, A. M., 32, 161
Lifshitz, S., 30
Lindblom, B., 123
Lisker, L., 149
Loud sentences, 99

Marked breath-group
  acoustic and physiologic correlates, 53, 73, 74, 76, 83–85, 87, 90–93
  division of sentences, 65, 108, 109
  minimal acoustic factor differentiating, 94
Mead, J., 21, 23, 61, 62, 193
Miller, G. A., 163, 164
Mimicking of adult intonation by children, 45, 46
Model for phonation, 18–22
Model of speech production and perception, 162–167
Molnar, C. E., 160, 161
Moore, P., 13, 21, 22
Motor theory of speech perception, 3, 4, 32, 60, 61, 161, 162, 167
Müller, Johannes, 8, 10–12, 21, 33
Myoelastic-aerodynamic theory of phonation, 14–18

Negus, V. E., 24, 40

Öhman, S., 97
Opening quotient, 13, 20–22
Ostwald, P. F., 41, 42
Overlapping acoustic correlates of articulatory gestures, 31

Pauses, 109, 122, 151–158, 184, 185
Perception
of intonation, 47–60, 104–107, 125–127
limits imposed by auditory system, 30, 125–128, 159–161
of prominence, 53–57, 104–107, 125–128, 144–161
of stress, 126–128, 144–161, 179, 180, 182, 185
of terminal fundamental frequency contours, 48–61, 126, 127
of yes-no question in Swedish, 58–60
Phonation
in chest register, 18–20
effects of extralaryngeal muscles, 37
in falsetto register, 12, 20–22
feedback control, 97
interactions with subglottal system, 32–35
interactions with supralaryngeal system, 35, 36
model for, 18–22
start and end, 94–96
Phonation delay, 69, 94–96
Phonation neutral position, 14, 15, 19, 21, 43, 93, 94, 104
Phonemic phrase, 2, 108
Phonemic pitch levels, 27, 28, 34, 35, 110, 123–128, 182–184, 188–191
Phonologic feature, 1–4, 39, 40, 46, 100, 104, 105, 107
Physiologic necessity for dividing sentence, 108, 114
Pickett, J. M., 164
Pike, K. L., 27, 35, 129, 145, 149, 184–187
Pitch perturbations, 36, 122
Pitch phonemes of Chinese, 101, 102, 130
Pleural pressure, 62
Pollack, I., 161, 164
Postal, P. M., 132, 133, 135
Proctor, D. F., 21, 37, 61, 62
Production component of the grammar, 166, 167
Production effects on intonation, 168–170
Prominence
acoustic and physiologic correlates, 30, 69–76, 79–90, 92–93, 105–107, 144–161
binary nature of, 144–161, 185
scope of, 52–54, 71, 72, 75, 107, 147

Q morpheme, 134
Question formation in several languages, 130–133
Questions, transformational analysis of, 136–140

Recoverability of deep phrase marker, 133, 134, 190, 191

Segmental tone features, 101–103, 107, 130–132
Semantic interpretation, 109, 124, 134, 188–190
Simplification of derived phrase marker, 120, 121
Slawson, A. W., 7
Sledd, J., 116, 125
Smith, H. L., 27, 35, 110, 123–129, 145, 188–191
Soron, H. I., 13, 22, 36
Sound spectrograph, 63
Speech production and perception, model of, 162–167
Stetson, R. H., 26, 35, 191–193
Stevens, K. N., 14, 30, 32, 160
Stockwell, R. P., 27, 111, 112, 115, 124
Stress
acoustic correlates of, 30, 144–161
cycle, 145–147
German, 153, 194
in linguistic analysis, 110, 123–128, 144–148, 179–182, 185, 188–191, 194
Studdert-Kennedy, M., 48–61
Subglottal air pressure
control of, 23–25, 93, 98–100
relation to esophageal air pressure, 62
Subjunctive mood, 138, 141–143
Sublaryngeal respiratory system, 6, 23–26, 33–35
Supralaryngeal respiratory system, 6–8, 29, 35–37

Suprasegmental phonologic feature, 2, 65, 66, 104–107, 191
Sweet, H., 145, 172
Syllable, 113

Tone analyses of intonation, 171, 172, 174
Trager, G. L., 27, 35, 110, 123–129, 145, 188–191
Transformational analysis
  of disambiguation by breath-group division, 109–119
  of yes-no questions, 133–143
Trubetzkoy, N. S., 36, 37
Tune analyses of intonation, 28, 171, 172, 175–180
Twaddell, W. F., 193

Underlying phrase marker, 109, 111, 120, 121, 124, 190

Van den Berg, Jw., 12–14, 16, 18–23, 33, 97
Vocal cords, 9-11
Vocal tract, 5–7
Vocoder, 28, 49, 194
Von Leden, H., 13, 21, 22

Ward, I. C., 28, 129, 169, 175–177
Wells, R. S., 35, 182, 187
Wolff, P. H., 42